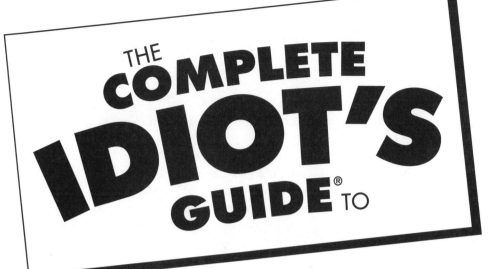

THE
COMPLETE IDIOT'S GUIDE® TO

Ballroom Dancing

by Jeff Allen

ALPHA

A member of Penguin Group (USA) Inc.

To my wonderful wife, Whitney, and my son, Joshua; my daughter Bethanie and her husband, Manny; my daughter Jessica and her husband, Sloan; Diesel and Snowflake—you are all my loves and inspiration.

ALPHA BOOKS

Published by the Penguin Group

Penguin Group (USA) Inc., 375 Hudson Street, New York, New York 10014, U.S.A.

Penguin Group (Canada), 10 Alcorn Avenue, Toronto, Ontario, Canada M4V 3B2 (a division of Pearson Penguin Canada Inc.)

Penguin Books Ltd, 80 Strand, London WC2R 0RL, England

Penguin Ireland, 25 St Stephen's Green, Dublin 2, Ireland (a division of Penguin Books Ltd)

Penguin Group (Australia), 250 Camberwell Road, Camberwell, Victoria 3124, Australia (a division of Pearson Australia Group Pty Ltd)

Penguin Books India Pvt Ltd, 11 Community Centre, Panchsheel Park, New Delhi—110 017, India

Penguin Group (NZ), cnr Airborne and Rosedale Roads, Albany, Auckland 1310, New Zealand (a division of Pearson New Zealand Ltd)

Penguin Books (South Africa) (Pty) Ltd, 24 Sturdee Avenue, Rosebank, Johannesburg 2196, South Africa

Penguin Books Ltd, Registered Offices: 80 Strand, London WC2R 0RL, England

International Standard Book Number: 0-02-864345-3
Library of Congress Catalog Card Number: 2002102219

07   06   05   11   10   9

Interpretation of the printing code: The rightmost number of the first series of numbers is the year of the book's printing; the rightmost number of the second series of numbers is the number of the book's printing. For example, a printing code of 02-1 shows that the first printing occurred in 2002.

Printed in the United States of America

Note: This publication contains the opinions and ideas of its author. It is intended to provide helpful and informative material on the subject matter covered. It is sold with the understanding that the author and publisher are not engaged in rendering professional services in the book. If the reader requires personal assistance or advice, a competent professional should be consulted.

The author and publisher specifically disclaim any responsibility for any liability, loss, or risk, personal or otherwise, which is incurred as a consequence, directly or indirectly, of the use and application of any of the contents of this book.

Most Alpha books are available at special quantity discounts for bulk purchases for sales promotions, premiums, fund-raising, or educational use. Special books, or book excerpts, can also be created to fit specific needs.

For details, write: Special Markets, Alpha Books, 375 Hudson Street, New York, NY 10014.

Publisher: *Marie Butler-Knight*
Product Manager: *Phil Kitchel*
Managing Editor: *Jennifer Chisholm*
Acquisitions Editor: *Mike Sanders*
Development Editor: *Nancy D. Lewis*
Senior Production Editor: *Christy Wagner*
Copy Editor: *Fran Blauw*
Illustrator: *Chris Eliopoulos*
Cover/Book Designer: *Trina Wurst*
Indexer: *Julie Bess*
Layout/Proofreading: *Angela Calvert, Svetlana Dominguez, Mary Hunt*

Contents at a Glance

Appendixes

Contents

Appendixes

Foreword

So you want to learn how to dance. In my opinion, you have found a great place to start. Jeff Allen is one of America's leading authorities on virtually anything and everything related to ballroom dance. In this very comprehensive book, he provides the novice with all the required information to make the transformation from spectator to participant.

The desire to dance is instinctive to all peoples in all cultures. There is something about human nature that compels movement in the body while listening to music. Music reaches into the depth of the human soul and demands action. This is why we dance. We are prisoners of our own humanity.

Ballroom dance is without a doubt the most versatile form of dance. Neither age nor infirmity is an impediment. The dance skills can be applied in both formal and casual settings. Spontaneity is encouraged. Infinite variation is available. The fundamentals are constant.

The capacity to dance is in us all not just the John Travoltas and Ginger Rogers of this world. As Jeff Allen so astutely observes, if you know how to walk and climb stairs, then you have already mastered many of the necessary fundamentals of ballroom dance. With a little bit of study and practice, the transformation from dance floor observer to active participant will be complete.

Please be forewarned. Many find ballroom dance addictive. Once they get started, they cannot get enough. More dances, more steps, more variations, more technique, more partners, more venues, more music, more fun. Fortunately, ballroom dance is one addiction with few if any negative consequences.

Ballroom dance, in fact, offers a plethora of side benefits that extend far beyond movement in time to the music. Ballroom dance works its magic in a host of ways. It offers respite from a sedentary lifestyle and provides an excellent cardio-vascular workout. It opens a world of social possibilities. It improves self-confidence and posture. It provides an outlet to the frustrations of everyday life.

Jeff Allen provides the rosetta stone that allows an average Joe or Janet to decipher the value of dance from the pit of ignorance. There is nothing rarified about ballroom dance. It is accessible to the masses. No special skills or talents required.

There is an old joke that has some application to the world of ballroom dancers. If a person speaks three languages, he is tri-lingual. If a person speaks two languages, he is bi-lingual. If a person speaks one language, he is American. The same phenomenon occurs in dance.

Europeans, Latins, and Asians view ballroom dance to be an integral part of one's education. It is never viewed as anything less than a cultural imperative. The well-rounded human being must learn to dance, especially partner dance. It goes along with speaking multiple languages, proper usage of eating utensils, good manners, reading, writing, and arithmetic.

As the founder of the Quickstart to dance program, Jeff Allen's professional focus has long centered upon getting beginners out on to the dance floor. He wants them out there dancing with a partner and enjoying themselves. He makes people understand that dance is less about where you move than how you move. And people already know how to move from their daily lives. With some help from an expert like Jeff Allen, the proverbial person with two left feet soon discovers they really match after all.

Whatever your motivation for wanting to learn dance, this book shall prepare you for when the moment arrives. Follow the instructions. Take the advice. Enjoy the thrills.

Michael Fitzmaurice
Dancing USA

Introduction

Our goal in this book is to help you be the dancer you want to be—Ballroom, Latin, Swing, or Hustle. Whether it is once a year or every night of the week, *The Complete Idiot's Guide to Ballroom Dancing* will provide the building blocks, insights, and skills needed to be successful.

Beginners and even more advanced dancers will find the answers to leading, following, physical performance, partnering, rhythm, and attitudes within the descriptions of every single pattern. Because the book is about building skills (creating a foundation, adding to it by learning new things, and fine-tuning your abilities), the material is appropriate for anyone who is taking lessons, studying to be a teacher, participating as a member of a college ballroom club or team, or preparing for a wedding day.

Maximum benefit will be achieved if you read the step patterns and related techniques *before* beginning your lessons or working on specific choreography. Then you will read the step numbers aloud as if giving yourself or a partner directions. Then follow your directions physically. In this way, you will be mentally prepared to begin by acknowledging all the elements that are key to the successful implementation of any dance step and its technique.

Visually, learning to dance can be very deceptive and prone to illusion. In physics we have learned that you only see the result of force and not what generates that force. For this reason, much about learning to dance remains a mystery to many. The words of this text will break you away from the illusions of dance and place your feet firmly on the dance floor.

This is a how-to book and *not* a novel. You must physically participate and at relatively small but frequent intervals. Learning to dance is a cumulative process and experience. Always keep this thought ahead of you: Others have done this, and so can I!

How This Book Is Organized

This book is presented in five sections:

As you might expect, **Part 1, "Before the Ball,"** is the preliminary and preparatory section of the book. You will enjoy and be motivated by this fast-paced and sometimes lighthearted expose about the beginnings of ballroom dancing right through to the present. Weddings are singularly the greatest concern for non-dancers, and you will find plenty of ideas here to get you through. Ballroom dancing will introduce you to a new threshold of social activity that can change your life.

In **Part 2, "Before Your Ball,"** we will explore the physical and intellectual requirements that will ensure your success. Dancing is all about physically expressing music, so we must fill your tool belt with the implements that will make it work for you. These tools include understanding music, timing, and rhythm. It will take a little time to keep time, but the analogies will surely help.

To conceptualize the dance couple is not an innate but an acquired skill! No one is naturally gifted in the art of moving with someone attached to them, so take all the time you need to develop. Do not compare yourself to others, be sure to put in the work, do not complain or be hard on yourself or your partner, and most of all, enjoy yourself. Like learning to ride your bicycle, suddenly one day your balance kicks in, and you are on your way!

In **Part 3, "Two Become One: Creating the Dance Couple,"** you will be introduced to my Quickstart to Dance Program©, which began in 1984 and has been responsible for teaching thousands to dance. It may not be what you expected, but it contains the primary and often missing components that will help separate failure from success. You will learn about the common denominator of ballroom dancing, which dynamically accelerates your learning curve.

The approach used in my writing is as if I am there with you teaching a private lesson. I will provide as much information as possible to help you succeed.

In **Part 4, "Fred and Ginger, Here We Come: The Smooth Dances,"** you will learn to navigate the ballroom and some of the common courtesies that show respect to your fellow travelers. Then we begin with the individual dances of Waltz, Foxtrot, Tango, and Viennese Waltz. Each figure described discusses the movement, timing, and direction of both the leader and the follower. Throughout the book, I will interrupt the actual choreography discussion when necessary to implement specific leading and following physical devices and mention other references to technique. This section includes hundreds of photos displaying the critical moments of each figure for easy visual and physical use.

Starting with the most basic patterns of Rumba, Merengue, Samba, Cha-Cha, Mambo, East Coast Swing, and Hustle, in **Part 5, "This Stuff's Hot and Spicy and Real Cool, 'Daddy-O,'"** you learn to dance five essential dance patterns. We will concentrate on very simple movements so we can exhaust the fundamentals that will make you look as natural and smooth a dancer as possible. These fundamental techniques are more important to keeping the infectious party rhythm and fun in your dancing than how many steps or patterns you learn.

Things to Help You Out Along the Way

Dancing is 90 percent technique (timing and balance) and only 10 percent choreography. Throughout this book you will encounter four types of information boxes.

Dancing Definition

On-the-spot translations of dance rhetoric will help your comprehension. Also refer often to the glossary.

Movement Memo

Lightweight yet prudent devices, ideas, and information that will assist you with your learning.

Ballroom Bloopers

This is advice about errors common to the learning process or elements on the social dance floor that you should stay away from.

Bet You Didn't Know

Anecdotes and trivia about the wonderful experience and history of ballroom dancing are found here.

Technique

Here are the "nuts and bolts" that will absolutely help you assemble the physical devices necessary to be successful on the dance floor. Technique, your foundation, is 90 percent of dancing with a partner, so treat it like the vowels and consonants of your speech!

Acknowledgments

I would like to thank the members of the Alpha Books family who behind the scenes provided time, information, and resources working tirelessly to bring this book to fruition. Special thanks are given to those with whom I worked directly—Mike Sanders and Nancy Warner. Also Jessica Faust, whose insight and patience was the catalyst for this project.

To my wife, Whitney Brown—no man could ask for a better life's companion and trusted partner in all I do!

To Joshua Allen, my son and a brilliant actor/performer committed to unstinting hours on both ends of the camera.

To Elizabeth (Liz) Nogueira—an extraordinary singing talent, my student, and Joshua's photo partner.

Special thanks to Diane DiSanto, whose creativity and kind insight have helped me learn more about the English language.

Trademarks

All terms mentioned in this book that are known to be or are suspected of being trademarks or service marks have been appropriately capitalized. Alpha Books and Penguin Group (USA) Inc. cannot attest to the accuracy of this information. Use of a term in this book should not be regarded as affecting the validity of any trademark or service mark.

Part 1

Before the Ball

It would not matter how far back in time we traveled or the region of the world we traveled to: Mankind has always danced! Dancing has always reflected the social condition and its need to change. Dancing combines our intimate desires with expressions of artistic movement, interpreting its magical source of energy—music.

We start by presenting two retrospectives of ballroom dancing. The first is the history from the Renaissance to the Age of Reform and then from the 1900s to the present. Most of all we glean, just as Solomon the Wise suggested, that no matter how much things change, they seem to remain the same.

This section continues with a bit of ballroom anthropology and sociology and then the ultimate climax to these aspects of getting us together—conducting your wedding dance.

We will then look at the lasting effects ballroom dancing has on your lifestyle. You will quickly see how it can improve your life socially, psychologically, and physically. Where you may have turned away from events and places with dancing before, you will now welcome the occasion. And who knows what may happen next!

Chapter 1

Past Ballroom Dancing Expressions: From the Renaissance to the Age of Reform

In This Chapter

- ◆ Early social dancing reflected early social mores
- ◆ The dancing queens of Europe
- ◆ The American colonist must follow the lead of the British
- ◆ The root of all evil: the Waltz

Ballroom dancing enjoys a rich history. As with most art forms, ballroom dancing has been influenced by and has been a reflection of the prevailing forces in a given society. Politics, economics, philosophy, and even ethics have played an important role in the development of ballroom dancing as we know it today.

In this chapter we will explore the highlights of the early days of ballroom dancing from the Renaissance Age through the Age of Reform—popularly known as the Victorian Era. I think you will find it an interesting trip!

The Renaissance Sets the Stage

The fifteenth century has long been considered the transition from the medieval world to the modern world. In this historical age of the Renaissance, Europe experienced a great revival of the arts, literature, and learning. During this cultural rebirth, social dancing was identified as court dancing. Numerous couples danced in formation, executing the same steps at the same time. While this dancing allowed for the interaction of men and women, court dances mirrored the strict social etiquette and dignity required of the era. One could say these dances reflected the attitude a gentleman was supposed to have toward a lady.

The European countries had different social standards based on the intricate relationships among the church, state, and military, as well as the events occurring at the time in each country. Although social standards and customs differed slightly within each country, decorum and behavior was much more reserved at the palaces and courts than in the agrarian areas.

If the times and locations warranted sternness in attitude, the dances became more subdued and less energetic. Dances were choreographed with complex patterns. The dance masters found this to be a favorable environment. The longer it took to learn a dance, the more students were dependent upon their teacher.

> **Bet You Didn't Know**
>
> The lower and middle classes often endeavor to copy the examples of the aristocracy and upper class. It seems that it has always been important and considered correct to do "what the rich folk do." At the same time, the upper class would closely examine the dance trends and fads of the lower classes. The dance instructors of this past era would then interpret these fads to make them fit for public consumption. Some of the more enterprising dance instructors in recent history made their fortunes doing the same thing. For instance, Arthur Murray did this with the dance called "The Big Apple."

When the attitude of the times and locations reflected a more relaxed social demeanor, simpler dances were used. Often these more vigorous dances were welcomed. As the lower and middle classes copied the simpler choreography more easily, these dances grew in popularity. The ability of the middle and lower classes "to let it all hang out" seems to be a recurring theme throughout history. The upper classes, often clandestinely, tried to incorporate the fun and social freedom of the lower classes into their world of society.

The First True "Dancing Queen"

Queen Elizabeth I, who began her reign in 1558, was a famous patron of the arts. The Queen loved men and spirited dancing. She prized the dance form called the galliard and particularly enjoyed a variation called Lavolta. During one dance sequence, the man placed one hand about his partner's waist, the other on her stomach, and boosted her high in the air with his thigh under her buttocks.

> **Bet You Didn't Know**
>
> A wonderful but reserved depiction of a galliard can be seen in the 1998 motion picture *Shakespeare in Love*. In this scene, Queen Elizabeth demonstrates her approval of this court dancing known as Lavolta. William Shakespeare picks up on this while courting his own love interest and includes the dance sequence in his play *Romeo and Juliet*.

Queen Elizabeth's high esteem for William Shakespeare is well documented. Shakespeare often honored her favor by including a galliard or two when performing his plays in her court. The more vigorous the dance, the more the Queen loved it!

The church was considered the protector and sanctifier of the social condition. The dance masters thought of themselves as interpreters of socially acceptable behavior. These dance instructors were the chief chaperones and upheld the standards of social propriety during special events. The social education of the aristocratic youth was also entrusted to them. Studying dance became a responsibility incumbent upon an aspiring social climber from the middle class. Dance served as the means to learn the customs, manners, and conduct attributed to social respectability.

The Dance Masters Create the Roots for Ballet

Just as dance instructors do today, these dance masters interpreted the popular dance trends of the peasants and middle class. These dances were then refined and subdued in order to be more palatable to any regal court. The idiosyncrasies of choreography differed from one region to the next and circulated via travel. The aristocracy traveled with a full complement of staff and servants, including the dance master. Observations were made on parallel social planes. The wealthy observed the wealthy; the dance masters exchanged ideas and notes; and of course at the taverns, the commoners enjoyed the local color. Exchanging social and cultural ideas was common in the courts of Austria, Germany, Italy, Spain, France, and England. The differences from country to country were essentially found in the music, since dance has always been and always will be the personification of music.

In addition to interpreting the various dances, these dance masters used a technique to portray refinement in dance. This technique consisted of five basic foot positions. One foot position was used to begin or conclude the dance's choreography. The dance masters referred to the normal walking position as *parallel feet*. In contrast, these foot positions were described as being positions of turnout.

The typical amount of *turnout* for these court dances equaled 45 degrees from the dancer's center, totaling 90 degrees; feet were placed at a right angle to each other. The dancers would proceed forward in fourth position or backward in fifth position. Although this 90-degree angle was not at all as extreme as today's ballet, anyone of normal physical capabilities could find it challenging. Toward the end of the 1600s, a shift in dance emerged. What had been a simple proletarian dance presentation in the courts of kings and queens actually became the beginning of professional ballet.

These five foot positions become the major demarcation between dance as an art in the performance vein, versus dance as an art to broaden the social spectrum of men and women. As the social dances that were known as court dances became more jovial, interpretive, and relaxed, they tended to use the five foot positions less and the parallel feet more. Understandably, the dance masters who wanted to maintain control of the social art were not thrilled with relaxing their standards. Even they suggested that these simplified dances with more hopping and joy would lead to social improprieties. The diversity and complexity of dance patterns upheld the proper social decorum and coincidentally protected the job of the dance masters.

Dancing Definition

Turnout is a dancer's ability to turn his or her feet, as well as the upper legs (thighs), out from the hip joints to a position of up to 90 degrees. Turnout is important in the dancer's ability to move in varied directions. Technically, turnout is the singularly most identifying position in modern ballet. In today's ballroom dancing, this technique is particularly useful in Latin American dancing.

Interpretation of the five dance positions presented in the style of a Dance Master.

The Scandalous Waltz

Not unlike any other time in history, dance soon became a social controversy. Individual expression and male/female interactions were at odds with the church and state. The dance masters added to the mix. They were obviously threatened by the simplicity of a new dance: the Waltz.

Ländler was one of the first of these simplified court dances. This partner dance originated from a traditional folk or peasant dance first seen in areas of Bavaria and Alpine Austria. The music was lively, using ³/₄ time, and frankly was much more fun to dance to. The dancers turned under each other's arms using complicated arm and hand holds, danced back to back, and grasped each other firmly to turn around and around. These figures and the triple rhythm have appeared in turning dances characteristic of German peasant dances from the Middle Ages. Ländler melodies became fashionable in eighteenth- and nineteenth-century Vienna, and the dance greatly influenced the evolution of the Waltz.

Lavolta, Lavatoe, or Levalto originated from the Italian "the turn" or "turning" and was a sixteenth-century leaping and turning dance for couples. The dance originated in Italy and was popular at French and German court balls until about 1750. Couples danced in a close hold in side-by-side fashion. This very close dance position was considered scandalous. Queen Elizabeth I, however, actually endorsed this dance and performed it frequently at social functions. She loved vigorous dancing (see the previous section, "The First True 'Dancing Queen'").

The popularity of dances like Lavolta and Ländler grew. The joy and freedom of movement could be expressed in a more personal style. The absence of strict adherence to the five foot positions was liberating. The gentleman had body contact with his partner. He supported her around the waist and had no complicated foot positions to learn. These dances were clearly far more intriguing and easier to grasp than the former court dances. Couples soon broke away from the traditional formations and danced as independent pairs. Needless to say, this dancing became quite popular among the youth and middle class! Owing to the circular and revolving nature of these dances, the term "waltz," from the German word *walzen* (to revolve) was natural.

The first recognized ball in the United States, simply called The Assembly, was held in Philadelphia during the Christmas season of 1748. Those who attended—most notably, George Washington—were among the highest ranking and socially conscious personalities of the time. The English dances that were considered "sanctioned dances" were the Schottische and the Minuet. Ladies remained under the watchful eye of their chaperones, and the ball itself was closely scrutinized. These formation dances were performed at arm's length. Both ladies and gentlemen wore gloves as etiquette required to prevent the pure contact of flesh, a great impropriety. Long-flowing full-length gowns were the style of the day. A bare ankle would have caused a scandal.

Bet You Didn't Know

George Washington wrote a documented letter strongly suggesting that his nephew be properly instructed in the art of dance. Dancing had become recognized as an indispensable social grace that ensured one's position in eighteenth-century society. Dancing was also considered preparation in the practices, customs, rituals, and disciplines of military training. Early Americans followed the same dictates as required by European customs and etiquette, specifically English.

In addition to teaching and interpreting the various court dances like Minuets and Schottisches, the dance masters had always served as officiates at society balls. They started a dance, called a dance, and prepared the overall program and timeline for the evening's entertainment. Since music education had become so prevalent for middle and upper class young ladies and gentlemen of the continent and England, they were able to begin the Waltz on their own. Imagine being able to start a dance all by yourself! These practices remained the same in colonial America. The dance master's control was clearly threatened, and his position as society's head chaperone was endangered!

As you read on, you will see that, when it comes to the history of dance, the past repeats itself. Change and the creativity and exuberance of youth have always been perceived as threats to the structure of society. The Waltz freed couples to enjoy the social and romantic aspects of dancing—a great departure from the regimentation of previous formation dancing.

During the summer of 1816, the society pages of *The Times* of London reported on the Prince Regent's grand ball. The writer was not as forgiving as his peers on the continent. The writer reported the following:

> We remarked with pain that the indecent foreign dance called the Waltz was introduced (we believe for the first time) at the English court on Friday last … it is quite sufficient to cast one's eyes on the voluptuous intertwining of the limbs and close compressor on the bodies in their dance, to see that it is indeed far removed from the modest reserve which has hitherto been considered distinctive of English females. So long as this obscene display was confined to prostitutes and adulteresses, we did not think it deserving of notice; but now that it is attempted to be forced on the respectable classes of society by the civil examples of their superiors, we feel it a duty to warn every parent against exposing his daughter to so fatal a contagion.

Interestingly, "voluptuous intertwining of the limbs," simply referred to the close dance position of the day. The gloved hand of the gentleman was placed gently on the waist of his partner at virtually full arm's length. The lady's left gloved hand quite possibly was delicately placed on her gentleman's shoulder, and she likely held a fan in that same hand. The left hand of the gentleman remained open and acted as the shelf for his partner's right-gloved hand. The really scandalous point of that reporter's observation was that the gentleman's foot disappeared from time to time under the lady's gown in the midst of the dance. The bodies of the dancers were never in contact!

If any readers are familiar with the English tabloids and their propensity for overstatement, the following quote from the English magazine *Belgravia* will amuse you:

> We who go forth of nights and see without the slightest discomposure our sister and our wife seized on by a strange man and subjected to violent embraces and canterings round a small-sized apartment—the only apparent excuse for such treatment being that it is done to the sound of music—can scarcely realize the horror which greeted the introduction of this wicked dance.

The Waltz had become the forbidden fruit of the bourgeoisie—the greater the scandal, the greater the popularity. The end of the French revolution (1787–1799) was a time of great growth for music and dance in Paris. Paris alone had over 600 dance halls, and the Waltz was king!

Age of Reform: Queen Victoria (Reign 1837–1901)

Like her predecessor, Queen Elizabeth I, Queen Victoria was a fanatic and proficient ballroom dancer. This fact was seldom mentioned, although the older generation voiced much disapproval. Victoria had a secret and special adoration for the Waltz!

The dance masters felt they had to stop the Waltz. Society and religion had tried and failed, so the dance masters took their turn. The control they enjoyed due to the complexity of the court dances was slipping away. The Waltz and its simplicity were gaining popularity. The reaction of the dance masters reminds this author of a very funny line from *Strictly Ballroom*, a 1992 Australian motion picture comedy: "There are no new dance steps." Plainly speaking, the more things seem to change, human nature never does. Even as D. H. Lawrence revealed that sex was the "dirty little secret" of Victorian society, suggestion of the human mating ritual began expressing itself in dance. Slowly, partners moved closer and closer to one another. To the chagrin of many, sexuality started to reveal itself in society. Partnered dances arose. The intrinsic human desire to dance was a means of celebrating life, courtship, and mating. The creative need to express art was too powerful. All efforts failed to halt the growth of the Waltz.

> ### Bet You Didn't Know
>
> The typical twentieth-century white, floor-length, full-skirted wedding gown was symbolic of the virgin-like qualities of the eighteenth- and nineteenth-century customs and attitudes. Queen Victoria herself was the first to don the white wedding gown. Because most upper echelon girls of society were educated in European monasteries, white attire was a natural choice. Today's gowns are actually much better suited for nineteenth-century dances. Because couples danced at full arm's length, stepping on the hem of the garment by either the gentleman or the lady was of little concern. A shorter hemline would be more appropriate for today's dancing, with its close holds. As ballroom dancing becomes more popular with each passing year, this author is of the opinion that the style will encourage a shorter hemline in the twenty-first century.

During the age of reform, labor laws changed radically, and the middle class suddenly had leisure time. Social activities previously available only to the upper echelons of society could now be readily enjoyed by the middle class. This included the pleasures of social dancing. The *music hall*, the common name for a ballroom, was open to anyone who could pay admission. Popular music and the orchestras that played this music were now available to the public.

Famous Waltz composers include Frederic Chopin (1810–1893), Peter Ilich Tchaikovsky (1840–1893), and Johann Strauss (1804–1849) and his sons. Johann Strauss the younger (1825–1899) was known as "the Waltz King." By today's standards, the idea of these classical composers producing music for dancing that could be construed as immoral is unimaginable. With all the rapid whirling around, was it centrifugal force or desire that caused the dancers to hold on tight? The clerics of the day would have certainly outlawed this dance if they had been able. The undeniable strict tempo of this beautiful music was predictable. The middle-class mimicked upper class activities but enjoyed a lifestyle of simplicity. People loved the music and expressed it through the Waltz, the most popular dance of the nineteenth century.

In an attempt to imitate the social behavior of society's elite, middle-class young ladies attended finishing schools where music, etiquette, and dancing were taught. Young men already had these opportunities in their secular and military education. Partner dancing had now become a staple of Western civilization.

Coming out parties became a popular practice both in Europe and the United States when a young woman reached the age of 16. This entree into society was her opportunity to be introduced to young bachelors. The party was quite formal, with elegant grand marches and plenty of ballroom dancing. This was the high point of life for a 16-year-old young woman.

Waltzing to America

European dance master Lorenzo Papanti gave the first exhibition of the Waltz in 1834 in Boston, Massachusetts. Boston would later ban almost every new social occurrence from the Tango to croquet. As one would have expected, the reaction was largely the same: The dance was viewed as shocking and vulgar. The early Waltz in the United States actually became known as "The Boston." Charles K. Harris' musical composition, "After the Ball," was considered a sentimental ballad by comparison to the very fast Viennese Waltzes composed by the Strausses. The introduction of forward and back steps to a much slower cadence was unique. Dancers could interpret the Waltz at an easier pace, which lead to the development of the American-style Waltz. As more music was composed in these tempos, the Waltz grew still greater in popularity.

The latter part of the nineteenth century spawned a great wave of American patriotism as Teddy Roosevelt and his Roughriders stormed up the slopes of San Juan Hill during the Spanish-American War. At sea, Admiral George Dewey defeated the Spanish Pacific Fleet. During the 10-year period between 1890 and 1899, John Philip Sousa composed stirring marches that still have widespread appeal by today's standards.

The dance that evolved in the ballrooms across the United States from these patriotic and bold cadences is called the Two-Step. The Two-Step really had more to do with a marching cadence and timing than the flowing style of the Waltz. This dance is definitely the predecessor to the dances we now call the Foxtrot, Peabody, and Quickstep. As the Two-Step spread to the rural and agricultural communities, it quickly became suitable for less regimented styles now called Country and Western music. Hence, the 1890's Two-Step still enjoys great popularity today in its present form known as the Country Two-Step. Most significantly, the practice of following the European customs and culture began to fade, and the United States initiated a social art of its own.

Movement Memo

If you want to find out more about the American-style Waltz, you should read *Dancing Till Dawn: A Century of Exhibition Ballroom Dance,* by Julie Malnig (New York University Press, 1992).

The Waltz still continued to grow as the most popular dance of the day. Composers and lyricists produced music representing fashionable events of the gay 1890s. Expressions of love and sentimentality typified songs like "After the Ball," "The Sidewalks of New York," and "Daisy, Daisy," all written in $^3/_4$ timing. This tempo is now described as the Viennese Waltz. The gay 1890s were truly a great time for society music and dancing!

The Least You Need to Know

♦ The earliest forms of ballroom dancing were formation dances with all couples doing the same steps.

♦ Early dance technique, particularly the foot positions taught by dance masters, helped produce a foundation for ballet.

♦ The emergence of the middle class led to a freer interpretation of traditional court dances.

♦ Queen Elizabeth I and Queen Victoria were both great proponents of social dancing.

♦ The Waltz changed dancing forever.

Modern Ballroom Dancing Expressions: From 1900 to the Present

In This Chapter

- ◆ Creature dances to the Castles
- ◆ Dancing to the radio and phonograph
- ◆ Latin beat and rock 'n' roll
- ◆ Solo dancing to Disco's Hustle
- ◆ Reagan era to the present

The twentieth century brought great changes to the world. Socioeconomic barriers were being broken down or simply ignored, and as is typical in history, it was the youth of the culture spearheading the movement. And also typically, it was the elders of society who tried to rein them in. The result of this pushing and pulling is clearly demonstrated in the changes that took place in the world of ballroom dancing. In this chapter we will explore these changes and learn how we got to where we are today.

1900: The Creature Dances

Teddy Roosevelt became president of the United States in 1901, following the assassination of William McKinley. His energy was certainly reflected in the ragtime music of the day. Like the young president, the music was robust and full of life. Although most of society was still dancing Waltzes and Polkas, inspirations for dance fads or trends were emerging.

New dances at the turn of the century took the names of creatures, not unlike the 1960s when dances were known as winged and other creatures (for example, the Bird, the Monkey, the Fly, and the Pony). The Bunny Hop, the Turkey Trot, the Horse Trot, and the Kangaroo Dip were the dances the young people were doing. These dances allowed the man to show off his manliness by using perilous dance positions that could only be rescued by his strength. Of course the young lady would retire helplessly in his arms. In other words, young people were not necessarily retaining their vertical alignment on the dance floor. After all, George Bernard Shaw said it best, "Dancing is a vertical expression of a horizontal desire."

New Orleans seemed ordained to be the trend-setting capital of the United States. Broadway Theater in New York reflected this robust ragtime sound with the great melodies of George M. Cohan, like "The Yankee Doodle Boy," "You're a Grand Old Flag," and "Give My Regards to Broadway."

The Turkey Trot attracted the disapproval of the Vatican as couples began to dip at the ends of the room. The Grizzly Bear, another fad dance, eventually became known as the Texas Tommy. The Texas Tommy is the second dance discussed so far in this book that appears to be the forerunner for the aerial tricks of the Lindy Hop. (The first was the Lavolta, a favorite of Queen Elizabeth I, as explained in Chapter 1, "Past Ballroom Dancing Expressions: From the Renaissance to the Age of Reform.")

At an alarming rate, young women were losing their balance and control for the sake of doing the dance. They went along with this as an expression of their new cultural freedom, an experience traditionally enjoyed only by men. Meanwhile, dancing cheek to cheek became common as partner dancing continued to break down social barriers and initiate new benchmarks. While the Wright brothers were trying to fly, women were pursuing other avenues of freedom. The dance floor had become the place to move in the direction of social equality. Good, bad, or indifferent, men needed women to consummate the dance.

1910: The Castles

Everything strikes a balance, and so it was with dancing. The older members of society had simply seen too much too soon. Committees to protect and enforce the social decorum of the young were formed. As one of its duties, these committees were to report the goings-on in recreation centers and dance halls.

Because society had the power to cancel dancing events, someone had to establish an acceptable standard. Enter the era of the show dance couple. In the way that Babe Ruth saved baseball from the darkness the Chicago Black Sox created, Vernon and Irene Castle rescued ballroom dancing. They exemplified elegance, charm, sophistication, and brilliant talent. Vernon was a choreographic genius! For 20 years, until his untimely death in a plane crash, Vernon and Irene Castle ruled the world of ballroom dancing.

The Castles recognized how dance appeals to the broad base of society. Vernon studied dances like the Tango that had drawn fire from social conservatives as too provocative for public consumption. He produced what is known today as the ballroom Tango. A standard of elegance had been set by the Castles' tasteful portrayal of each dance. Responsibly, dancing came out of society's closet to assume a place of respectability. The trendy fad dances with names taken from the local zoos died down. The stylish presentation of the Castles's Tango and the Hesitation Waltz were welcome replacements. Everyone emulated them. Dancing greats Fred Astaire and Ginger Rogers later portrayed them in *The Story of Vernon and Irene Castle* on the movie screen in 1939.

In 1913 Harry Fox and Yanszieka Deutsch of the Ziegfeld Follies formed an exhibition team and slowed the pace of that ragtime music. This couple smoothed the stride of the marching cadence to develop what was destined to become the most popular ballroom dance of the twentieth century. Harry Fox lent his name to this dance, known then as Mr. Fox's Trot. Of course we now call that dance the Foxtrot. Music composers and publishers responded quickly. The old tunes were converted from $^3/_4$ increments to $^4/_4$ increments, and new tunes were penned with lightening speed. The hemlines rose an inch, and the unthinkable female display of ankles was now in vogue.

Argentina's Influence

Paris, the world's threshold to the Argentine Tango, expelled those same Argentineans who had been sent abroad to experience European culture and society in the finest schools. Argentina had aligned with Germany for economic reasons. Germany, for example, was Argentina's best customer for red meat. Argentina's isolation was a direct result of World War I and destined the Argentine Tango to develop in a vacuum apart from the influences of other dance forms.

A *renaissance* of the Argentine Tango has occurred in the past 10 years. This expressive, eccentric, and often dramatic dance has long been a theatrical favorite and has been depicted by numerous movie stars—from Rudolph Valentino to Arnold Schwarzenegger. And how could we ever forget actor Al Pacino in *Scent of a Woman?* But in recent years, there has been an increase of interest among the dance community and, as a result, the general public. For the first time, Tango Argentino (as it is referred to with a Spanish flavor) has actually become an active social dance in the United States. Argentine Tango classes are offered at many studios, and it has become a popular category in ballroom dance competitions. To find out more about the theatrical and social development of Argentine Tango, consult *Quickstart to Tango*, by Jeff Allen (QQS Publications, 1998).

Cuba's Influence

From the early post-colonial days, the United States had invested heavily in Cuba. The disastrous economic situation brought on by wartime destruction made land and labor cheap for American companies.

After the United States won the Spanish-American War in 1898, it granted Cuba independence in 1902 following four years of U.S. occupation. U.S. companies owned 75 percent of the sugar industry and 60 percent of Cuba's land. The wealthy Cuban elite grew richer, but the poor continued in poverty.

On January 16, 1920, the Volstead Act officially took effect in the United States. When the country went "dry," the tourist business in Cuba boomed. Havana, with its gorgeous beaches and tropical weather, became a popular destination for Europeans and Americans alike. The influences of Cuban music and dance were brought back to the United States and Europe. The Rumba was the first of these dances seen around 1913. The Bolero, Mambo, and the Cha-Cha followed. These dances were very adaptable to the dance floors of nightclubs, hotels, and resort environments. Most Americans found Latin American dances easier to learn than those fast-paced Waltzes and very energetic Swing dances.

As the popularity of the Mambo rose, there was fierce competition among the Mambo orchestras for audiences. These orchestras were continually trying to compose music that was bigger and better than the other guy's. Dancers became more proficient at the dance and were looking for more of a challenge on the dance floor. As a result, the tempo of the popular Mambos got faster and faster!

Dancing Definition

The general usage of the word **syncopation** in dancing has come to mean splitting the beat into two parts. In the case of the Cha-Cha, the forth beat of the measure is split into two even segments—the quarter beat is danced as two eighth beats. Musicians refer to this as shifting the accent from a stronger beat to a weaker one creating a new standard rhythm within the composition.

This was fine for the youngsters, but the older dancers found this pace a bit too much and rebelled. In response to the demand for a slower pace, Cuban and Mexican orchestras began to split or *syncopate* the fourth beat of music in what they called "Polite Mambo." The Latin percussion instruments made a certain sound when performing this syncopated or "split" beat. That sound was cha-cha-cha (musical counts 4 and 1), and the Cha-Cha was born. The dance retained its sensuality and the basic diamond-shaped form of the Mambo but was much more manageable for a wider audience of dancers.

1920s: The Radio and the Phonograph

While America may have been dry, women were exerting their rights and freedoms both socially and economically. The new dance called the Charleston, along with the Black Bottom, the Shimmy, and the Varsity Drag, stirred the ire of the clergy once again. The flicking knees both opened and closed were hardly considered ladylike. But the dance was exuberant with plenty of room for freedom and individual interpretation.

On March 26, 1926, the Savoy Ballroom opened its doors, and once again lifts and aerials returned to the dance floor. Swing dancing was far more athletic than any dance form to date. America searched for a name for this new dance. In 1927 Charles Lindbergh hopped across the Atlantic Ocean and supplied the image! The Lindy Hop was the perfect name for the rhythmic flying style of this new Swing dance.

In Chicago, Joe Oliver emerged as the "King of Jazz." His group included such notables as "Baby" Dodds on drums and Louis Armstrong on trumpet. They began to entertain both white and black audiences. Xavier Cugat formed a marvelous Latin American orchestra. Wayne King, who was crowned affectionately in America as "the Waltz King," whose preference was three-quarter timing and Guy Lombardo, whose music was considered "the sweetest music this side of heaven" became hugely popular in the hotels of New York City. All of these orchestras could be heard on the radio.

In addition, the newly invented phonograph and its flat heavy disks whirling around at 78 RPMs provided listeners and dancers with music according to their own taste whenever they wanted it. Now the most popular music would represent the most popular dance. Dancing could be criticized but could never again be influenced by the aristocracy, upper society, or the clergy.

America prospered in every area of its economy, entertainment, and sports. But a dark cloud loomed at the end of this decade. On Wednesday, October 30, 1929, the stock market crashed.

1930s: America Cuts a Rug

The repeal of the Volstead Act in 1933 started the liquor flowing again, but the venues for dancing were closing all over America. Americans still needed forms of recreation and enjoyment. They wanted to turn their minds away from the bitter times they had to endure. The radio turned out to be a cheap form of entertainment. People danced at home in their living rooms and parlors. American vocabulary coined a new phrase: "cutting a rug." People entertained at home and enjoyed the new jazz rhythms filtering across the United States. Swing flourished, and the young Jewish musician Benny Goodman was crowned its king!

Ballroom Bloopers _____

Just because you see it in the movies doesn't mean you can do it! Please remember that aerials and acrobatic dance tricks, which involve the female partner leaving the surface of the dance floor to elevations higher than her partner's head, are very dangerous. Careful and controlled practice is required to perform these movements. Although these tricks are quite popular among Lindy Hop competitors today, they should never be attempted by the inexperienced on the social dance floor or at a nightclub. This is particularly true if alcohol has been consumed. When these tricks are practiced, spotters should be available and padded surfaces used at all times to prevent injuries. Permission from the venue's management should be requested and granted before such tricks are executed to limit liability and prevent injury or even death.

During the depression, the movies were an inexpensive and welcome diversion. For dancers, none better than Fred Astaire and Ginger Rogers graced the screen. The public clamored to emulate their idols on the dance floor. Fred Astaire was a notorious perfectionist. Typically, Fred spent six months of perfect, repetitive practice to meet his own standards before filming his choreography. Needless to say, making it look easy does not mean it *is* easy!

From the glamour of Fred and Ginger to the darkness of the depression, we find the unseemly side of dancing: the dance marathon. Enduring to the end, the last man standing—or in this case, the last couple dancing—was the simple goal of the dance marathon. Dancers literally died for a chance to cash in on the prize.

> **Bet You Didn't Know**
>
> In 1969 director Sydney Pollack made the film adaptation of Horace McCoy's novel, *They Shoot Horses, Don't They?* This film more than adequately depicts human degradation and humiliation. These conditions were the outgrowth of the dance marathon during the depression.

1940s: The Latin Beat and World War II

The Great Depression of 1929 had all but subsided by 1939. The nation was on the road to recovery and economic prosperity. Toward the end of the depression, New York held the World's Fair. Someone must have alerted Hollywood that something very special was going on at the Brazilian exposition. It was called the Samba.

Earlier in the 1930s, Fred Astaire and Ginger Rogers started collaborating on the motion picture *Flying Down to Rio*. This movie depicts the Samba and Tango. Carmen Miranda and several notable leading men danced the Samba into the hearts of America. The music and the notion of the "Latin lover" or "heartthrob" reinforced America's love for Latin American music.

The war, which began across the Atlantic in 1939, made its way to the shores of America on December 7, 1941, when Japan attacked Pearl Harbor. Uncle Sam put out the call "I want you." World War II had begun. American men by the countless thousands joined the armed forces to protect their liberties. Once again the hemline on skirts began to rise!

On the American music scene, one person embodied all that was fashion, music, and slang. Cab Calloway was a pure entertainer. As he asked his orchestra, "You all Reet?" they responded, "Yes, we're all Reet!" Turning to the audience, he asked, "Hey now hey now, are you hep to the Jive?" Cab may not have created the zoot suit or the big fedora, but he sure took the show on the road. As a result of all that jargon, Cab was known as "The Professor of Jive." The Swing culture was born!

The American GIs brought the exuberance of Swing, Jitterbug, and Jive to the European war theater. The nuances of the American Foxtrot and the beginnings of Latin American dancing also jumped aboard and made the trip across the Atlantic. Once again the European dance masters took some offense to the unstructured style of the American dancer.

British dance instructors did their homework in interpreting these dances. They produced what would be called the standard or international technique. Following awkward, confusing footprints had outlived its usefulness. British instructors contributed standardization of technique and consistency of choreography to the world of dance.

1950s: The Rock and Roll Invasion

The 1950s had more to do with the music than with dancing. The music was called rock 'n' roll. The various adaptations of Swing dancing fell into the category of the Jitterbug. American youth sought it out, at times defiantly, to express themselves. Rock 'n' roll music highlighted the need for racial equality in the United States. White artists and black artists sang the same music while the dancers of either color responded. As usual, the social and political scene was critical. The 1960s were destined to be tumultuous.

Notable exceptions were the dances called the Mambo and the Cha-Cha. During the 1950s and into the 1960s, the Mambo and Cha-Cha (its slower syncopated version) were among the most popular dance rhythms in the world. In 1957 Jerome Robbins brought his smash hit, *West Side Story*, to Broadway. The show was released as a film in 1961, reaching a very broad-based audience. This twentieth-century version of Shakespeare's *Romeo and Juliet* was set against the backdrop of New York City. The story portrayed the struggle between the newer Puerto Rican community and the more established immigrant community in the streets of the west side. The show included a theatrical version of the Mambo. This promoted the growth of Latin American dancing throughout the United States. Later on in the 1970s, we will highlight the Hispanic community's contribution to the American dance scene.

1960s: Solo Dancing

A yearning for personal expression turned into solo dancing in the 1960s. A new dance called "the Twist" took the world by storm. Ballroom dancers of the 1940s asked themselves if this marked the end of touch dancing. Once again in dance history, a trend or fad rose to prominence.

Singer-songwriter Wilson Pickett described it best in his recording "The Land of a Thousand Dances." Every week a new dance appeared named for a bird, insect, beast, tribal warrior, food type, or anything at all, including names that defied description. The unrest of the 1960s is well documented. America endured the assassination of President John F. Kennedy and Dr. Martin Luther King Jr. Through the latter half of the decade, we had the socially and politically unpopular Vietnam War. By the time we got to Woodstock, ballroom dancing was something only your grandparents did!

> **Bet You Didn't Know**
>
> The dance craze of the early 1960s, "the Twist," was the first partner dance in which no one touched each other! Even during the early development of dance, partners touched each other—if only with a gloved hand. But the wild and crazy 1960s brought a new focus on personal expression and "doing your own thing." As is typical throughout history, dance reflected the prevailing social environment, and "free-style dancing" became the rage. Luckily, there were enough proponents of "touch dancing" to keep the concept active, though out of the mainstream.

1970s: Disco and the Hustle

Through the 1970s the Hispanic community of New York grew tremendously. The youth struggled to belong. Something exciting was happening within their culture. The Latin American dances of the 1940s, 1950s, and 1960s were termed "classical Latin dances." The youth wanted to be part of New York's nightclub scene, not do their grandparents' dances. With the heavy influence of jazz music and the repetition of computerized percussion, a new music was on the horizon. They called this music Disco. Somehow Mambo and Cha-Cha did not quite fit.

The American Hustle was the first form of the Disco dance. However, this version was admittedly boring, and Latin club-goers added their own flavor to this Disco sound. The sensual hip action indigenous to the Bosa Nova and Rumba plus the repetitive eight-count movement of Merengue were soon added to the dance.

This dance, the Latin Hustle, was in vogue for about six months to a year. Through it, the Hispanic community experienced the challenge of restrictive floor space in New York style discos. The Puerto Rican sound is still the music of choice by the Hispanic community. Mexicans and Colombians also flocked to New York City, adding to the Hispanic culture of this cosmopolitan environment. Each had their cultural dance influences.

Adding the flavors of Mexico, Columbia, Cuba, and Puerto Rico, a new sauce was in the making. The music and the dance called Salsa is a blending of many herbs and spices. Salsa is primarily Mambo with spatial restrictions. Elements of Cumbia from Columbia and cucaracha, a Mexican side-breaking action (*cucaracha* means "cockroach"), added to the sauce of Salsa.

> **Bet You Didn't Know**
>
> Although Disco music had a short-lived popularity on the music charts, the music and the resulting part-ner dance—the Hustle—found a permanent home among ballroom dancers. While Disco may not be your choice for listening music, it remains an outstanding source of dance music. The "boom boom boom" of the bass is easily heard and identifiable. In fact, this same bass line is found in many of the songs re-leased in the last four or five years. It is no wonder that the Hustle has experienced and great resurgence and is being enjoyed by a whole new generation of dancers! Broadway has actually re-created its version of the movie *Saturday Night Fever* and is touring the United States as of the writing of this book.

The final evolution of the Hustle was called the New York Hustle or three-count Hustle. The Latin Hustle included elements of the older dance the West Coast Swing. These characteristics included a slotted action with many underarm turns. The Disco music increased in tempo and the dance added syncopation.

1980s: The Reagan Era

Ronald Reagan was the fortieth president of the United States. He and his wife Nancy brought both conservatism and elegance to the White House. The President was an advocate, sponsor, and friend to ballroom dancing. Reagan proclaimed the third week of September as National Ballroom Week.

The 1980s suffered the consequences of the promiscuity of the 1970s. Two dangerous social diseases, herpes and HIV-AIDS, came to the fore with heightened consciousness. By comparison to the 1970s, human relationships slowed to a snail's pace. People were now taking precautions in their sexual activities as never before. They wanted time to get to know each other before engaging in sexual relationships.

The political and social atmosphere was conservative by former standards. The slowdown in physical relationships led couples to seek alternative ways to express physical contact and enjoyment. Ballroom dancing has been and always will be the means to do that. Dancing together is the best way to create chemistry between two people.

1990s to the Present

A proliferation of ballroom dancing, Swing dancing, Tango, and Latin dancing has marked the end of the twentieth century and the beginning of the twenty-first. Virtually every college campus in the United States is forming ballroom dance clubs and competitive ballroom dance teams. The complement of these dances will be the continuing conversation in this text.

The Least You Need to Know

- Partner dancing helped promote social and sexual equality.
- Tourists brought Latin music and dance rhythms back to America.
- After entertaining at home during the depression, America returned to the ballrooms to Swing!
- The dichotomy of the 1960s revealed itself on the dance floor.
- The experimental 1970s resulted in the more conservative 1980s, and once again, partner dancing became a great way to "get to know someone."

Chapter 3

What Makes Us Dance

In This Chapter

♦ The birds and the bees have it easy!

♦ Exactly what does separate us from the animals?

♦ Turn up the volume!

♦ Ahhh—that human touch

It often appears that dancing has been a part of the human experience forever! Artifacts found in archeological digs, drawings on the walls of caves, and ancient manuscripts all contain at least some small reference to or depiction of dancing. But what makes us dance? What is it that inspires human beings to rhythmically move their bodies in response to some internal or external stimulus? While a thorough exploration of this topic could fill volumes, in this chapter we will explore three of the reasons we dance: to initiate the mating process, to fulfill our need for human intimacy and contact, and to express art.

As you move through this chapter, please bear in mind that when I mention "mating" or "mating ritual" of human beings, I am using this terminology in the broadest possible context. I am not assuming procreation or sexual intercourse as the ultimate result of dancing! I am using these terms to express a greater level of intimacy—which may simply be a smile and a "thank you" when the dance has ended. Let us look at why we dance.

Mysterious Instinctual Desire

When I was a kid I used to watch Marlin Perkins and his TV show *Wild Kingdom*. In grade school and junior high school we welcomed the feature films from the National Geographic Society in place of class time. We learned that there were common threads that tied races of people together regardless of their level of cultural development and education by Western standards. Animals, too, seemed to share one of these common threads. That common thread—no matter where, no matter when, they all danced! Let's explore why.

Yes, Survival

Survival is the most important primal instinct. Very simply, if we do not mate, the species will be extinct within one or two generations. This fact remains the same for all living creatures on the planet. Biologically, all members of the animal kingdom have a physiological device that triggers when mating is most appropriate. In addition, our five basic senses—seeing, hearing, smelling, tasting, and of course, touching—are always active.

Clocks and Calendars

The five senses help us to make choices and are always operating. We like what we see, we like what we hear, we do not like the taste of that, and so on. At times on the internal male and female calendar and clock, these senses heighten or signal greater alert. During this alert, our hormones are on active duty, and sensory stimulation may trigger those physiological devices. Given the green light, mating and its related ritual may begin.

> **Bet You Didn't Know**
>
> Balance and timing govern our personal survival instincts. Our brain continually searches for the physical security known as balance. This continual monitoring supervises the patterns developed during the course of events in our lives. These patterns are the timing of our lives. The instinct to survive causes the human race to instinctually search for, set up, and follow the conditions for mating. The individual's personal security is a prerequisite to allow for this. You should not be surprised that balance and timing are the two most important elements in dancing!

Compared to humans, the creatures of our planet have it easy! As long as a female and a male of the species are around when that biological clock sounds the alarm, mating season begins. The female always knows when it is time to mate. She sends out an invitation. Each of the species is specifically attracted to that physiological message. Those messages are transported to entice the senses generally by sound or by fragrance. The guest list is nonspecific. If you are a male, you are invited! Regardless of his appearance, each male has an equal chance. When the boys show up, the competition begins. Depending on the species, some of the boys share similar time clocks as their female counterparts. They dress for the party by changing their feathers or their fur.

Boys Will Be Boys

All the boys seem to be in a good mood when they arrive. They come curious about their hostess and excited about the challenge. Stalking about, they initiate confrontation by checking out the competition. They howl; they beat their chests; some of them even begin to perform. These boys can prance about to impress their prospective mates. Others bear gifts. Freshly killed meat may be used to demonstrate what a good provider they would be.

This solo parading around often becomes combative. When this happens, the most physically powerful or the most durable of the boys will win his lady's favor. Sometimes the most intelligent or resilient, the one that knows how to get up and fight again will emerge as the winner. Regardless of the technique or ritual, one of the guys is going to get lucky, and the result will be new offspring.

Different yet the Same

A human analogy to what I have described plays itself out in any roadhouse café or bar in the country or city. Some gentlemen will wear gallant attire and others will not concern themselves with their appearance. Some men will flash a bankroll while others will flex their muscles. A ridiculous recent TV commercial showed a foolish man in the restroom practicing his come-on lines while strutting his stuff! Although somewhat effective, females usually regard this as the seedier side of courting.

Yes, we often attempt mating by instinct just like the animals, but success requires more on the human level. Human beings have emotions, intelligence, and reason. This combination makes the selection and attraction of a mate much more difficult. I believe the word to use here is "refinement." Refining our instincts, emotions, and senses helps us to be more discerning when selecting a person for mating and companionship. This refinement is also a matter of trial and error.

The Stage Is Set

The designers of successful nightclubs must know how to create an ambience that heightens the senses and at the same time helps to break down the barriers between men and women. The selection process often begins by watching someone dance in this atmosphere. The music and lighting excites the senses and provokes the imagination. Actually, the same scenario exists at high school dances; ballrooms across the country; and social dances sponsored by dance studios or DJs familiar with ballroom, Latin, and swing music.

As we watch, we begin to imagine what that person would feel like in our arms. On the other hand, we may just know we would never want to touch a certain person. Animals do not have imagination and, therefore, do not need their emotions or intellect nurtured. Humans do! One thing is certain; the mix of music and dancing provokes the instincts to begin the human mating process.

Why Men Dance

As part of my research for this book, I called my 26-year-old son and said "Josh, I need you to answer this question spontaneously." "Okay," he replied. "Why do you dance?" Without hesitation his answer was simple: "Women!" Uniformly whatever surveys I have read or situations I have observed as a dance instructor, the overwhelming evidence is clear that men dance because of women. Men dance with women as a response to social obligation or as the first step in the selection process of the mating ritual. To a lesser degree, men will dance to experience romance and express artistic qualities of dance.

Bet You Didn't Know

Comedienne Joan Rivers once told a story about a group of women planning to attend a dance party. They mentioned three of four male names whom they all knew. Another female simply said, "Didn't you hear Harry died last week?" To which Joan responded, "Bring him anyway. We will prop him up!" Although I cannot verify where I got this number, I believe there are 70 women waiting for one man who knows how to dance. You may go to a party where there are three women to every one man; the other 67 have simply given up!

Earlier in my dance career, my professional dance partner and I performed at a large local nightclub. The public relations manager of that nightclub asked me to contribute some ideas for increasing the number of patrons on Wednesday nights. After banging our heads together for a few hours, we kept returning to the concept of a ladies night and a plan emerged. Ladies would receive a red rose at the door, a welcome gift of sorts, and would not be charged admission. It would be up to my partner and me to perform a different show each Wednesday and then teach a free lesson after the performance. The dance lesson was for beginners and carried the same theme or characteristic as our dance performance. Once this scenario hit the radio waves, the population at the club swelled. Before Ladies Night, the average on a Wednesday night was 70 to 90 patrons and no one paid a cover charge. Within a short period, the count went up to 700 to 900! The results were remarkable. Despite the $5 cover charge for the men, a steep price for that time on Wednesday night, 25 percent more men than women came to dance! My contract was extended for 2¹/₂ years.

Good Dancing Will Get the Girl

Envy, resentment, and even mild hostility always lurked around me when performing or after a show when I was dancing with one of several partners. One night a stranger proceeded to tell me that I was not very popular with many of the guys in the club. They were tired of hearing from the women, "Look at that guy dance," "Will he dance with me?" etc. He also said, "But to be honest, when you're dancing we are living vicariously through you." My embarrassed response was, "Thank you, I think." As I continued my conversation with the stranger, I explained that I thought women were more attracted to good dancing than just the dancer. Good dancing was not an accident. Good dancing was a matter of training, time, and energy. I discovered long ago that every dance class I ever attended included many attractive women. No matter what type of dance form we were studying, more often than not I accompanied an attractive woman. In college, I originally studied ballet because while waiting for a study companion to finish her ballet class, I observed the class. Not only did I see beautiful girls, I saw that dancing amplified the beauty of every woman in the class. The decision to attend with great frequency was easy!

I learned four lessons at those classes:

1. Women love to dance.
2. Women love men who can dance because they are so scarce. The numbers always favored the men.
3. Not only did I learn how to dance with women, I also learned how to communicate with women through dance.
4. And most important, women appreciate men who join them in the study and sharing of an art form that they love.

The stranger thanked me for my willingness to share this information with him and assured me that he would join us next week for the dance classes. The same man continued to study partner dancing and many years later danced with competency and enjoyed the company of many women!

You Can Lead a Horse to Water, but You Can't Make Him Drink

At the club, the music format was essentially "oldies," which meant plenty of Rumbas, Cha-Chas, Mambos, Jitterbugs, and even a few Foxtrots. A small percentage of the patrons occupied the dance floor—essentially only those who had studied these various ballroom dances. When a slow song was played, everyone else who could not dance did the Penguin Shuffle! Of course, girls always danced with girls and the guys leaned on bar rails watching, frozen in their shoes.

Many attractive women danced, but the men were overwhelmed and speechless when these women left the dance floor. The potential for ridicule was there. Perhaps they were told at one time they had no rhythm or could not dance. That fear may even have kept them from attending a dance class. These men had not learned yet that the better way to "break the ice" was ballroom dancing!

> **Bet You Didn't Know**
>
> A man can easily be overwhelmed by the presence of a beautiful woman. He can actually lose his ability to become conversant and coherent. Dancing is a physical skill. When practiced, the outcome will be predictable, as if directed by the music itself. Good muscle memory, not intellect, ensures this! Once the body begins to sense balance and poise, the man may come to his senses and begin to converse intelligently and effectively.

He Can't Dance, Has No Rhythm—Ridiculous

Although rhythm is often thought of in the context of dance or music, rhythm is really a measured physical response. My definition of rhythm is simple: the ability to consistently repeat a familiar or acquired skill. Any regular sequence of muscle contraction and extension that recurs while completing a skill is rhythm. Consider simple tasks like brushing your teeth, going up the stairs, or even signing your name. These are examples of physical skills done essentially the same way each time. Sometimes you rush to do them. Other times you do them at a more leisurely pace. Sometimes you stop all together and resume the tasks later. The variation of your timing has no bearing on your ability to complete the recurring skill!

Do you really believe that someone who is athletically inclined and participates in sports as a novice, amateur, or professional—in competition or simply for recreation—has no rhythm? Of course not! Learning the skills, practicing the skills, then using the skills in real-time situations are what it takes to participate in the game!

Think about yourself for a moment. Every physical skill you now take for granted, you had to learn. If the skill was popular and accompanied by strong peer pressure for acceptance, you worked harder to master the skill. At first, you probably failed frequently, but you got up and tried again. Learning to social dance is just like that.

The physical skill required most for ballroom dancing can actually be pinpointed in the human anatomy. The ability to use the upper leg muscles is key. This is the region of the leg controlled by the knee and the ball socket joint at the hip. Therefore, if you can ascend or descend a staircase, ride a bicycle, or swim, nothing should prevent you from learning to dance. You will need a good beginning, a good teacher, and frequent repetition. With *The Complete Idiot's Guide to Ballroom Dancing*, you have a good beginning. So gentlemen, whether you are looking for a committed relationship, a casual one, or some intimate physical conversation, the path known as ballroom dancing is a great shortcut!

> **⚠ CAUTION**
>
> **Ballroom Bloopers**
>
> Suggesting that someone has no rhythm is never wise! This just serves to belittle and discourage that person from learning to dance. Many individuals who have experienced such ridicule cannot specifically recall when this took place, but the result is in their subconscious. Though the memory is clouded, their lack of participation in social dancing remains the same. Dancing with a partner and learning how to partner is an acquired skill. Remember, although undeniably enjoyable, moving with someone physically attached to you is not natural.

Why Women Dance

When I asked my wife why she danced, she looked at me with a quizzical expression. So I asked again, and she responded as if it was a silly question, "Because of the music!" This response was not a blow to my ego; in fact, it was perfect. Women often respond to music with rhythmic movements and feelings of romance. Images include being held in the arms of an often faceless lover. Dancing can outwardly express a woman's imagination about things like courting and lovemaking. Dancing may be a means for women to express art and decorate life.

The rhythmic impulses of music reveal themselves through the body as an almost instinctive invitation to celebrate life, love, and finally mating. Music seems to bring into recall past pleasurable events for women that they may desire to repeat. Dancing allows them to recount the story using hand gestures and body movements. This musical interpretation has actually become an art form in China, the Hawaiian Islands, India, and many other lands throughout the world.

If Music Be the Food of Love ... Play On

While listening to music, your heart is beating, blood is circulating throughout your body, and you are breathing (hopefully). The style, volume, and rhythm of the music have the ability to heighten the sympathetic actions. When this happens there is a greater need to express muscular activity. A finger starts snapping and your toes start tapping. Your muscles become restless and you experience the need to get up and start moving. This is the same for both sexes. The storytelling and the need to be romanced separate the reactions of women and men while listening to music. For a woman, dancing seems to be a method of filling in the blanks between the sound of music and the act of mating.

Women need much more information about a prospective lover than do men. Dancing provides a woman with a physical, social, psychological, and cultural overview of a man. Questions are answered about her feelings of security in a man's arms. Is he sincere, attentive, and courteous to her? To move with another person requires patience and forgiveness. These traits are necessary in oneself as well as the partner. A woman evaluates this fact, even if subconsciously, while she dances with a man. Lastly, does he move well? The woman will learn much from the man's body language. His body language is not only important when he dances with her but also when she observes him dancing with other women. If it were not for the social pressure imposed on men by women, most men would be happy to ignore things like romance and dancing. Thank goodness women will not allow men to miss out on this very important part of the mating ritual.

Desire and Romance

Mankind has found that the next best things to the physical act of making love are the expressions of desire and romance found in dancing. A woman's desire to dance with the man is really a form of invitation. She is asking him to join her on the dance floor in this romantic expression of art. Ballroom dancing brings people into close proximity. In order for a couple to move together, both a physical and intellectual commitment must be made. While the gentleman is evaluating his partner physically, the lady has begun an overall evaluation. If chemistry exists during this intermediate stage of physical conversation, then chances are very good that a relationship including the sexual conversation will be more enduring.

Deepening Relationships with Dance

Both new and established relationships need nurturing to grow and to maintain their vitality. When a couple has the ability to dance, their social calendar will never again be empty. Dating or married couples will no longer have an empty look when their partner asks the $64,000 question, "What would you like to do tonight?" To which the response is generally, "I don't know. What would you like to do tonight?"

Turning down invitations to important social events, fundraisers, family get-togethers and, of course, weddings, will no longer be necessary. The fear of being asked or required to dance will no longer exist. The holiday season filled with Christmas parties climaxing with New Year's Eve will take on a greater air of excitement. The sheer romance of dining and dancing will replace the movie theater or staying at home to watch videos or DVDs. Where a night out was formally noncommunicative, genuine excitement and very pleasant exercise can now fill it!

Approaching Social and Physical Equality

Activities that present an opportunity for social and physical equality are few and far between. However, by reading this book, you will discover that ballroom dancing is just such an activity. The reality is you cannot Ballroom, Latin, Swing, and Tango without your partner. Partner dancing needs a partner!

The dance couple becomes powerful on the social dance floor, not just the individual. Unfortunately, usually only one or two couples out of hundreds are remembered at the conclusion of a social occasion. You have overheard this before: "They move together as if joined at the hip," "They glided across the floor effortlessly," "They looked as if they had been dancing forever, so natural and graceful." You may have even uttered those phrases yourself!

The couple is an entity that demonstrates its own personality and playfulness in a way that cannot be duplicated by a solo dancer. Dancing gives couples the opportunity to exhibit genuine feelings of love and affection for each other. Everything that is correct and desirable in a marriage or relationship exists on the ballroom dance floor. The partners complete each other in their response to the music. These comments are not exaggerations. My goal is to help you apply them to you!

Another wonderful aspect of ballroom dancing allows our physical strengths to complement each other. The physical commitment to each other is unlike anything else. The dance couple does not leverage strength from each other, but rather the individuals contribute to the strength of the couple. Due to the innate strength and differences between a man and a woman, we do very few sports or physical activities on an equal plane.

While bowling, playing a round of golf, or tennis together is nice; rarely do a man and woman compete at the same level. One partner or the other often complains that he hits the ball too hard or too far while she does not hit hard enough—"You're always walking ahead of me," "Try to keep up." The difference generally lies in the strength factor. With ballroom dancing, we need only our intrinsic strength to support ourselves. Leading and following in the dance is spatial reciprocity rather than physical strength. Each partner is responsible for carrying his or her own weight. The result is the wonderful entity known as a dance couple. Such response and interactivity can only make a happy couple happier and a strong relationship stronger.

> **Movement Memo**
>
> The skills of cooperation, kindness, patience, and forgiveness are vital while dancing together and learning to dance. Two egos are involved in this process as well as two opinions and two levels of physical capability. Thus, I do not recommend that a couple experiencing personal difficulties begin learning to dance, although it may seem like a good idea at first.

A New Type of Foreplay

An evening of ballroom dancing can excite every aspect of the human condition. Through dance, we can play out human fantasy on a public dance floor that will pass the test of public scrutiny. Holding and touching each other in response to music can bring the desire to make love to new levels. Small gestures, not directly part of the dance but still resulting from it, further enhance the moment. Leaning on each other while exiting the dance floor, walking arm in arm, gently wiping the sweat from your partner's brow, or a kiss on the hand or cheek to say thank you, bring additional intimacy to the couple. These acts of chivalry and common social courtesies take on a special meaning.

Here is a list of courtesies compiled by a gentleman who was married for 56 years and had spent 40 of them ballroom dancing. They will assist you in your journey around the dance floor.

Courtesy on the dance floor:

1. Do not criticize your dance partner.
2. All rules of courtesy apply on the dance floor—respect, trust, cooperation, and politeness.
3. Smile. Every aspect of the dance contributes to your relationship with your dance partner.
4. When dancing, you are not going anywhere, but you have to be on time.
5. If you get in trouble with your partner, see courtesy No. 1.

The Least You Need to Know

- We are not alone: Dancing is enjoyed by every species.
- Men and women may start dancing for different reasons, but mostly to enjoy each other.
- Believe it or not … you do have rhythm!
- Little else provides the common pleasure we share with each other during the dance.

Chapter 4

Dancing Through Your Big Day

In This Chapter

- ◆ Plan ahead
- ◆ Dance to the music
- ◆ Keep it simple—make it beautiful
- ◆ Everybody dance now

Virtually everyone goes to a wedding at least once a year—as evidenced by the number of calls any ballroom dance studio receives on Monday morning. There are two types of callers. The first will be the couple engaged to be married, with their date set. Over the weekend, they suffered a panic attack at their friends' wedding. The couple knows that without help, the first dance holds more potential for disaster and glory. Callers of the first type have determined that the first dance will be a source of pride rather than embarrassment at their wedding.

The second type of callers will be those who attended a wedding and became enamored with the memory of that magical "one couple" that danced the night away. Callers number two have resolved to become unglued from their chairs when the dance floor harkens.

The Magic of the First Dance

Your "first dance" should be memorable and emotionally touching. Historically, the first dance is symbolic of the consummation of the wedding vows and marks your first cooperative engagement and joint endeavor. When the bride accepts her dance with the groom, she accepts him for the rest of her life. The frame and posture of the groom when he proposes the dance to the bride speak of the source of strength, love, companionship, and guidance he offers his bride. It is no wonder that the tradition of the first dance has continued throughout history as one of the most important facets of the wedding day.

Highlight or Low Light

Many weddings do not have a good plan for the first dance during the reception. Consequently, what should be a very beautiful time often crumbles into a haphazard, silly, ineffective, and boring affair that brings the wedding reception to an embarrassing standstill. The bride and groom are haunted by the memory for decades to come. Unfortunately, they often have the wedding video as photographic evidence.

To avoid wedding dance purgatory, you must first learn to dance. Take lessons, study this book or a video, but do not go out there with your partner unprepared. For many, a wedding represents the largest single financial and emotional investment of their life. The bride and groom are unquestionably the stars of the production. This is not the time to just rock back and forth in a huddled mass like monkeys seeking shelter from the rain!

Movement Memo

Plan to prepare for your first dance several months in advance of your special day. Take the opportunity to dance out in public at a club, cruise, or perhaps someone else's wedding reception as often as possible before your big day. Get used to dancing with one another in front of others. This will help immensely in reducing the pressure or nervousness you will experience on your wedding day.

When we are talking lights, camera, and hopefully some action, it is show time! No distracting or dim lighting to afford lovers or "wannabes" moments of intimacy during a love ballad. Not a professional show, but a few minutes of simple concentrated rehearsed action that in and of itself demonstrates the affections of the newlyweds and their ability to cooperate with one another. As the stars of the show, the first dance is like the opening production number on Broadway. The first dance is crucial for setting the tone of all that ensues.

The Penguin Shuffle

The penguin has often been thought of as a waterfowl that appears ready for a formal occasion. Its black and white feathers look like a tuxedo. The characteristic movement of the penguin is waddling awkwardly from side to side from the top of their body. The formally attired wedding couple that rocks side to side is not far from the appearance of two very cold penguins! We have all been bored by this rocking style; I have seen guests even turn away from this monotony and begin chitchatting. No respect—"Oh no, not five minutes of this again." After about one minute of being center stage, the bride and groom start to get that pained, "I can't wait for this to be over look," having realized they are in front of 200 people in a well-lit environment. A forced grin—"We should have done something and now it's too late."

By contrast, in working with this text, you prepare for your first dance. Expect an enthusiastic greeting. The guests know something is different as soon as the groom regally escorts his new bride out to the dance floor and presents her to all present. At the weddings that I have attended or from the reports by the attendees, all were standing and cheering by the conclusion of the bride and groom's first dance. The feeling in the room is magical as many stand applauding with tears of joy in their eyes! This memory becomes unforgettable.

The Perfect Song

Picking the perfect song is no easy chore. Let me tell you why. When considering the selection of the song for the first dance at their wedding, a couple needs to consider two factors: *mold ability* and *danceability*. Mold ability reflects the musical and emotional photograph a song imprints upon your mind. Your song's lyrics should express special meanings of all your hopes and dreams, particularly on your wedding day. Some couples have a song that unalterably reminds them of that special person. Many do not.

The danceability of any given piece of music is dependent upon the rhythm or tempo, which is measured by *bars per minute* (BPM). Specific dances have unique characteristics and are tied to a music's tempo and rhythm. For example, the Waltz and the Foxtrot shown in this book will fall in the range of 28 to 32 BPM. Moreover, in my experience, couples find the slower the tempo, the more difficult to dance. Think in terms of the difference between running on a track or through mud.

Movement Memo

The Wedding Dance Music List at www.QuickstartBooks.com is a comprehensive and up-to-date listing of the most popular music for the wedding dance scenario. The wedding dance music list includes more than 500 songs for your first dance. Also included are selections for the father-daughter dance, mother-son dance, and any other relatives. Each title is listed alphabetically followed by the artist, BPM, album title, and most important, the dance type that best suits the song.

When asked as the dance instructor and educator my preference for dance tempo, I direct a couple toward the Waltz or Foxtrot. By the way, many people think the act of dancing slowly with a partner means they are "Waltzing, together. Waltz music must be present for the Waltz to be taking place. These two dances offer long- and short-term benefits. Both the Waltz and Foxtrot lend themselves to choreography that can look highly polished in a compressed timeframe. Therefore, you can give a strong performance at your wedding. Second, the Waltz or Foxtrot affords you the opportunity to dance with a broader spectrum of people over a wider range of time in circumstances ranging from fundraisers to anniversaries to corporate dinners. These two dances also help you narrow down the musical selections to a more manageable level. Overall you learn a valuable life skill instead of learning something just for your milestone date.

Bet You Didn't Know

The *Waltz* and the idiomatic expression *waltzing* are very different. Waltz music is written in three-quarter time and is the dance that is presented in this book. "Waltzing" is a term that many use to describe slow dancing to a romantic ballad.

Now after giving you my advice about the use of a generic dance, I want you to know that I would never suggest that you change your favorite song even if it happens to be a slow rhythm ballad. When your song is a slow rhythm ballad, which means it is less than 26 BPM, you will have to dance slowly to it. I have developed a curriculum for slow dancing that uses ballroom dance figures adapted for this type of dancing. That curriculum is presented in both booklet and video format and is called *The Complete Guide to Slow Dancing*. Please refer to the website www.quickstartbooks.com.

Movement Memo

As part of the wedding dance scenario, both of you dance with a parent or surrogate. This dance partner will be 20 or more years older than either of you. Parents are someone you love, but they are not love interests! When you dance with an individual who is not a romantic interest, the comfort level is best with a generic dance like Waltz or Foxtrot. The standardized closed dance frame is preferable to a romantic dance position.

How Soon Is Soon Enough?

Successful dance couples, like good marriages, require cooperation, commitment, patience, and forgiveness. These attributes must be found in both partners. I am always amazed at how much of a student's true personality is revealed in the process. I have always recommended that any couple embarking on a serious relationship take dance lessons. It exposes chinks in any armor!

Preparation (i.e., lessons) for the first dance should begin six months in advance. This schedule allows plenty of time to learn and practice choreography. It also means that in the weeks leading up to the wedding, the first dance will not be a source of anxiety but confidence.

Is There Any Hope for Me?

Many people hate dancing (or at least vocalize that belief, especially to wives, fiancées, and girlfriends). Dance-haters tend to fall into two categories. The first category is ignorance-based. These people do not know how to dance. Their left-brain-dominant wiring tells them that shame follows exposure of underdeveloped skill on the dance floor and helps create a nightmare that features an ego shattering like Humpty Dumpty.

Movement Memo

Always bring your music with you. Whether it is in your car, at the dance studio, or practice space, you should become familiar with every word and every note. Once you have established the correct dance rhythm, I suggest that you find other music that matches this rhythm. The reason for this is simple: No matter how good your song, you can become tired of it.

The second category is fear-based and offers a demonstration of the Pavlovian theory of negative reinforcement. These people have a negative dance experience in their past. It's kind of like a kid who is sick with the flu, eats a banana, throws up, and is forever nauseous at the sight, smell, or mention of bananas. The bananas take the blame without just cause. The desire to dance is part of the human condition, and powerful psychological forces must come into play to suppress that desire.

In either scenario, knowledge is the key! Learn to dance and keep it simple. Beginners should restrict the wedding dance routines to five or six figures. Knowledge always eases the burden of fear in ignorance. Even four left feet can handle five figures without incident. At the end of either the Foxtrot or Waltz section of this book, you learn a routine that suits your wedding dance.

Learning Curves Are Unique

Leading is more difficult and comes with greater responsibilities than following. Therefore the leader is likely to have a slower learning curve than the follower. Mr. Groom, I want you to learn your part and be able to dance it by yourself. I do not want you to depend on your bride for your choreography. That would be like looking at the passenger while you're driving—it is simply not a good idea! Practice all alone so that no one has to watch.

It is incumbent upon the follower to prepare well in the area of body flight, or carriage of the torso. An inexperienced driver will always be safer and exhibit much better control in a Lincoln or a Cadillac than that of a jalopy—the suspension system is all-important!

Give the Guy an Even Break

All too often women have actually intimidated men with these statements: "I can follow anyone with a strong lead!" or "I already know how to dance—he needs the lessons!" I personally feel that it is *not* a natural or innate experience to move well with someone attached to you, and therefore everyone needs lessons to partner each other.

In Part 2, "Before Your Ball," pay particular attention to the section on the challenges you will face. This section was placed before the choreography in this book to prepare you to learn all the requirements as either leader or follower. What is easy is learning the steps of choreography; what is difficult, is learning to move together!

Keep the Moment Brief and Let the Magic Last

Many of the most popular first dance songs are at least three to four minutes long. Although three minutes does not seem to be a long time, when you are the only couple on the dance floor it can seem an eternity!

The optimum time for a first dance should be 2 to 2¹/₂ minutes long. Due to the length of some of the songs popular among wedding couples, this will require some coordination between the wedding couple and the DJ.

> **Movement Memo** _____
>
> Work with your DJ to plan the music list for your wedding reception. Dinner and dancing is an activity making a strong resurgence in the USA; therefore, have your DJ play Foxtrots, Rumbas, slower or bluesy Swings, and Waltzes during dinnertime. From that point on, as the reception grows older, the music grows younger! After all, this will be a great opportunity to take advantage of the skills you've learned in this book.

Rather than depending upon the DJ to fade the music in and then out, prepare a custom audiotape or CD. You'll be pleasantly surprised how easy it is to pare away parts of the song, yet retain all the vital lyrics and pacing. This way you can dance to your exact preference, including if desired segueing to more than one song. In addition, by keeping the songs shorter and more meaningful, all attention will remain focused on the dance floor.

Funny, on the Way to Their Wedding, We Learned How to Dance

A child's wedding is certainly the inspiration that many parents finally need to learn to dance. Make the use of this book a family affair. Dads, practice with your daughters—knowledge replaces fear, and a plan is always best. This is the honor dance and the second-most-important event at the wedding reception. By the way, the honor dance with the bride is generally reserved to the individual who accompanies or presents the bride at the wedding ceremony.

Mothers, dance with your sons—the more he practices the skills of leading, the better he and his bride will dance. Once again, it may be a little more difficult to learn a Waltz or Foxtrot, but in the long run, the parent will feel much more comfortable with their child. If the song selection is a slow rhythm ballad, then please refer to my video and booklet, _The Complete Guide to Slow Dancing_.

> **Bet You Didn't Know** _____
>
> Many customs at the wedding reception are changing to reflect better taste, dignity, and respect for all present. Couples are now eliminating elements like removing the garter, the bouquet toss, and the dollar dance. The dollar dance evolved from much less affluent societies where guests could not afford gifts for the bride and groom. Your guests have already given you gifts. Additionally, the atmosphere that often surrounds the dollar dance can be on the unseemly side. If you do not want to eliminate the dollar dance, announce that the proceeds collected will go toward a named charity. Removing the garter and the bouquet toss are being replaced by what is called the "anniversary dance." All married couples are invited to the dance floor. The MC or DJ announces that anyone who has been married less than a day must sit down. The bride and groom sit down, and everyone laughs! Then in five-year increments, couples are eliminated from the dance floor until the longest married couple remains. They dance to a suitable song and are presented with the bride's bouquet and garter.

The Groom Presents His Bride

The following list is a very successful formula I have developed for instructing my wedding couples. This formal and elegant presentation is designed for maximum effectiveness and emotional impact. There is nothing difficult about presenting the bride. Mr. Groom, follow these simple directions, and they will work beautifully for both of you, adding sophistication to these very special moments:

1. The bride and groom come into the room and move to the edge of the dance floor. You can arrange for an overture or introductory music for maximum effect in gaining the attention of the room.

2. The introductory music stops. The groom steps to the left of his bride. Her left arm is lifted and placed under the elbow and over the forearm of the groom's right arm. The groom's right forearm is parallel to the floor at the level of the bride's bust line. With your best posture, walk forward starting with the groom's left foot and the bride's right foot.

3. The groom escorts the bride to the center of the dance floor and presents her to the guests at least two sides of the room. This gives all the guests at the reception an opportunity to see her and take photographs of the couple.

4. Once this has been done, the groom faces his bride and takes one or two steps backward. There should be a pause and a glance of adoration and a smile from the bride. You'll know this was effective when family members pull out their handkerchiefs!

5. The groom offers the bride his left hand while asking her to dance.

6. If the music is not already playing, begin it now.

7. The bride steps forward to accept this dance for the rest of her life!

8. Dance through to the end of your music and dip or lunge for the end of your dance. The groom helps his bride recover gracefully to a full standing position. The couple acknowledges the wildly cheering crowd, and the groom escorts his bride to her seat offering her his right arm as described in step 2.

9. Now sign the wedding certificate. Congratulations!

Movement Memo

It is a good idea to keep the time duration of your dance from two to three minutes. If you wish to use more or all of your song, begin the music of your selection as you enter the dance floor. Keep the music playing while posing briefly for pictures and following all the other elements described in the presentation of the bride. Make sure you have worked this out with your DJ or MC!

Recommended Timelines for the Wedding Dance Scenario

First, and most important, conduct the bride and groom's first dance immediately after their announcement into the reception hall from the receiving line and before dinner. It is good etiquette for the king and queen (a.k.a., bride and groom) to open the dance floor. You may want the DJ or orchestra to play ballroom dance music all night long instead of slower, nondanceable elevator music during dinner. With the dance floor open during the early part of the reception, this is now possible.

Older guests commonly leave earlier in the evening. Unfortunately, when the first dance scenario occurs after dinner, these guests miss their opportunity to "cut a rug." The music and its tempo should become more youthful as the evening continues, leaving the opportunity for all to have a great time dancing or simply watching those who are.

Ballroom Bloopers

An announcement should be made about three to five minutes before the bride and groom enter the room. This allows time to clear the dance floor and passageway for the wedding couple and the bridal party. The service personnel should be cautioned by the maitre d' to avoid moving about or clamoring serving trays during the bride and groom's first dance. No one wants to hear service personnel or kitchen noises on their video. Guests with cameras will also have an opportunity to get ready to take those pictures.

Toast at the beginning of dinner, once the drinks have been served. The best man generally offers the first toast to the wedding couple. The groom responds with a toast of thanks. The ceremonial cutting of the cake follows dinner and precedes dessert.

After cutting the cake, introduce the father of the bride (or surrogate). He should proudly escort his daughter from the head table to the dance floor. Once father and daughter conclude their dance and emotions subside, the father escorts the bride back to her seat.

Introduce the mother of the groom (or surrogate) while the groom rises and proceeds to escort his mother to the dance floor. At the end of the dance and, once again, after emotions subside and candid cameras stop clicking, the groom escorts her back to the family table.

By separating the bride and groom's dance from the two parent dances, these three distinct moments of the wedding reception become more significant and meaningful. At their conclusion, invite the entire wedding party and immediate family to dance. About a minute into the music, the DJ or MC requests that all those on the dance floor ask someone who is seated to dance. This snowball dance generally gets everyone up for a short period, whether they are dancers or not. It is a lot of fun and everyone has a good time! This happens quickly. No attention is drawn to nondancers so they are not embarrassed. Now the real party begins.

The Least You Need to Know

- Learning to dance for your wedding will add elegance and pizzazz to this special event.
- Chose a dance appropriate to the rhythm of your song.
- The optimum length of your First Dance song is 2 to $2\frac{1}{2}$ minutes.
- The groom should practice "presenting" the bride as described in the chapter.

Part 2

Before Your Ball

Everything and every day in your life presents new challenges, and with these challenges come opportunities. So it is with ballroom dancing. We begin in this section by setting down some ground rules and giving some perspective as to what this dancing stuff is really about.

You will start with some reasonable explanations to center your thinking about the real issues—the necessary quality of movement and the poise required. Each of us has tried to dance at one time or another whether with or without a partner. Based on that experience, some ideas have become preconceived notions about the art of ballroom dancing. Some of those may have been correct, others incorrect. However, you will experience from my teaching that the priorities and sequence of events may change so that you can become a successful partner.

Because ballroom dancing is all about the music, we have provided some wonderful selections for you. They are chosen to best suit your beginning experience. *The Complete Idiot's Guide to Ballroom Dancing* will finally bring clarity to the issues you may have had with music, rhythm, and timing. You will be given a blueprint for working comfortably with your partner on the road to successful and enjoyable ballroom dancing.

Chapter 5

Lifestyles Improve Socially, Psychologically, and Physically

In This Chapter

- ◆ Opportunities to dance are everywhere
- ◆ Dance the stress away
- ◆ All that fun and a better body, too
- ◆ Achieving the proper balance

Take a moment and applaud yourself for reading *The Complete Idiot's Guide to Ballroom Dancing!* Some event or an individual gave you a wonderful gift by motivating you to learn ballroom dancing. This opportunity is much more than the fulfillment of an immediate goal. Every aspect of your present life will change once you learn to dance. You will no longer shy away from social functions that include various forms of partner dancing. Instead, you will look forward to them.

Before you were a passive onlooker; now you will become an active participant. Your confidence level around people, especially in social situations, will soar. This chapter explains how to prepare for dancing, both physically and mentally, and discusses a variety of social functions and activities where you have the opportunity to dance.

No Longer a Couch Potato, Your Dance Card Is Full

The benefits of improved health from the physical activity of ballroom dancing are tangible. Just think—every time you practice your dancing, it is like going to the gym. You are exercising your major muscle groups as well as giving yourself a great cardiovascular workout. Did you ever think a night on the town would be as beneficial as a trip to the gym? Relieving stress is one of the major health issues in today's society. Every dance in any situation is like taking a small vacation! Your stress can disappear. Speaking of vacations, you will have the best time of your life! Some vacations cater specifically to dancers at every level of experience. The best part of all is sharing it with someone else.

Incentives and goals are very important to education. An invitation to an anniversary party, political event, charitable fund-raiser, holiday or New Year's party, and many other affairs are motivation for improvement and diversity. Whenever people interact on a social level, music and dancing usually occur.

The venues and events fall into these broad categories:

- Weddings and anniversaries
- Nightclubs with live or recorded music
- DJ-sponsored ballroom dances
- Resorts and cruises
- Fund-raisers with dancing or period themes
- Family and cultural events

Come Celebrate with Us

If you are the guest of honor at an anniversary party, you should learn to do the Waltz. Chances are very good that "The Anniversary Waltz" or any of the other popular Waltzes will be played for you at a designated time. Second, it would be nice if you knew when that time would be, unless of course it is a surprise party! My timeline preference is the same as that used for the bride and groom (see Chapter 4, "Dancing Through Your Big Day"), dance as soon as you're introduced to the room. Any specialty dances such as those with grandchildren or children should be done after dinner.

> **Movement Memo**
>
> Regardless of the type of event or location, knowing some general information as it applies to your dancing is always wise. Live or recorded music makes a big difference! Type of music, diversity of dance rhythms, and, of course, quality of music make big differences to dancers. Trained dancers usually prefer strict tempo music because the timing is always perfect. In other words, they like a recording as opposed to the varied timing of a poor-quality band. The quality of the dance floor should be important to you. A nonsuspended floor (meaning no floor or basement below) tends to be very hard. For example, a surface of tile over concrete would be very tough on your feet. You will definitely limit the amount of dancing you do.

A guest at a wedding or anniversary reception should be prepared for what we call general dancing. General dancing is nothing more than the garden variety of ballroom dances. The two most popular of these are Swing and Foxtrot. This is particularly true if the music is live and the classification of the orchestra is known as a jazz combo, a swing orchestra, or a general business orchestra.

If there is a DJ at these affairs, the musical taste of the guest of honor usually determines the type of music. However, the flexibility of a DJ allows you to make requests for specific songs or dance rhythms such as Cha-Cha, Tango, Disco Hustle, and so on. Experienced ballroom dancers will often call the venue hosting the occasion to find out the size of the dance floor and its surface type. Do not expect the guest of honor or host to know this information—unless they are experienced dancers!

The Nightlife Beckons; There Is Something for Everyone

Nightclubs are responsive to their patrons' musical preferences. This is particularly true in smaller cities and towns. In larger cities, musical tastes often reflect the ethnicity of the population as well as the most popular musical trends of the day. Big cities can produce a smorgasbord of dance excitement—something different every night of the week! Quite often restaurants provide an opportunity for dancing either after or during dinnertime. Tango or the perennial lounge lizard is popular in these venues.

When we actually begin our step-by-step approach to each dance, I will often use the expression "Less is more." At the beginning stages, ballroom dancers all have a tendency to exaggerate the size of dance steps and patterns. This is normal. In a nightclub situation, learning to dance each figure with a rhythmic approach, as opposed to a spatial one, will be in your best interest. The nightclub dance floor holds a microcosm of personalities in a very confined space and often under the influence of alcohol. Due to the close proximity on a nightclub dance floor, you need to be able to limit and control the size of your dancing. This will allow you to dance all your figures in a small area and avoid invading others' space.

Dancers always attract dancers at a nightclub. Once you gain some proficiency, you will find this a big plus. Traveling together, meeting and establishing "dance buddies" will amplify any experience you have had at a nightspot.

Movement Memo

If an advertisement or the restaurant maitre d' tells you there will be a jazz combo or group, this generally means listening music, not dance music! The difference lies in the intent of the host venue. Very often a group of this type is hired for listening entertainment—dinner music—rather than dancing. Call ahead and ask so you will not be disappointed.

Ballroom Bloopers

As I have mentioned in an earlier chapter, just because you saw it in the movies, doesn't mean you can do it! Please note that aerials and acrobatic dance tricks—any movement when the female partner leaves the surface of the dance floor—are very dangerous. Careful practice is required and these tricks should never be attempted on the social dance floor or nightclub. When these tricks are practiced, spotters should be available at all times to prevent injuries. Special permission by the management of the venue should be granted before any trained dancer attempts to execute these tricks. This is necessary to limit liability and prevent injury or even death!

Here Is Where the Dancers Go

Owing to the rise in popularity of partner dancing, a relatively new phenomenon has occurred wherever people are taking lessons. These are dances that are sponsored by dance instructors, amateur dancers, and other dance enthusiasts. Sometimes they take place in rental halls or nightclubs. Frequently dance studios will offer their space to the public. By simply checking the calendar section of the newspaper, you can easily locate these dances in your area, or any area you may be visiting. Checking the Yellow Pages under "Dance Studios" is also effective. Inquire as to what they know about public dances. An Internet search for dance instructors, dancing, and arts and entertainment calendars will often be quite fruitful. Individuals, groups, or dance societies that hold these dances make sure they are well publicized. If they hold them, they will make them easy to find!

Movement Memo

Business travelers and vacationers alike find an Internet search very effective. A full description of the dance is generally given. This will include the type of music, the cost, whether a complimentary lesson is given before the dance, whether smoking is allowed (generally not), and whether the dances are primarily for singles or couples.

More often than not these events offer the best available dance music. For example, at a Swing dance, do not necessarily expect a lot of Latin music. At a general ballroom dance, expect everything. Another great feature is that you will be able to dance all night long, if you can hold up. Recorded music is nonstop. Properly run dances will include mixers where everyone is encouraged to dance with everyone else.

Most of these dances offer a complimentary dance lesson before the actual start of the dance. The effectiveness of this free dance lesson is contingent upon the quality of the instructor. Most attendees are beyond the beginner's stage. Beginners are better served by taking dance instruction in a controlled environment. The more experienced dancers use these lessons to break the ice with new partners, as a social practice time, or as an opportunity to learn a new dance step. Free is what it is, and as you know, you get what you pay for!

The Love Boat and Hernando's Hideaway

Cruise vacations are second on the list of reasons why people call dance studios. If you learn only one dance in preparation for a cruise, make that dance the Merengue! I have always referred to this dance as the cruise-ship dance.

A cruiseship may have three or four nightclubs operating at any given time. Each nightclub usually has a theme—hot Latin, oldies but goodies, Disco, and of course Ballroom. Here is a list of dances applicable to each theme or music type:

- **Latin:** Merengue, Cha-Cha, Mambo, Salsa, Rumba, and Samba
- **Oldies but goodies:** Any Swing dance, Cha-Cha, Rumba, Foxtrot
- **Disco:** Hustle, Swing, Cha-Cha, and slow dancing
- **Ballroom:** Anything and everything

Dance lessons are frequently available on a cruiseship. These lessons may be conducted in a group or in a private lesson format. Cruiseships have recently begun offering what they call *dance cruises*. The cruiselines market these dances through travel agencies, dance studios, teachers, and dance periodicals. The cruiselines will hire a competent dance team or couples that will host dances every night, teach a series of dance seminars during the day, and quite frequently perform at the evening dance. The emphasis is on fun and not competency. Technique is reserved for the dance studio. These dance cruises are increasing in popularity and have many repeat patrons. Cruiseships are also noted for what they call *dance hosts*. These are moderately experienced dancers whose job it is to partner single patrons. Check with your travel agent, on the Internet, or even your local dance studio for these types of cruises or resort trips.

A resort vacation is not unlike a cruise. The resort areas also offer dance weekends with a format similar to the dance cruises. A resort location will rarely have more than one nightclub or ballroom. Checking the hours of operation for the resort's nightclubs and ballrooms is important. Additionally, be sure to inquire as to whether the music is live or recorded. Vacation resorts generally gear the musical formats to the locality. For instance, in the Caribbean islands, you are likely to hear what is known as a steel band playing Reggae and Merengue music. In the Catskills or the Poconos, you will generally hear ballroom music. In Las Vegas, San Francisco, New York, Chicago, or Los Angeles, every type of musical format is available within a close proximity.

Politically Correct

Charitable and political fund-raisers are very popular formats for ballroom dancing. Unfortunately, the preponderance of attendees cannot dance. As you read in earlier chapters on the history of ballroom dancing, the monarchs, politicians, and upper and middle classes learned dancing as part of their education and social responsibility. I am happy to report that because of the standardization of ballroom dancing, more people than ever are taking lessons and once again learning how to interact on the dance floor.

At these fund-raisers, you will probably have more room to dance than at many of the previously mentioned venues or vacations. The bigger the budget for the fund-raiser, the more money they expect to raise. When dancers do not know how to dress up the dance floor, the sponsors of the event often hire professionals to entertain the guests. Quite frequently they will find an orchestra to suit a theme, outfit the professionals, plan the room's decor to match that theme, and ask the guests to come suitably attired. I know because I have personally performed at hundreds of these!

Once the show is complete and the evening is still young, the attendees who are prepared to dance to the theme can really have a ball. Beginner dancers can actually be mistaken for Fred and Ginger! Normal folks who learn to move well together look exceedingly good to those who cannot. You will know the theme by the beautiful posters and invitations that promote the event. If the event has no theme, expect plenty of the good old-fashioned American dances like Swing and the Foxtrot. If a particular ethnic group is prominent in the constituency, then the music and dancing are likely to represent that culture.

Viva la Familia—Long Live the Family

Family and cultural events are not unlike anything previously mentioned. The United States is a bastion of religious and cultural diversity. While we are all brothers and sisters of a great family, most of us are citizens of a specific country. However, our families may have their origins in a completely different country. Although the United States is the ultimate melting pot, it is very important to us to uphold, respect, and learn about our ethnic backgrounds!

Each ethnic group is steeped in tradition—much of which centers on dancing. My advice is to study the dances of your heritage and culture. Perform these dances at least once at every family gathering, festival, and holiday meeting. You will be pleasantly surprised at the response.

Poise and Power Meet Elegance and Romance

Great exercise is one of the intrinsic benefits of ballroom dancing. In the normal regimen of your life, you practice and repeat many mundane activities. You do not think about timing and balance while moving from place to place. The normal human being is an intellectual creature. If you are like the rest of us, you tend to look for shortcuts in each and everything you do. This is natural. In terms of movement from place to place, getting where you want to go is the important element. Slouching, hunching over, or rocking from side to side is of no consequence in reaching your desired destination.

As a dancer, the quality of movement found in your day-to-day activities will simply not be good enough. A dancer's movement must be better than normal, and as you learn to dance, your *normal* movement will improve greatly. Later on in this chapter in the section "Let's Get Physical … with Nonmovement Activity," I will teach you a very effective exercise to prepare yourself for ballroom dancing and improve the quality of your movement. The exercise will include a partner, but it can be done alone.

Bet You Didn't Know

Many of my female students are thrilled and excited to find their legs becoming shapelier after a relatively short time of dancing. I have had many women in their 40s see their legs return to the firmness and condition of their early 20s. Some women have experienced more overall improvement in the size and strength of their legs than they had ever possessed at any other time in their life. Fat tissue burns away, and muscle tissue responds quickly, especially in the upper thighs. This is true for both men and women. As you continue learning to dance, you will experience a proportional increase in the strength of your legs. This process is self-serving; you will need more strength to achieve a higher quality. The good news is that the exercise is motivational, intellectually challenging, and artistically creative.

When you dance, transferring weight from one foot to the next, you lift the weight equal to your torso and head. Imagine how many squats in the gymnasium are the equivalent of three to five minutes of dancing. Consider the boredom of working your legs and abdominal wall using repetitive motion on some apparatus. Now imagine how much fun and interesting the exercise of moving with someone attached to you will be. Especially since you will be doing this with music. Ballroom dancing is where poise and power meet elegance and romance!

The Mayo Clinic Loves Ballroom Dancing

The Mayo Clinic reported that dancing is not only a great way to have fun and socialize, but it also offers several health benefits:

- **Burning calories:** Dancing continuously for 30 minutes burns 200 to 2,400 calories, which is the same as walking, swimming, or cycling.
- **Cardiovascular conditioning:** Consistent social dance exercise leads to a slower heart rate, lower blood pressure, and improved cholesterol levels. The degree of cardiovascular conditioning depends on how vigorously you dance, how long you dance continuously, and how regularly.
- **Strong bones:** The side-to-side motions of many ballroom dances, such as Mambo and Swing, strengthen the tibia, fibula, and femur. This also helps in preventing or slowing the loss of bone mass associated with osteoporosis.

Quality Movement Becomes a Lifestyle

While learning to dance, greater benefits result when you apply the elements of balance, timing, and carriage of your body to your normal routine. In other words, when you walk, walk tall. In Parts 2, "Before Your Ball," and 3, "Two Become One: Creating the Dance Couple," we will establish the exact requirements for the quality of movement necessary in the art of ballroom dancing. Practicing just a few hours a week or taking a lesson or two a week is not enough to offset the casual and often erroneous *normal* movement qualities developed over the course of a lifetime. Your goal will be to practice the error out of your muscle memory, replacing it with correct postural movement.

Portraying a Better Image

The human neck is quite possibly the most elegant part of your body. When an individual portrays confidence and poise during normal movement, the full neck is visible. The way we communicate ourselves to others in a physical sense is called *body language*. The expressiveness of body language frequently dictates the way others respond to us.

Do you look like someone who can be taken advantage of because your head is slouching and you do not look confident? Many experts will tell you that communication is 80 percent physical. What you say or do may not be as important as how you look while saying or doing it. To express positive body language, you must feel good about yourself. Nothing enjoins self-confidence like physical success. Think of how many professional athletes are also wonderful public and motivational speakers. They perform well in front of others because they have confidence in their appearance and have enjoyed success as a result of their own movement.

As you begin to dance and conquer the demons that have prevented you from dancing before, you will experience many emotional highs. These emotional highs will translate to physical confidence. Your body language will definitely improve.

Bet You Didn't Know

Many people begin ballroom dancing with a specific milestone in mind, like dancing on a cruise, and then come to realize many more important benefits. Their body language, physical confidence, and communicative skills all seem to improve proportionately with their improvement in ballroom dancing. Over the course of my teaching career, I have witnessed examples of students improving the quality of their lives. The self-fulfillment of conquering loneliness and finding a life partner or moving from job insecurity to owning one's own business is immeasurable. When they initially came to the dance studio, they may have had these issues in the back of their minds but lacked that certain something to overcome them. Ballroom dancing improves the quality of every participant's life.

Everyone Can Benefit from Reduced Stress

I do not need to remind you of the stress that exists in today's world. Life's complications create unavoidable stress. How stress and stress-related issues can diminish the quality of your health is well documented! Finding diversions or stress relievers is of primary importance to our overall well-being.

Ballroom dancing has the capacity to transport us from our world of problems to a world of virtual make-believe. On the dance floor we can be anyone we have ever dreamed of being. We enjoy the images of the art while we are free to create the art ourselves. Dancers need not be good to do this; they just need a good imagination.

Movement Memo

Make the physical benefits of ballroom dancing cyclic. Work hard to improve your physical stamina and strength. Strive to move better and look better. Portray self-assurance and improve the quality of your life. Watch the cycle evolve within you and then work harder, move better, and enjoy more confidence.

I found out a long time ago that the preparations needed to improve dancing were wonderful diversions from stress. And that practicing what I learned, although difficult, was like taking a vacation. I liked being on a vacation in the middle of the afternoon. I loved dancing. The better I became, the more I loved it. Nothing made me feel better. Dancing helped me escape from trying or difficult circumstances. Preparing for competition heightened all of those feelings and chased the stress away!

Let's Get Physical ... with Nonmovement Activity

A very simple, pleasant warm-up exercise for ballroom dancing can be done alone or with a partner. However, doing this exercise with a partner will yield a fuller benefit. For convenience, the partner's gender does not matter. For motivation, begin with Foxtrot music, and then as you become familiar with other forms of music, use them as well. You will find the timing description of rise and fall at the beginning of each dance.

While you practice, please note the exertion of energy necessary in your legs and abdominal areas. This energy secures your balance while extending your legs. I want you to note these feelings so that you will be able to reproduce them on command. From now on, as you learn a physical skill, think of your muscles as a blank tape and your brain as a VCR. Everything you do while learning to dance has a consequence of reproducing a good image or a poor one.

Although moving up and down is easy and very simple in concept, adding the dimension of a partner reveals both the vulnerability and the sophistication inherent in moving with someone attached to you. Right now I just want you to have fun with this exercise. Use this exercise frequently and note your improvement as you continue to study this book.

To begin, you and your partner join arms in the practice position shown in the accompanying photographs:

1. The leader's hands should be lightly clasped under the partner's elbows. The poise of both dancers is erect and at a right angle to the dance floor. The dancers will not use each other for balance but join arms together strictly as a guide.

2. Brace or flex into your knees, keeping your feet 10 to 15 inches apart from each other.

3. Keep your knees braced while you pulse (move) up and down slightly. I remind my students to keep energy—a slight tension—in their quadriceps while dancing and while doing this exercise.

4. Create this rhythmic pulsing or pressure from the hips to the knee while lowering to a flat foot and then the knee to the hips while rising to the balls of the feet.

5. Begin this exercise using both feet, and then as you build leg strength and power, alternate from right to left and then left to right.

Step 1.

Step 2.

Step 3 up with ribcage lifted.

Step 3 down with ribcage lifted.

While engaged in this exercise, the pulsing you feel from the hips to the knee will apply pressure against the supporting foot. Allow this pressure to pass through your ankle by releasing any tension in that ankle. Allow the residual effect, which is governed by Newton's third law of inertia (for every action there is an opposite and equal reaction), to return vertically through your body until the right-angle alignment previously described is achieved.

Do not concentrate on your ankles or feet. Focus your concentration in the areas of the quadriceps, hamstrings, and your gluteus. Maintain good elevation of your ribcage using the muscles in your back and around the ribcage to maintain its balance and elevation. Do not allow one side of the ribcage to lower more than the other. Use the abdominal wall to control the balance of your ribcage, which will result in the balance of your body. Do not allow one shoulder to lower more than the other. If you have a momentary loss of balance, do not use the shoulders to correct it. Instead, learn to use the tool for balance that dancers use: their abdominal wall (the tummy).

> **Movement Memo**
>
> A physical analogy comparable to this exercise is the feeling of being at the end of the diving board. Your toes are folded just over the edge of the diving board while you are flexing up and down vertically as if you have no intention of actually diving off the board. The difference here is that you are doing this pulsing using four beats of music in the rhythm of the Foxtrot.

I call this exercise *nonmovement activity*. The force passing through the vertical center of your body is not something that your eye can see. The vertical movement of energy from the dance floor through the top of the head is the source of your balance. This is much more important than any type of lateral movement across the dance floor. It is within the context of vertical energy that the head, and more specifically the brain, is supported and made to feel confident and secure.

Once your brain feels this newfound confidence, the messages sent to the intellect and muscles of the body are simple: "Go! Go! Go! Go!" This balance translates into the needed ability to swing your legs without the necessity of hanging onto your dance partner. If you were to hang onto your partner while ballroom dancing, you would prevent your partner from moving properly!

Now you have learned the first rule of ballroom dancing: Never use your partner for balance. Instead, supply all of your own energy to move all of your own body!

The Least You Need to Know

- Many venues are available for dancing if you take the time to look.
- Physical fitness and an improved self-image are two great side effects of dancing.
- Dancing increases your self-confidence and reduces stress.
- Never use your partner for balance!

Chapter 6

The Challenges of Ballroom Dancing

In This Chapter

♦ Go vertical

♦ Speaking the physical language

♦ Deep cleansing breathes

♦ The Dynamic Duo rules your legs

♦ It takes two to Tango

Now that you have decided to learn ballroom dancing, we will begin by addressing the first important issue: how you should apply yourself! Your physical and mental approach to learning ballroom dancing is vital and will have considerable bearing on your success. Your good attitude toward learning both the physical skills and mental priorities will ensure a fruitful and happy experience.

Like many other skills, ballroom dancing is a very cumulative one. Think of playing with building blocks. It is important to place the first blocks in order to begin constructing anything. You need to work on the first block, and that is you. In this chapter, we will explore the challenges you face in your dance education, both physical and mental, with and without your partner.

From Jalopy to Ferrari

Movement and balance are the foundation of dancing, so you will need to start with these two "blocks." You already know how to walk, run, and ascend or descend a staircase. Now we will work on the quality of the movements you use to perform these acts. We will then apply this quality of movement as an approach to ballroom dancing. The more you bring to the table in terms of balance, the better partner you will become.

Your present muscle memory does not include moving with someone attached to you. When you move in your daily life, getting from point A to point B is simple: You just do it! The art of dancing is more dependent on the vertical alignment of your body, and therefore, how you travel from point A to point B is more important! I want you to make a conscious effort to work on retooling the movements of your body. No matter how expensive or beautiful your automobile may be, if the tires are flat, the shocks are shot, the front end is out of alignment, your buggy is a no-go showboat! You are your own vehicle, and the quality of the ride is up to you.

Clarity in speaking is rooted in the way you articulate your words. Dancers speak to each other and to the public with the articulation of controlled body movements. This communication is totally nonverbal, and adding words often spoils the effect. Speaking with good body language is the beginning of mastering the skill of nonverbal communication in the art of dancing.

Since words cannot move you physically or even help your partner, you must discover other means to transmit information. This communication is not "heady." It is quite elementary in nature and strictly physical. The best mindset for this type of learning is to recall the attitudes of your youth when your ego was less dominant. Many times I have seen successful businesspersons, lawyers, doctors, and teachers come in for dance lessons, confident of their success, only to walk out with their heads hanging low. Somewhere along the way, they were led to believe that moving with someone attached to them was going to be easy. Unfortunately, they only set themselves up for a big fall!

Why should that be? I do not believe that the skills to move with someone attached to you are intrinsic. Additionally, we are self-preservationists and resist the notion of moving dynamically into another person's space. Whether dancing or otherwise, every one of us has attempted to move with another person attached to us in some way. Whether in a game or holding hands, we quickly found out that it was not easy. If you have had the occasion to try dancing, your single imperative thought was probably to avoid stepping on your partner's feet.

Each of us needs a teacher to learn techniques for overcoming the physical and intellectual notions that have been roadblocks in the past. Overcoming these notions will allow us to move in the art of ballroom dancing. So now we begin with half the dance couple: you! Later when we build the dance couple, we will want to ensure that all the apparatus functions correctly and has no faulty parts. Let's begin.

From top to bottom the spinal column moves, essentially, at one rate of speed while you dance. These four physical techniques will permit that to happen successfully:

1. The top of your head should be extended from the top of your spine. The joint at the top of the spine is known as the *atlas axis joint*. When the head is lifted, this joint works better. You will need to rotate your head during dancing. You want to be able to do this without your head falling off balance or out of alignment. Your head is the heaviest single object on your body and must be kept in balance. Without your head in balance, other parts of your body will be forced to compensate, which will adversely affect your dancing.

   Sometimes dancers have difficulty perceiving the top of the head and often move their eyes instead. One suggestion for learning the feel of the extension of your neck is to put a hardcover book on your head and try to push upward. You must concentrate on keeping your jaw level (parallel) with the floor and your ears centered over your shoulders. Vertical lift is what balances the book on a model's head. The book is trying to fall directly down, and the level head prevents that from happening.

2. Relax your shoulders by letting the center of the *deltoids* (the muscles at the uppermost portion of the arms located at the corner of the shoulders) fall evenly under your ears.

3. Widen the space between your shoulder blades by flexing your *latissimus dorsi*—the muscle at the back upper left and right side of the ribcage—and the pectorals in the front upper left and right side of the ribcage. When this is done properly, you will experience stretch through the armpits and gain flexibility and range of motion in your upper arms.

4. Your ribcage should remain lifted at all times. The wrong way to maintain lift in your ribcage is by holding your breath. Preventing yourself from breathing will likely produce a poor physical performance. The muscles need oxygen to function, as does the brain. The breathing technique used while dancing is called *diaphragmatic breathing*.

Here is a simple way to apply these four items. Inflate your chest with air while at the same time shrugging your shoulders upward toward your ears. Now I want you to roll your shoulders back and down while maintaining the lift of your ribcage. Now allow the air to exit from your lungs while contracting your abdominal wall.

> **CAUTION** **Ballroom Bloopers**
>
> Avoid looking at the dance floor, particularly when learning your steps. Dropping your head to peer at the dance floor adversely affects your balance both alone and with your partner. You need your eyes looking ahead of you to move with competence and confidence. I often tell my students that the brilliant concept at work here is *look where you are going!* Please work hard at this. If you learn to feel a step with your head down, lifting it up will always be difficult, because your muscles remember it another way.

Breathe Better for Effective Dancing

Breathing affects the quality of performance and the state of mind in virtually every physical activity. Tai chi, a Chinese martial art form, sites breathing as its undergirding and foundational experience. Natural and continual breathing is a means of relaxation and optimization of physical performance. *Diaphragmatic breathing* is the fancy technical description for the breathing to optimize mental and physical performance in virtually every aspect of life.

Baseball players are taught to exhale to clear the mind and relieve stress as they wait in the batters box for the pitch to be thrown. This allows the concentration level and vision to be optimized. You will notice that basketball players do the same thing just prior to releasing the ball at the free-throw line. A cleansing breath can calm the nerves and prepare you in situations that require great concentration. Taking such a breath is one key to success and performance. Students taking examinations find this to be an excellent technique to calm down, allowing their brain to function clearly.

> **Dancing Definition**
>
> **Diaphragmatic breathing** is created by exhaling frequently, letting the normal usage of your muscles (contractions and extensions) naturally accomplish the intake of the air. Muscle usage will always draw in a proportional amount of oxygen. This happens easily as long as your lips are not sealed. This is a good excuse for smiling while you dance!

This type of breathing must be practiced until it becomes natural. You will always find that exhaling has a cleansing effect on your mind and body. Exhaling keeps stress to a minimum, therefore allowing your body to perform "to the max" or in the way you have trained it.

Whatever Goes Up Wants to Come Down

Now that you have achieved the lift of your ribcage, let's work on maintaining that carriage. If I ask every one of my students if gravity is the most influential and powerful force on the planet, they will say yes. Continuing my examination I will ask, "Do you believe that gravity exists in all places for all time?" Once again they will agree. I will then tell them that they must realize that to a large degree, good dancing means providing a continual offset to the forces of gravity. The ability to dance or to sustain the art of dance movement is the muscular application of support and

> **CAUTION** **Ballroom Bloopers**
>
> Never use the shoulders forcibly to correct the balance of your ribcage. The tendency here is to counterbalance rather than to create balance. The use of the abdominal wall is far more effective to repair momentary losses of balance and to sustain that balance. The abdominal wall is the best means for the human body to maintain a good vertical alignment of the spinal column.

balance to the human body while moving to music. The key barometer to quality movement is the lift and balance of the ribcage.

On the planet Earth, the best means for supporting an object is from underneath. The legs, pelvis, and abdomen are below the ribcage. Therefore, we derive support from these areas. First we structure the *gluteus* (your hind side) and *hamstrings* (leg muscles in the rear of the thigh) by squeezing or flexing them. This flex will drive the spinal column upward and away from the hips.

Next we contract the abdominal wall as discussed earlier. The toning and flexing of the abdominal wall will be used to prevent loss of elevation on either side of the ribcage.

The Suitcase Method

Here is a simple way to illustrate the physical feelings I have described in this chapter. I will call this the *suitcase method*. Simply lower your body evenly to pick up one of two suitcases of equal weight. Take the handle while bracing your leg muscles and begin to rise. We all know what happens now: The ribcage inherently tilts to the side of the first suitcase, necessitating the use of the abdominal muscles to level our bodies while supporting our ribcage, shoulders, and the suitcase with our legs. Now repeat the process and pick up both suitcases. Once again, use your abdominal muscles to level your body and the two suitcases. While managing the additional weight of the suitcases, relief for the stress exerted on the spinal column can be obtained by contracting the abdominal wall to push up the pelvis. You can feel your tailbone move closer to the center of your legs.

Correct ribcage position during "pick up."

Many top professionals will agree that proper and continuous use of the abdominal muscles is at first more important than correct use of the dancer's feet. The reason is simple: Without control of the body's center (abdominal wall), the dancer's feet cannot possibly perform properly or feel comfortable!

Correct ribcage position during "lift."   *Incorrect ribcage position during "lift."*

Now I want you to put down those two suitcases, whether they were imaginary or real. But I do not want you to let go of the internal power and strength you used to sustain your balance while maintaining the carriage with those two suitcases. Dancers carry their bodies at all times. This body carriage is not passive; the body carriage is passive when we move through our daily activities. A dancer's carriage is active! While ballroom dancing, the carriage of our body, and specifically the ribcage, is similar to the added weight of those suitcases. To be an effective ballroom dancer, we must carry our bodies as if they were actually heavier and more burdensome than they are. Having an active body carriage is most desirable for the ballroom dancer.

Gravity pulls everything to the Earth at the rate of 32 feet per second. This is happening at all times and in all places. Gravity is seeking to pull over anything on or in your body that is unsupported every single moment you are on the dance floor. Dancers must remain vigilant about the support of their ribcage! An onlooker observing good dancing never sees the continual application of this vertical energy and lift. The same casual onlooker would be amazed at how much energy a dancer uses just at standstill. Observers often seem perplexed at the amount of sweat a dancer exudes in just a few moments. We work hard to maintain the vertical alignment of our body, as if the atmosphere is more like hurricane winds trying to stop us or blow us over.

Without constant support, our bodies do not move in balance; instead we move counterbalancing. Excessive counterbalancing will not lend itself to good timing and rhythm. Counterbalancing and lack of support make new dancers feel like they are chasing the music rather than moving with the music. Counterbalancing can make a dance partner feel like a sack of potatoes or a brick wall. If we do not support our ribcage and uphold our half of the bargain, then who will? Why, our partner will, of course. The problem is that when your partner is holding you up, who is holding your partner? As a result, we spoil not only our movement, but our partner's as well! While passive movement may suffice in our daily routine, it seldom works in ballroom dancing.

In the opening paragraphs of this chapter, I stated that you already know how to run, walk, and ascend or descend a staircase. Now I want you to try any of these three activities and include the application of lift and carriage of your ribcage. You should experience a whole range of new feelings. Your walking stride should feel effortless; ascending a staircase should feel balanced even without the handrail; your running stride should move with greater ease and actually feel more powerful. Your power should be concentrated toward the center of your body. If these results are true for you, then congratulations are in order! You have embarked on the right path to ballroom dancing.

What Is a Dance Step?

What constitutes an actual dance step? The definition of a dance step is the dancer's movement (body flight) from one platform, the *foot*, to the next platform within the designated period of time, the timing of the music. In other words, you must exit an existing vertical position entirely and achieve a new vertical position with all of your weight over the next foot. At this point, you have created a new supporting foot. Simply placing your foot in another location is not enough. You must *complete* the transfer of all your body weight over the new supporting foot.

Dancing Definition

The **foot** of the dancer is merely a horizontal platform that is responsible for keeping the body in the vertical position. The upper legs, which are closer to the body's center, are responsible for the body's movement. Your feet have been holding you up for as long as you have been walking. Do not try to teach them something new. They know more than you think they do, so let them work effectively for you.

The Body Is First

Your brain is much happier if you begin a dance step by moving your body toward the new location just before moving your feet. This way, legs and feet accommodate the movement of your body every single time. Here is an example. Pick up an object from anywhere in the room and bring it to another place in the room. Did you think of your feet while doing this? Of course not! Let's take a closer look at this and try another exercise. Place your hand solidly on your sternum and repeat the process. Notice that you first felt pressure at the contact point of your hand at your sternum. Your body moved first! Your direction of travel has more to do with your body than foot placement.

Over my years of teaching, I have had the opportunity to witness very intelligent and successful people stymied in their attempts to learn to dance. Why? They try to learn a dance pattern without feeling their body weight covering their foot!

Learning a dance step just the way you will feel the step while dancing it is important. Never be afraid to commit yourself to movement. Errors of omission are more difficult to correct than errors of commission! This approach to a dance step will allow you to feel the step even as you read about it, view it, or even learn from someone else. Professionals learn steps and patterns very quickly because part of their mental imaging includes a sense of what the new step will feel like. The feeling, not the thought, is everything!

Ballroom Bloopers

The act of touching or tapping your foot will not teach your brain what is necessary to achieve a new point of comfortable balance and the completion of the desired choreography. You must remove the former foot from the floor to have completed a dance step. Never finish a dance step with two feet on the floor! The result of this "touching the floor method" will frustrate you because your brain will not learn the feeling of the body over the foot.

It All Begins with Your Body and Ends with a Free Foot

In *The Complete Idiot's Guide to Ballroom Dancing*, whenever a command such as "left foot forward" is given, please move your body as well as your left foot to the position directed using the rhythm of the dance you are studying. To illustrate this point, I often tell my students to think of their feet as empty glasses and their bodies as a pitcher of water.

The pitcher is lifted and suspended over the glass. The water contained in the pitcher is poured into the glass, freely and unrestrictedly until the glass is filled. The water in the pitcher is not impeded in any way from being delivered to the base of the glass. Likewise, your body is lifted from one location toward another location and is delivered to your empty foot without impedance or restriction.

Just as the pitcher is a solid controlled container for the water, so must your ribcage be.

Your body is suspended over the free foot long enough to load your foot with the body's weight. The location from which you begin lifting your body is known as your supporting leg and foot. In the case of the pitcher, your hand and arm supplied this lift. In the case of your body, your legs and lower torso will supply the lift required. The lifting process (a.k.a., dance step) is not complete when the empty glass is filled but when the pitcher is emptied. So it is with a dance step, one foot full and one foot empty.

Remember to prioritize the use of your body as you study each dance step through each of the 11 dances described in this book. You will learn quickly and more effectively.

Movement Memo

Stiffening your ankle will prohibit your body weight from fully entering your foot. To avoid this, keep your energy in the center of your thigh muscles and calf muscles. Beginners and nondancers often experience soreness in their joints because they tax the small muscles around those joints instead of applying the natural and proportionate power of their leg muscles.

Movement Memo

When dancing, treat your ribcage as you would carrying a cup of hot coffee! Balance it while letting it move. When the distance between the pelvis and the base of the ribcage is constant on all sides of the body, the ribcage is level. The dancer delivers a balanced and complete dance step.

"The Dynamic Duo" Legs in Action

One of the beautiful things about ballroom dancing is that you use the same body and the same legs in all the dances! We have discussed the proper body carriage; now let's look at those legs. The use of our legs in every dance can best be described by what I call the "Dynamic Duo." The duo is made up of two coincidental actions broken into two parts:

◆ The first segment is what I refer to as *impact and correction*.
◆ The second segment is what I refer to as *compression and leg swing*.

I firmly believe that an understanding of how your legs work will aid you tremendously in achieving a higher level of accomplishment.

Segment One: Impact and Correction

Impact occurs when the first supporting contact point of your foot meets the dance floor. Because your muscles located below the knees absorb impact, dancing with very pliable ankles is preferable. Your platforms (feet) must fully accept the body's weight. Positive impact cannot occur if the ankles repel your body's weight. Simultaneously with this impact comes correction. Correction means fixing your body so you maintain your vertical position and proper elevation. Impact and correction are needed for every single

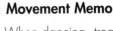

dance step where a weight change occurs. It is imperative that no inadvertent or intentional loss of elevation occurs. The loss of elevation and vertical position occurs naturally when your body is in flight between your feet. Your attention to the support of the ribcage will minimize or prevent this loss of elevation.

This correction instantly brings your body to its desired position for your next dance step. Correction should happen virtually coincidentally with impact. No matter how good you may get, gravity will influence any unsupported area of your body. Thus, upon foot impact, instantaneous correction of your elevation and vertical position is vital. Another measure of your ability will be how quickly you can correct a dance position. Loss of position is inherent, so taking control of a dance step becomes a process of continual correction!

Segment Two: Compression and Leg Swing

Compression is the event that occurs after correction. By compression, I mean the development of muscular power sufficient to propel the body to the next dance position. Compression is the muscular contraction of the portions of the leg above the knee up to the hip. Compression also occurs when you feel the spreading of the muscles and bones of your supporting foot. This spreading action of the foot is due to increased pressure caused by the body's weight plus the contraction of the muscles above the knee. It is of the utmost importance for dancers to feel the expansion of the foot on the dance floor so that they know there is a stable and active platform from which to begin body flight. Through this compression, you will often experience the greatest feeling of musicality and rhythm. Without compression following impact, the dance movement becomes suspect, erratic, and stilted or static.

Bet You Didn't Know

The growth of a dancer from the newcomer or beginner level can be measured by the frequency and depth of muscular compression throughout the leg and foot. A good teacher possesses the skill to take a student from visual perception to the compressive and physical level of dance feeling. New dancers both male and female are often amazed at the physicality and athleticism that are required to dance with even moderate success. Once you learn a correct feeling, sustaining the feeling with physical and mental concentration is absolutely vital. Because of gravity and other physical forces, momentary losses of concentration will inadvertently alter the position of your body.

The coincidence that occurs during the act of compression is the swing or positioning of the free leg and foot. The optimum time to swing the leg will always be the moment that the dancer's supporting foot feels the greatest compression and spreading within the dance shoe. This is your moment of greatest floor contact and connection. You will also notice that this becomes the point of greatest partner connection and contact. This is the moment in your dancing when you have the greatest ability to create transition and retain musicality between your partner and yourself. While moving into compression, you possess the greatest amount of control—to rotate, to lead, or to position the free foot and leg. When compression is complete, the body begins accelerating and traveling.

Patience and Kindness Are Virtues

Like any other human relationship, a dance partnership will have ups and downs. You will find that the key to successful partner dancing lies in your ability to be kind, patient, respectful, and forgiving. This attitude applies not only to your partner but also to yourself!

To negotiate properly, you need three partners:

- Someone to lead or follow.
- The dance floor to provide stability and energy.
- The music that becomes a partner to both of you.

After all, without the music and its sensuous interpretation, you and your partner cannot dance. And as described in Chapter 5, "Lifestyles Improve Socially, Psychologically, and Physically," you derive energy from the dance floor by virtue of Newton's third law of inertia—for every action, there is an opposite and equal reaction.

When learning and practicing with partners, I find the dominant personality of the couple tries to control the other partner. Frequently this ends the dance or partnering relationship before it can begin. Remember, in partner dancing, "a couple" is really a singular animate object. The attitude and personality of each of the members make up a component of the dance couple but should not dominate it. If your arms dominate your legs, you cannot walk. They must exist harmoniously.

To achieve even a moderate level of success in any form of partner dancing, both partners will have to face the same trials and tribulations. At the top of the mountain, both of you will experience the same joys of achievement and pleasure. Each member of the dance couple must really do some soul searching to understand this and then allow for each other's frustration, errors, growth, and adaptation to partnering. Neither member could possibly know it all. Nobody does. You could not possibly know how you feel physically to another person. How could you? A clone of you would have to exist with a complete and a continuous transmittable sense of feeling. You are trying to become a perfect building block or that certain piece of a puzzle that fits just right.

Be very kind to your partner, and remember, you are learning, too. When you take a moment to teach him or "just show him what to do," you are taking responsibility for knowing what you are showing. More often than not, this can become your undoing. Because you are not an expert, you can only correct your partner with a negative rather than a "how to."

The best way to teach a partner the proper steps is to be proficient yourself. When you get better, your partner always seems to have gotten better! Remember, ballroom dancing is not just about you anymore; it is about the two of you moving as one.

You and your partner will learn at different rates of speed during your ballroom dancing experience. While this can become frustrating, you have to remember that dancing can be like learning to walk all over again.

While learning, you and your partner will—and I mean *will*—hit roadblocks. You will also achieve many rewarding threshold experiences that will more than offset your struggles and failures. As you embark on this adventure called partner dancing, please enjoy all of your growth. Many others with fewer skills and tools have tried and learned to dance successfully. I promise you will, too!

> **Bet You Didn't Know**
>
> Ballroom dancing may be the most revealing indication of the overall compatibility of any two people. For engaged couples taking lessons, learning to dance is often their first joint goal requiring mutual effort. The kindness, forgiveness, and mutual respect required to work together to achieve the dance relationship is very revealing.

The Least You Need to Know

- Attaining good vertical position and control of your ribcage will make dancing much easier to learn.
- Never finish a dance step on two feet.
- The leg action used to dance is not made up of small, separate movements, but rather a series of coincidental actions.
- Building a dance couple is a cooperative effort, and both partners enjoy the rewards equally.
- Everyone has a different approach to learning something new, so be kind to yourself and to your partner!

Chapter 7

Music and More Music: About the Music on Your CD

In This Chapter

- ◆ Do the same thing—not your own thing
- ◆ Finally! I can hear it
- ◆ Fred and Ginger liked it smooth and dreamy
- ◆ The rhythm's goin' to get 'cha!

The very heart and soul of dancing exists within the music. In addition to a physical form, dancing is also the personification of music. Simply stated, dancing comes from music. I know of no social dance that was first choreographed and then followed by the creation of a suitable musical composition. Each dance expresses the characteristics of the music it was fashioned for. You will learn about those characteristics and each song selection on your CD compilation as it matches the dances we will study.

Frequently beginner students are frustrated by the music played at a nightclub, public dance hall, or DJ-sponsored social dance. The music is too fast, too slow, lacks variety, or is just not danceable! Dancing within acceptable tempos always makes the dancer's experience more enjoyable. In this chapter you will learn what tempo of music works best for you in each dance at each stage of your dance development. If you are a DJ or a dancer sponsoring or hosting a dance function, reading this material will definitely help you play better music suitable to the level of your dancers' abilities!

Your Music for Dancing

Included with *The Complete Idiot's Guide to Ballroom Dancing* you will be pleased to find a wonderful CD compilation produced and directed by Dance Vision International and Winrod Productions. The music selected is designed specifically for dancers. This CD can be used for practicing or for general dancing enjoyment. I have selected these music tempos to benefit any beginner learning to dance in the ballroom style. The difference between instructional music and popular music is the dancer's ability to clearly hear the rhythm of the music.

In *The Complete Idiot's Guide to Ballroom Dancing* we will cover two complements of dances. They are the American-style smooth dances and the American-style rhythm or Latin dances. The major characteristic of smooth dances is that they travel around the dance floor in line of dance (see the Line of Dance diagram on the reference card and in Chapter 14, "Your Best Directions"). In contrast, the rhythm or Latin dances are localized and danced within a limited amount of space. An analogy would be dancing around your dining room table versus dancing on top of your dining room table.

Popular music is often produced in popular rhythms, which can be close to strict tempo but can become erratic. Sometimes during a composition a vocalist or a portion of an instrumental will depart from the basic timing of the song. For instance, guitar or saxophone players may highlight their musical talent during what is called a *solo*, *riff*, or *highlight*. This portion of the song may actually become undanceable. At times there are breaks in the music where there is no audible sound or rhythm at all. While this might be popular for more advanced dancers, allowing them to be playful or theatrical, a beginner can become very confused and actually stop dancing.

From a dancer's point of view, the big band and swing sounds of the 1930s and 1940s were the biggest offenders of this undanceable interlude. This fabulous music, among my favorites, was often lacking in *strict tempo*. Popular American jazz music grew up in the big band era, but jazz music is not widely held as being good dance music. Jazz is often improvisational; good dance music cannot be! Glenn Miller was a captain in the United States Air Force and military bandleader in Europe during World War II. Perhaps it was this military experience with so much emphasis on cadence that influenced him the most. More than any other of the famous big band leaders, Miller seemed to understand the importance of strict tempo for dancing. His songs are still very popular for ballroom and Swing dancers because of their adherence to strict tempo. The rhythmic approximation of Miller's music suits the average dancer.

Dancing Definition

Strict tempo is a consistent and dependable beat structure. Every beat of music in the bar or measure of music is like every other beat of music in the same bar. This structure continues for the remainder of the composition. The accent or highlight beat, known as the *downbeat*, is also the same in each bar of music. The number of beats and bars in a minute does not vacillate and remains the same throughout the composition.

Your music sampler included with this book is produced in strict tempo. The rhythm from the bass, percussion, or rhythm section of the orchestra is easily heard. The discernibility of this music answers the beginner's common question, "How can I learn to hear the music and learn what dance to do?"

Dance instructors agree about the importance of strict tempo music as a teaching tool. To a large degree, dancing has become standardized, and the tempos that suit each dance have as well. This is good news for all of you who are studying this text and now own your CD sampler.

Standardization = Acceptance

The standardization of any activity represents and produces broad-based acceptance, including accessibility by an increasing number of participants. This is absolutely the case with dancing and dance music. The choreography in this book is standardized and has been recognized by the National Dance Council of America. The music you now possess falls within the parameters of the tempos recognized by the National Dance Council of America.

Grandma and grandpa or their parents (depending on your age) never had standardization in dancing or music. When the big band era subsided, there was a significant decline in the number of ballroom dancers. Most of them who bragged about being ballroom dancers were really "doers of their own thing" in a contact position.

Unfortunately when this older generation lost a dance partner, they were sunk! There was no one else to dance with—or at least no one who understood his or her own style. This older generation frequently could not tell the difference between a Rumba and a Cha-Cha. Interpreting the differences in Swing or the Foxtrot was often a mystery. Was waltzing an idiomatic expression, or was it the Waltz in $^3/_4$ timing?

Many of this generation used the same steps to the same rhythm regardless of what music was playing. Unfortunately while they were having a good time, they were eliminating many people from their dance equation. A dancer without the ability to discern one music type from another and then what dance is suitable is like an automobile and a driver without anywhere to go!

The good news is that you can hear the differences between a Foxtrot and a Tango on your CD. Each dance was developed in character to match its own music. While you listen to this music, you will be studying the differences from one music type to the next. The more you hear, the easier it will be to identify the music type and what dance to do to it. This is absolutely part of your dance education! Soon you will listen to the radio, an orchestra or band, or a DJ and know the dance type that suits the popular song. This becomes exciting in and of itself. It opens up a whole new realm of possibilities and opportunities to dance! Let's begin to study the music.

Ballroom Bloopers

"Doing your own thing" on the dance floor is fine for the individual but generally does not work with a partner. When you find a partner who does it with you, you had better not lose him. He may indeed be irreplaceable! Standardization of dance instruction and dancing allows you to learn in New York and dance in L.A. with any partner in any dance.

Bet You Didn't Know

From 1998 right to the present, America has enjoyed the explosion of Latin American dance rhythms on the pop music scene. Not since the 1940s and 1950s has the intrigue and sensuality of these Afro-Cuban rhythms invaded our diverse culture. Much of this music has been categorized as Salsa—a dance that is essentially a derivative of the Mambo. The untrained dancing public has lumped the following songs into the Salsa category: "Bailamos," performed by Enrique Iglesias, "Livin' La Vida Loca," performed by Ricky Martin, "Smooth," performed by Santana, "Let's Get Loud," performed by Jennifer Lopez, and "I Need to Know," performed by Marc Anthony. The reality is that the first two of these songs are really a Samba rhythm, and the latter three songs are all Cha-Cha rhythm. During the 1940s and 1950s, Cha-Cha and Samba were extraordinarily popular in the United States. These two dances have experienced exceptional growth in the last several years.

Track One: Waltz

Song title: "Time in a Bottle"

Album title: *Anyone Can Dance* (CD214)

This song is 30 measures per minute or 90 beats per minute.

The basic timing is $^1/_4$, which means three $^1/_4$ notes to a measure of music. The down or accent beat is the first beat of the measure. The music rises to a crescendo from the first beat to the third and halfway through the third beat falls to diminishment. This rise and fall is consistent with every Waltz regardless of tempo.

Movement Memo _____

Dancing is the personification of music. Music is beautiful, so you must be as well. Dance is beauty and if done correctly makes you beautiful—remember that! Concentrate on your musicality and movement across the dance floor. This is essential to express the art of ballroom dancing.

The Waltz is included in the American smooth complement of dances, and the measure per minute range is 28 to 36. For social dancing the best range of Waltz music occurs from 30 to 32 measures per minute. This selection of 30 measures per minute makes this Waltz work best for the beginner level. Like the Foxtrot, beginners should be first concerned about timing and footwork prior to the need to express greater amounts of rhythm forced by the slower Waltzes. While beginners generally find it easier to deal with the faster Waltzes, this is only true to a point. When the music is faster than 32 measures per minute, difficulty arises in the action of closing the feet and making various kinds of rotations.

The Waltz is certainly the most romantic of the smooth dances. At the slower tempos, dancers are able to express the dreamy qualities invoked by the music of the Waltz. A good Waltz seems to stir the imagination whether it be of love lost, love found, or happily ever after.

Track Two: Foxtrot

Song title: "I Left My Heart in San Francisco"

Album title: *Fabuloso American Rhythm & Smooth Vol. II* (CD208)

This song is 31 measures per minute or 124 beats per minute.

The basic timing is $^4/_4$, which means four $^3/_4$ notes to a measure of music. The down or accent beat is the first beat of the measure. The Foxtrot is included in the American smooth complement of dances. For social dancing, the best measure-per-minute range of the Foxtrot is 30 to 33. Foxtrots can actually range from 28 to 34 measures per minute.

At 31 measures per minute, this Foxtrot selection works best for beginners. Beginner dancers should be first concerned about timing and footwork before advancing to the need to express greater amounts of rhythm dictated by slower music.

New dancers find it easier to glide between their feet on slightly faster tempos in the smooth complement of dances. Once you get better, begin to use Foxtrots that are a bit slower. It is within the slower rhythms that the wonderful fluid romantic feeling of the Foxtrot actually exists. In these slower Foxtrots, you hear the music begin to *crescendo* from the first beat in the measure to the fourth and then diminish halfway through the fourth beat.

Dancing Definition _____

A **crescendo** is when music gradually increases in loudness or intensity. The listener senses this as a rise or climax in the measure of music. Dancers personify the music by expressing these crescendos in elevation changes commonly called "rise." From crescendo comes diminishment and in dance we express that through lowering to our normal elevation. This is commonly termed as "fall." I have never like the usage of the word "fall." Dancer's never fall, they are always in control of the lowering action!

The faster tempo Foxtrots have a very bright, robust tone and produce a feeling similar to a party atmosphere. The music in these Foxtrots will sometimes have a more up and down movement not unlike swing music. However I believe that while the first two beats and the second two beats of the bar have an up/down feeling, the second two beats are somewhat lighter, distinguishing it from swing music. Do not be surprised if during the faster tempo Foxtrots many on the dance floor feel and dance the Swing.

Movement Memo

The slower tempos are expressed more in the knees than in the extension of the legs. That means there is a slight bounce through the knees and ankles. This is called *rhythm dancing* and effectively uses up the time of the music. Rhythm dancing does not travel very far and is preferable on the very congested ballroom or small lounge-size social dance floors. The same timing is maintained in all figures. For more of an explanation of the time of music (or time signature), refer to the section "Time Has a Signature" in Chapter 8, "Timing and Rhythm for the Layperson."

Track Three: Tango

Song title: "Tango Jack"

Album title: *Fabuloso American Rhythm & Smooth Vol. II* (CD208)

This song is 32 measures per minute or 128 beats per minute.

The basic timing is ⁴/₄, which means four ¹/₄ notes to a measure of music. The down or accent beat is the first beat of the measure. In a sequence of eight beats (two measures) of music, the first measure will be bolder or more intense than the second of the two measures. You might say the Tango is written in two connecting measures totaling eight beats. These eight beats form what is called a *phrase*. At the end of the phrase, the music seems to stop or drift off. This is exactly the way that dancers express Tango music—they dance to stop! We will cover more of this in the choreography section for the Tango.

The Tango is included in the American smooth complement of dances. The measure-per-minute range of the Tango is 26 to 34. For social dancing, the best range of Tango music occurs from 30 to 32 measures per minute. This selection of 32 measures per minute makes this Tango work best for the beginner level. The intensity of ballroom Tango music will always wake up a room. Its strict military cadence seems particularly appealing to gentlemen! The cat-like eccentricities of the dance and staccato (cut) music make the Tango a theatrical favorite. The Tango is not hard to do, it just requires attitude and posturing!

Bet You Didn't Know

In this book, we are covering the very popular ballroom style of Tango. Ballroom Tango progresses around the dance floor unlike its predecessor the Argentine style of Tango. Ballroom Tango found its roots in Paris and was adapted to the style of movement similar to the progressive nature of the Waltz. From Paris, the dance made its way to America. Tango Argentino frequently pauses its progression in favor of extended physical conversations and interludes between the dancers. You will see very sophisticated in-place circling and provocative interactions of their legs and feet. Tango Argentino is more closely akin to Latin American dancing with more enduring Moroccan and Creole influences. We have included the ballroom Tango, although unique in music and dance style, with the American smooth complement of dances because of its progressive nature. For more information on the Argentine and American Tango, please consult the reference and instructional book *Quickstart to Tango* by Jeff Allen (QQS Publications, 1998).

Track Four: Viennese Waltz

Song title: "My Favorite Things"

Album title: *Fabuloso American Rhythm & Smooth Vol. II* (CD208)

This song is 54 measures per minute or 162 beats per minute.

The basic timing is ³/₄, which means three ¹/₄ notes to a measure of music. The down or accent beat is the first beat of the measure. The music rises to a crescendo from the first beat to the third and halfway through the third beat falls to diminishment. This rise and fall is consistent with every Viennese Waltz regardless of tempo.

The Viennese Waltz is the oldest of all the partnered dances and is included in the American smooth complement of dances. The measure-per-minute range of the Viennese Waltz is 50 to 62. For social dancing, the best range of Viennese Waltz music occurs from 50 to 54 measures per minute. This selection of 54 measures per minute makes this Viennese Waltz work best for the beginner level.

Beginner dancers of the Viennese Waltz will use many of the balance steps described in the choreography section of this book. When the music is faster than 54 measures per minute, difficulty arises in the action of closing the feet and making various kinds of rotations. A good DJ will announce to the dancers that they are about to play a Viennese or sometimes called a Strauss Waltz. The advanced dancers should be requested to use the outside of the dance floor while the beginners, who will not travel nearly as much, should restrict themselves to the center of the dance floor.

Bet You Didn't Know

Wedding couples frequently select Viennese Waltzes for the wedding dance. However, they often make these selections unknowingly unless they are experienced dancers or are very familiar with music. Songs like "Can't Help Falling in Love," by Elvis Presley, "Color My World," by Chicago, "Ebb Tide" or "Unchained Melody," by The Righteous Brothers, and "(You Are My) Special Angel," by The Vogues are all Viennese Waltzes. Although I have presented a beginner level in this book, the Viennese Waltz is not really considered a beginner dance. At one time dance studios only taught this much faster version of the Waltz to their intermediate and advanced level students. If you are a beginner or a wedding couple, an alternative to the Viennese Waltz is a hesitation Waltz. This alternative form is described in *The Complete Guide to Slow Dancing*, by Jeff Allen (QQS Publications, 1997). This form of Waltz allows dancers to use the very fast Waltz without too much effort. As a result, the hesitation Waltz becomes slow even though the musical tempo is very fast.

Track Five: Rumba

Song title: "My Rumba"

Album title: *Fabuloso American Rhythm Vol. II* (CD207)

This song is 32 measures per minute or 128 beats per minute.

The basic timing is ⁴/₄, which means four ¹/₄ notes to a measure of music. The downbeat occurs on the first beat of the measure. The accent, crescendo, or highlight beat of the Rumba occurs on the second beat of the bar and then diminishes through the remainder of the measure.

The Rumba is included in the American rhythm complement of dances. It has a wide range of tempos and a measure-per-minute range of 26 to 36. For social dancing, the best range of Rumba music occurs from 28 to 32 measures per minute. This selection of 32 measures per minute makes this Rumba work best for the beginner level. In the Latin dances, the expression of Cuban motion, or hip action, takes a period of time and experience to develop comfortably. The slower of the Rumba tempos require more of this body music to maintain its timing. Therefore it is easier for beginners to concentrate on their footwork, closing action, and figure selections at the early phases of their experience with the Rumba.

Whether in English or Spanish, Rumba music speaks of love and sensuality. Many artists like The Drifters, Stevie Wonder, Smokey Robinson, Elvis Presley, and Michael Jackson have expressed their best lyrical efforts using this rhythm. Whether provocative or subdued, the Rumba is a favorite throughout the world.

Track Six: Merengue

Song title: "El Meneito"

Album title: *Anyone Can Dance* (CD214)

This song is 29 measures per minute or 116 beats per minute.

The basic timing is $^4/_4$, which means four $^1/_4$ notes to a measure of music. The Merengue can also be written in $^2/_4$ timing, which means two $^1/_4$ notes to a measure of music. The downbeat occurs on the first beat of the measure. Merengue music and the dance is phrased into measures of eight $^1/_4$ notes. The basic steps change weight on every beat of music.

The Merengue is included in the American rhythm complement of dances and has a wide range of tempos. The measures per minute can begin at 29 and top out at 52. Deejays often play a moderate tempo and then a very fast tempo Merengue. This will always satisfy a diverse group of dancers.

Merengue music has two major styles. The first is commonly used by ballroom dance studios and is Haitian. It is a bit more subdued and slower than the second styling, which is from the Dominican Republic. An example of this Haitian style would be the song "Hot, Hot, Hot," by Buster Poindexter. The Dominican Merengues are at times exceptionally fast. These are designed for very congested dance floors with very little progressive movements. The slower Merengues are very sensual, and the faster Merengues are very sexy!

The beginner dancing the Merengue in the ballroom style will find the tempo of 29 measures per minute easy to negotiate using the dance figures found in this book. This tempo will work well with respect to timing, footwork, and Latin motion. It is conceivable that on any given Saturday night there are more people dancing the Merengue throughout the world than any other dance!

Movement Memo

One shortcut to help discover the first beat of any musical composition or measure of music is to listen for the moment a vocalist begins to sing. Generally a vocalist will begin on the first beat of the bar. Also, you may discover that many of the instruments cut in at the first beat of music, distinguishing themselves from the base or percussion instruments.

Track Seven: Samba

Song title: "Hot Hot Hot"

Album title: *Fabuloso American Rhythm Vol. II* (CD207)

This song is 50 measures per minute or 100 beats per minute.

The basic timing is $^2/_4$, which means two $^1/_4$ notes to a measure of music. Samba music is quite different from those previously mentioned. The downbeat is on the fourth beat of the measure. Samba is phrased like Merengue and Tango in eight-beat increments, with the latter four beats being slightly less intense than the former four beats of music. Accents occur on every even beat of the music.

The Samba is included in the American rhythm complement of dances. This Brazilian dance has strong roots in African rhythms. The atmosphere of the Samba is always festive and can be quite provocative. Samba at 51 measures per minute is very good for beginners, but like Merengue, authentic Brazilian Samba can be extremely fast. A trip to Rio de Janeiro would reveal how fast and provocative the Samba can be, especially during their festival period or Carnival! Socially Samba is comfortable from 48 to 52 measures per minute.

Samba rhythm is very popular in contemporary American jazz music. It is one of the few if not the only danceable jazz rhythm. Great Samba music of the past includes "Brazil" and "The Girl from Ipanema." In the 1980s, Madonna charted number 1 with her popular "La Isla Bonita." As previously mentioned, Ricky Martin and Enrique Iglesias have recently had big hits using this rhythm.

Track Eight: Cha-Cha

Song title: "Me Gusta Estar Viva"

Album title: *Fabuloso American Rhythm Vol. II* (CD207)

This song is 30 measures per minute or 120 beats per minute.

> **Bet You Didn't Know**
>
> The musical instruments that create the sounds of syncopation and rhythm in Latin American music are the claves (two sticks of hardwood), the maracas (gourds on wooden handles with seeds that rattle inside them), the cencerro (sometimes called a Cha-Cha bell), the timbales (the Cuban drum played with untapered dowels), and the conga and bongo drums.

The basic timing is $^4/_4$, which means four $^1/_4$ notes to a measure of music. The downbeat is on the first beat of the measure. The accent, crescendo, or highlight beat of the Cha-Cha occurs on the second beat of the bar and then diminishes through the remainder of the measure. Cha-Cha music is very staccato, with syncopation or split on the fourth beat of every measure. This is what makes the Cha-Cha distinct from the Mambo or Rumba. Cha-Cha music developed from Mambo music. When the Mambo got faster, musicians slowed down the Mambo tempo and added the syncopation to give the dance pace or interest. The result was the Cha-Cha.

The Cha-Cha is included in the American rhythm complement of dances. Its Afro-Cuban rhythm ranges from 26 to 33 measures per minute. The best social range for the Cha-Cha is 30 to 32 measures per minute. During the 1950s and 1960s, the Cha-Cha was frequently called the most popular dance in the world. It still retains its versatility with an uncanny ability to accept any of the characteristics that arise from street or jazz dance trends and fads.

Track Nine: Mambo

Song title: "Mambo Cinco"

Album title: *American Rhythm Vol. I* (CD202)

This song is 47 measures per minute or 188 beats per minute.

The basic timing is $^4/_4$, which means four $^1/_4$ notes to a measure of music. The downbeat is on the first beat of the measure. The accent, crescendo, or highlight beat of the Mambo occurs on the second beat of the bar and then diminishes through the remainder of the measure.

The Mambo is included in the American rhythm complement of dances. Also an Afro-Cuban rhythm, the Mambo has a range of 44 to 51 measures per minute, with the best social range being 45 to 47 measures per minute. Mambo was the predecessor to Cha-Cha and has been so popular that the word itself conjures up ideas of sexy playfulness and sensuality. It is in this dance where men and women portray the best elements of Latin American dancing by characterizing the war of the sexes as a provocative cat and mouse game.

> **Bet You Didn't Know**
>
> From the 1950s to the present, the highest-ranking and largest-selling pop hits in music history have used Cha-Cha, Rumba, and Mambo rhythms. Roy Orbison's song "Pretty Woman," Michael Jackson's song "Billie Jean," and Santana's two huge hits "Oye Como Va" and "Smooth" use Cha-Cha rhythm. You can hear the Mambo rhythm in many of the "British invasion" hits—most notably, "She Loves You" by The Beatles. The Dave Clark 5 used the Rumba tempo in their smash hit "Because."

Track Ten: East Coast Swing

Song title: "Blue Monday"

Album title: *Fabuloso American Rhythm Vol. II* (CD207)

This song is 32 measures per minute or 128 beats per minute.

The basic timing is ⁴/₄, which means four ¹/₄ notes to a measure of music. The downbeats are on the second and fourth beat of the measure.

The East Coast Swing is included in the American rhythm complement of dances. This form of Swing dancing is the most diverse and adaptable of the Swing dance family. Since the inception of Swing dancing in the 1930s, every conceivable musical format has had some form of swing music within its parameters. The East Coast Swing has something for everyone, with an acceptable social range of 34 to 46 measures per minute. So in this case, a DJ would simply have to know his audience of dancers and their skill level to determine what tempo to use.

Simply stated, "It don't mean a thing if it ain't got that swing!" Americans really know how to "Jump, Jive, and Wail."

Track Eleven: Hustle

Song title: "Queen-a-Licious"

Album title: *Anyone Can Dance* (CD214)

This song is 28 measures per minute or 112 beats per minute.

The basic timing is ⁴/₄, which means four ¹/₄ notes to a measure of music. The downbeat is on the first beat of the measure.

The Hustle is included in the American rhythm complement of dances. The measure-per-minute range of the Hustle is 27 to 32 measures per minute, with a comfortable social range of 28 to 30 measures per minute.

Sometimes the Hustle is referred to as the disco Hustle because it was first danced in the venue called a disco nightclub and was danced to disco-style music. The disco-style music at the time used vinyl records only. It had elements of rhythm and blues, Latin, and American rock music. The most notable characteristic of disco music is the use of a computerized beat structure. This perfect repetition may produce monotony for some listeners but nevertheless is absolutely fabulous dance music. The consistent computerized bass beat is a great tool for beginners learning to keep time with the music!

The Least You Need to Know

- ◆ Smooth dances move counterclockwise around the perimeter of the dance floor and include the Foxtrot, Waltz, Tango, and Viennese Waltz.
- ◆ Rhythm or Latin dances are done in a smaller, localized area and include the Rumba, Merengue, Samba, Cha-Cha, Mambo, East Coast Swing, and Hustle.
- ◆ Your CD contains music for each dance type covered in this book at tempos appropriate for the beginner dancer.
- ◆ The accent beat and the tempo of the music will identify the music type and appropriate dance type.

Chapter 8

Timing and Rhythm for the Layperson

In This Chapter

◆ Keeping time is more than looking at your watch

◆ Rhythm—easy as digging a hole!

◆ Fast or slow—it's up to the tempo

◆ "Beat" me eight to the bar!

This chapter promises to be a revelation for those who have shied away from dancing because of an unfriendly relationship with music. This revelation comes in the form of knowledge, and with that knowledge you will lose your fear and gain confidence. You are going to learn the differences between timing and rhythm. I will also teach you how to keep timing and express rhythm. You will quickly find that the skills to keep timing in dance are not foreign to you. In fact we will use such simple examples that you will be surprised you didn't learn how to dance long ago.

Please do not rush through this chapter, particularly if you perceive yourself as musically challenged! You are not going to learn how to read sheet music. You are going to learn how to keep timing while dancing. It may be a very good idea for you to work on this chapter all by yourself, in peace and quiet. Using simple, easy-to-understand examples, we will break down the barriers that have kept you from the dance floor.

Once you have become comfortable with the aspects of timing and rhythm as a functional skill (used in ordinary daily life), we will move on to their applications with music and expressing them through your body and legs.

Music and You

The dancer does not have to know how to read music. Many experienced dancers and teachers that dance with great expertise have no clue how to describe the dancer's relationship to the mathematical structure of music. Even fewer have the ability to read music. Think of it this way: We learned to speak long before we were able to read or write. Through the course of daily life, we continue to converse with others even though most of us are far from grammatical experts. I consider myself an expert in dancing and teaching dance with a fair understanding of grammatical structure in the English language. I write books about dancing but I am not a grammatical expert. When I need help, I turn to people who make their living correcting errors made by writers like myself. You do not need to be an expert in speech to make your point known, and you do not have to be a music expert to dance.

Think of music in the same way you think of language. It is a means to convey a thought or action. When you speak with someone, you definitely use timing. You decide when and what to say as a result of what you have heard, read, seen, or felt. You learn to react to music in the same way you react during conversation. In order to know what to do, you will have to become a good listener and respond properly. The gravity or force of what was said to you determines the speed or intensity of your response. This is your rhythmic relationship with your conversationist. In music, your response will be in rhythmic movement.

Bet You Didn't Know

Every dancer has three partners. Your first partner must be the music. The music is the source of inspiration for the dance and the "when" of the movement. The music tells you when to begin to dance, how fast to dance, and even when to stop dancing. Your second dance partner is the dance floor itself. The dance floor provides the spatial feelings of welcome resistance and support. The "how" begins with the dance floor—without it, the dancer could not move or carry his body. The third partner is the human one. This is your traveling companion or the "where" of the dance couple. They follow you, and you follow them. The relationship is really amazing, as each individual brings two other partners, and together the dance couple creates a cycle of connecting feelings and forces!

The music is the boss and the real leader of a dance couple. Think of music for dancing like you would think of a benevolent dictator. You have the same freedoms of choice as you would in a democracy, with the exception of when you make those choices and the speed at which you make them. As a dancer you must be subservient or obedient to the music. Since ballroom dancing is danced as couples, both dancers must be subservient to the same music. This consistency allows us to respond and communicate together.

Life itself flows with timing and *rhythm*. The word *beat* comes from the action of your heart—a heartbeat. Sometimes life is exciting and moves faster, and sometimes life is docile and slower paced. Your heart reacts with a change in rhythm and timing. The situation determines the rate of speed your heart beats. We identify these situations by labeling them as joy, excitement, danger, and so on.

Dancing Definition

Rhythm is the interplay of the timing of a sequence of events. It is the way in which the events are aligned with each other and includes any empty or unoccupied moments within the sequence. It also includes the recurring blueprint of heavier movements within softer movements. In music, rhythm is a consistent pattern of beats with the emphasis or accent recurring on the same beat throughout a specified period (measure or bar).

Music has identified these situations as rhythm and timing. When rhythm and timing characteristics become dependable, consistent, and cumulative, we begin to recognize them as a standard form of music. We are able to label this standardization as a dance rhythm—for instance, the Foxtrot. We could have labeled music by the feelings expressed, like exciting, upbeat, boring, romantic, heavenly, masculine, feminine, and the list goes on. Instead we have given musical rhythms names like Waltz, Tango, Mambo, and Cha-Cha that portray a composite of many feelings. Each of these musical rhythms expresses a mood, tempo, or feeling that is recognizable. As a dancer, you will learn to hear and feel what characteristics create these differences. The good news is you will not have to learn how to read or write music to do this!

Let's Take a Break from Music

When I receive a phone call from a prospective student, I am often greeted with the following statement: "I need lessons because I have no rhythm or timing." I always respond with amazement as if never having heard this before. "You say you have no rhythm? Then how do you brush your teeth in the morning?" Or "Are you able to travel up and down a staircase the same way each time?" Or "Can you ride a bicycle or swim?" Or "Can you sign your name the same way each time?" Or "Are you proficient in or have you played any sports?" It would be very rare to receive an answer of "no" to any or all of these questions!

The caller is now curious and wants to know what these things have to do with either dancing or expressing rhythm in dance. The following response is my layperson's definition of rhythm:

> Rhythm is the ability to repeat a skill the same way each time. Sometimes you repeat that skill slower or sometimes faster. Sometimes you add emphasis to a portion of that skill and sometimes you change the place of that emphasis.

I go on to tell the caller that it would be very difficult to exist and perform the functions of daily living without having rhythm. The caller's general remarks are "You're right, I never thought of it that way. Maybe you *can* teach me to dance!" Let's move away from musical expression for a while and find out how some ordinary skills require rhythm, timing, and accent.

Gardening for Rhythm and Timing

The illustration that I like to use while teaching rhythm and timing is that of a gardener shoveling dirt. Forgive me if the following seems very remedial—it is intended to be! I can best create physical analogies by using the remedial skills that you are familiar with. I have already stated that the best thing for you to do when learning to dance is to remove your ego from the equation.

Turning over your garden, planting bulbs and shrubs, or even shoveling the snow in your driveway will never be the same again! Do you have your shovels ready?

Movement Memo

It is imperative that before you begin any physical activity, including dancing, you warm up your muscles. Always begin stretching slowly; athletes, coaches, and trainers have learned that you can actually become injured while stretching if you do so too vigorously! Here is a simple series of warm-up exercises. Gently twist from the waist clockwise and counterclockwise. Gently lift your arms up and down from the shoulders. Spread your legs apart with your arms lifted in the air and sway to the right and left. After doing this a few times, you may increase the intensity of each movement. Use one arm to support yourself from a stable structure like a wall or rail, and with the other hand, bend down and grasp the front of your ankle. Gently bend your knee so that the back of your heel is almost touching the back of your thigh. If you are able, gently swing your leg forward and back in this position.

Digging the Beat

Here is a list of directions to follow, figuratively or literally, that represent the physical use and distribution of time:

Step 1. Choose a place where you can begin digging.

Step 2. Stretch out a little bit and warm up those muscles gently.

Step 3. Penetrate the garden bed with your shovel and scoop out a shovelful of dirt. Now toss the dirt away.

Step 4. Repeat step 3 at the same rate of speed and intensity. Maintaining the speed and intensity is very important!

Step 5. Repeat step 3 again at the same rate of speed and intensity.

Step 6. And, for the last time, repeat step 3 at the same rate of speed and intensity for a total of four shovelfuls of dirt.

In theory what you have done is created a series of actions where each action took exactly the same amount of time. In other words, each shovelful of dirt and the speed at which you dug and tossed the dirt away were exactly the same. In layperson's terms, one "dig and toss" would be the equivalent of a consistent period of time equal to any other "dig and toss" period of time. Each shovelful began and ended in the same way—with an empty shovel. The empty shovel was the result of concluding the action. There was the start to this action ("the dig"), and the conclusion to this action ("the toss"), and together they took a period of time. You repeated this action a total of three times. If you were to repeat this measured process in its entirety, it would in theory take exactly the same amount of time. The dig and toss was a sequence of events that took time to accomplish. This accomplishment was finalized when the shovel was emptied.

The Same Thing over and over Again

I know this process must seem very redundant, but that's just the way timing is. Timing is any sequence of events that occur and conclude in a specified period. There is also a minuscule period of time that exists between the sequences of events. We do not have to dwell on this but it must exist.

Let's call the "dig and toss" one beat. The accumulation of four "dig and toss" actions will be referred to as a measured period of four beats. The passage of four measures would include the same 16 beats as any other four measures. Now if your neighbor asks you how long it would take to dig a similar-size hole for him, you have an established precedent and theoretically the exact amount of time that would pass to accomplish the task. In other words you have established a recognizable and dependable timeframe for any "dig and toss" process. You and your neighbor know exactly how long this process will take from start to finish.

We are not done with this "dig and toss" model, but let's explore what you have learned in terms of your usage of time with respect to the physical activity of ballroom dancing. You have learned from this model that timing is a physical sequence of events rather than just a moment of time. The physical sequence of events described in the model has mathematical precision, physical standardization, and its movement had ongoing physical consistency.

Ballroom dancing is the personification of music, a physical activity performed within the particular dance characteristic. Therefore, the need for the same mathematical precision, standardization, and consistency as any other physical endeavor is paramount to the dancer and the dance couple. Without these, the ballroom couple could not depend on the music or each other. It is compulsory for the ballroom dancer to develop consistency in the "when" or timing of their physical expression.

Time Has a Signature

Let's begin to translate that "when" to the language of music and dance. First we will discuss what the $^4/_4$, $^3/_4$, or $^2/_4$ fractions symbolized in the previous chapter regarding your music. In music those fractions are called your *time signature*. The denominator of that time signature—the number 4—simply means that a quarter note in music equals one beat. For example, count the following out loud: "1, 2, 3, 4, 1, 2, 3, 4, 1, 2, 3, 4," and so on, while saying the numbers at the same speed each time.

Ballroom Bloopers _____

Always be careful to observe Jeff's Eleventh Commandment of ballroom dancing. "Thou shall never finish a dance step with weight on two feet!" The action of the dig and toss model was completed when the shovel was emptied, signifying that one full beat was complete. When you completed a "dig and toss" you did not stop, lean on your shovel, and rest. The end of your toss became the beginning of your next dig. The moment between is so indistinguishable that it becomes coincidental. A dance step is never complete until you are able to remove the former foot from the dance floor. If you finish a dance step with two feet on the floor, you will always be perplexed by which foot is next. This would be like resting between each dig and toss and having to start over again from a dead stop. Music moves along too quickly for you to have to deal with this indecision or stop and start.

The denominator of the fraction is much less important to the dancer than the numerator of the fraction. For most of the dances we cover in this book, the numerator is 4. This means there are 4 "digs and tosses" in each measure. You will notice three exceptions to this: Waltz ($^3/_4$), Viennese Waltz ($^6/_8$), and Samba ($^2/_4$). Remember that we called a "dig and toss" one beat. So you now understand that there are four beats in any measure of your $^4/_4$ music. If you were to "dig and toss" at a greater rate of speed, you would still have four beats to your measure, and the same could be said for moving more slowly.

Musically, *speed* refers to the number of bars of music per minute. Regardless of the speed of the music, in order to complete a dance step, you must load your foot up with your body weight and then discharge that weight—the same way that you empty your shovel. Such a dance step would take one beat of music. In dancing, the speed at which we operate is known as the *tempo*. Tempo is simply how fast you are traveling or how fast the music is traveling in terms of time.

Slows and Quicks

We can quantify timing in dancing the same way we can quantify the "dig and toss." Suppose we dig and toss with a shovel that has twice the capacity of our original shovel. In theory it should take twice as long for the "dig and toss" to be completed. Relax for a moment and think about this: More capacity takes a longer period of time!

In dancing we have terminology that represents the difference between a bigger shovel and a smaller one. The bigger shovel, which could now handle two beats, we will call a "Slow" shovel. We will call the smaller, standard one-beat shovel a "Quick" shovel. If we understand our fourth-grade mathematics, two Slow shovels equals the same timeframe as four Quick shovels. Your shovelful will represent your entire body weight, and each dance step represents a change of your full body weight. We can cut the time it takes to dig and toss by moving quicker, or we can increase the time it takes to dig and toss by moving slower.

You will soon begin learning to take dance steps. The terminology you'll become familiar with will be the same that you have just learned. The increment of a Slow count in dancing will be two beats of music, and a Quick count will be one beat of music. It is also possible that a Slow could be one full beat of music and a Quick could be one-half beat of music. So the equation is simple: A Slow takes twice the time as a Quick. In this book we will use the terminology of "Slows" and "Quicks" to describe the value of time for each dance step you'll learn.

For the foreseeable future, this is all you need to know about the physical application of time in ballroom dancing. Now we are going to return to our model of digs and tosses and talk about musical characteristics, down beats, and accents.

Since you already understand the physical basis of a measure, let us add emphasis to a beat, known as a "dig and toss," within that measure. First, what is generally called the *downbeat* refers to the first beat of the measure, and each measure definitely has a first beat. Like musicians, dancers begin at the first beat. This would be called starting together in time with the music. A dance couple must begin together in time, or the consequences might be the same as the front wheels of your automobile moving forward while the back wheels stay put!

Movement Memo

Here is one way to find the first beat. The first beat will have greater intensity or volume than the others. The second, third, and fourth beats generally diminish in intensity through the bar of music. A simple trick that helps many new dancers find the first beat is to listen to when the vocalist begins to sing. Ninety-nine percent of the time, the vocalist will begin singing on the first beat of any new phrase of music. Lyrics always begin following at least one bar of instrumental play or "intro."

Stressful? Not Really

Now let's talk about creating rhythm to add to your new understanding of timing. Each measure of your dig and toss began with the first dig and toss.

Once again for your convenience, here are steps 3 through 6 of the "dig and toss" model:

Step 3. Penetrate the garden bed with your shovel and scoop out a shovelful of dirt. Having done this you will toss the dirt away.

Step 4. Repeat step 3 at the same rate of speed and intensity. Maintaining the speed and intensity is very important!

Step 5. Repeat step 3 again at the same rate of speed and intensity.

Step 6. And, for the last time, repeat step 3 at the same rate of speed and intensity for a total of four shovelfuls of dirt.

Step 3 will always have greater emphasis. Your first penetration of the garden bed should have a bit more power but no different speed for the dig and toss. This is your downbeat, as this is your beginning.

Let's create an accent beat or what is sometimes called a *highlight beat*. On step 4, which is your second beat, I want you to penetrate the soil with more intensity and power. Now you've created an accent beat. As you repeat the process from measure to measure using a slightly intense first downbeat and then a second accented beat, you create a consistent rhythm.

Bet You Didn't Know

The term "tone deaf" does not refer to rhythm or the ability to hear music. Actually, tone deaf generally describes an individual who cannot reproduce musical pitch accurately when attempting to sing. Pitch defines the number of vibrations of a musical note. The higher the note in frequency, the greater the amount of vibrations, with the opposite being true. Pitch has nothing to do with rhythm. The speaking or singing voice has pitch; therefore, if you are tone deaf, you will often have difficulty understanding some spoken words. While someone who is deaf may be unable to hear pitch, they can certainly feel rhythm. A deaf person would distinguish rhythm or rhythms by the differentials of physical pressure through any sequence of events. Physical events like taking dance steps exert pressure or, as we described, have greater or lesser degrees of stress or emphasis.

While you repeat this process, you will feel greater and lesser moments of stress. Stress in this case refers to physical pressure. In dancing we pressurize the moments of accent or highlight. All of this exists within the normal beat structure of a standard measure. So it is the differences of intensity, as in our illustration for penetrating the soil, that produce rhythm!

Each type of music on your CD has these characteristics. Listen to your music often and try to pick them out. As we describe a dance, we will make you aware of the accents and the downbeats of each. Once you have listened to a particular selection several times, you will begin to hear what we have described. In time, you will be able to recognize the same musical characteristics in any and all of your favorite music. Like learning the dance steps, this is an important process of learning to ballroom dance.

Using the Time to Count Time

The standard form of timing that you and I are both familiar with in our daily lives is the one the clock tells us. For our next exercises you'll need either a clock or a watch with a second hand. We are going to create a model that will not only teach you but also prove to you that you can tell time like any other dancer.

Three of our five senses are used continually while dancing. In this model we will use seeing, hearing, and touching. The more senses you activate and are conscious of while learning an art form, the more expeditious your learning curve. Sensual perception stimulates our intellect and our emotions. These senses create recognizable situations from encounter to encounter.

Let's begin with a sequence of counting exercises:

- **Counting Exercise 1.** Watch the second hand on your clock and begin as the second hand reaches 12; say "one" (1).

  You always have to begin somewhere, and making the first beat the first second is your best bet.

- **Counting Exercise 2.** Begin counting consistently and audibly for 20 seconds as follows: 1, 2, 3, 4, 5, 6, 7, 8, 9, 10, 11, 12, 13, 14, 15, 16, 17, 18, 19, 20.

  In this exercise you develop the skill to count in an even tempo while hearing your own voice in a perfect and controlled cadence.

- **Counting Exercise 3.** Begin counting aloud and tapping your foot on each beat of the clock as follows: 1, 2, 3, 4; 1, 2, 3, 4; 1, 2, 3, 4; 1, 2, 3, 4; 1, 2, 3, 4. Again, do this for 20 seconds.

  In this exercise you learned to feel the pressure of your foot tapping in coincidence with the sound of your voice. You are speaking and tapping in strict tempo. You also learned to do this while naming each beat of each measure for a total of five measures.

- **Counting Exercise 4.** In dancing we usually count the number of bars or measures of music as follows: 1, 2, 3, 4; 2, 2, 3, 4; 3, 2, 3, 4; 4, 2, 3, 4; 5, 2, 3, 4. Do this now for 20 seconds.

  This type of counting structure assists the listener or dancer in counting how many measures per minute exist in any song. The first numeral of each measure indicates the number of measures in ascending order. In this case there are five measures.

Ballroom Bloopers

I have purposely avoided using handclapping or finger snapping to develop your rhythm and timing. You will dance with your feet, so you need to get your feet used to feeling the music. Using your hands and then sometimes your shoulders for timing on the dance floor would be very, very distracting. For the most part you'll be using your arms, hands, and shoulders for leading or following.

For our example, we are using a $^4/_4$ time measure. There are four beats to the measure, and we have counted five measures. There are 60 seconds in a minute, and we have used up 20 seconds or $^1/_3$ of a minute. That must mean that the tempo of what we have counted is 15 measures per minute or 60 beats per minute (5 measures × 3 = 15, and 20 beats × 3 = 60 beats).

You will note on your CD included with this book—and in Chapter 7, "Music and More Music: About the Music on Your CD," in which I list the songs on the CD—we have indicated the measures per minute.

Movement Memo

> One of the ways to make music more user friendly is to count aloud when taking your lessons or practicing. I have found that my students who count aloud have a much-accelerated learning curve. When you count aloud, you are expressing confidence in the audible expression of tempo. The sound of your voice matches the baseline of the music, so be sure to count in a strong, crisp voice. Later, when you count in an inaudible fashion, you will still be able to hear that strong inner voice. This will be a valuable tool as you learn more and more dances.

Now you want to try a few counting exercises of measures per minute on your own. On your CD, select the Foxtrot. A stopwatch is helpful for this. Wait till your clock's second hand reaches 12, and begin to count as detailed in the exercises. Watch the clock for 20 seconds, stopping right on the twentieth second, and determine how many measures you have counted. If you have listened to the beats correctly, you will have counted slightly more than ten measures of music. Multiply by three, and you'll see that your Foxtrot has a tempo of 31 measures per minute. The number of beats per minute is determined by multiplying the number of measures by 4. This means your Foxtrot equals 124 beats per minute.

The tempo of this Foxtrot is exactly twice as fast as the speed of your clock. By using simple arithmetic, you will determine that each beat of this Foxtrot equals one-half second. You can see why dancing is such good exercise! You will be taking between 62 and 124 steps per minute. This is owing to the fact that some of the steps will be Slow counts (two beats) and some will be Quick counts (one beat).

◆ **Counting Exercise 5.** Now let's create rhythm by adding an accent on the second and fourth beat of each measure. You will do so by counting aloud and tapping your foot with greater emphasis and volume on the second and fourth beat of each measure.

Remember we are still keeping the same cadence or tempo with your clock's second hand.

As follows: 1, 2 (loudly), 3, 4 (loudly); 1, 2 (loudly), 3, 4 (loudly); 1, 2 (loudly), 3, 4 (loudly); 1, 2 (loudly), 3, 4 (loudly); 1, 2 (loudly), 3, 4 (loudly).

Let's get physical by using Counting Exercise 5 to march in place with the preceding cadence. Start with your left foot for all odd counts—1 and 3. Then your right foot will be used for all the even counts—2 and 4. You know the drill—heavier with your right foot than your left.

The accents of this particular counting pattern would be the same accents you would find in Swing music. Take your music CD and choose the Swing dance selection. Listen for the accents on the second and fourth beat of each measure.

Listening and Learning

To easily distinguish the timing of the music, listen to the bass line. Pay no attention to the melody or lyrics. Dancers must dance to the rhythm of a song, not to the melody or words. Listen for the consistent "boom, boom" of a drum, or the "da, da" notes of the bass guitar. In fact, new dancers find it helpful to adjust their stereo to full bass and no treble in order to clearly hear the timing. This definitely brings out the bass line and helps them practice listening for the rhythm.

Songs with the dance characteristics of Tango, Merengue, Hustle, and Waltz are the easiest tempos to practice your counting exercises with. Again do not become frustrated counting music! It is an acquired skill, just as dancing is an acquired skill.

The Least You Need to Know

- You do not need to be able to read music to become an accomplished dancer.
- Every physical act has elements of rhythm and timing, so everyone has these skills—they just have to recognize them!
- Use as many of your senses as possible when learning to dance.
- Counting aloud in a strong, clear voice will accelerate your learning curve.
- You can find the *timing* in music by listening to the bass line—not the melody or lyrics.

Chapter 9

The Plain Truth About Practicing, Expectations, and Prioritization

In This Chapter

- ◆ Privacy, please
- ◆ Less is more
- ◆ Mirror, mirror on the wall
- ◆ Get it up to speed

Every dancer and dance couple develops on three levels: pupil, practice, and performance. Whatever level your public or performance level may be, social dancer, world finalist, or anything in between, you will discover how to achieve a higher level of dance during your time as a pupil and during your practice.

In this chapter you will learn to organize your practice time, make it effective, and prioritize not only the physical but emotional issues that may come up between you and your partner. Decisions such as suiting up and when and where to practice your lessons are very simple choices that will help you gain insight and make ballroom dancing very approachable for you.

The Three Ps of Dancing

There is no getting away from it: You the dancer exist in three ways:

- ◆ You are first a pupil. And you will always remain a pupil.
- ◆ You are a practitioner of the art you are studying—practice, practice, and practice!
- ◆ You are a performer. Social dancing is by definition an activity that happens in the midst of others. Others will see you and may watch you dance.

The Pupil

You must be a student of dance to learn to dance. As you step onto the studio floor, allow yourself the luxury of believing you are a dancer. And remember the time spent there is to become a better dancer. Take a trip outside the everyday happenings of your life and step into our fantasy for a while. It will be time well spent! If you do not yet believe in yourself as a dancer, then believe you are someone else who is! That dancer, your fantasy, is not traveling down the city streets dancing; they too wait for their moments at the studio or rehearsal hall. To a dancer, these places should not just be fun. These places should be desired above all else—yes, almost sacred.

For the present, consider this book your teacher. As you progress beyond this book, and you will, be sure to have the reference card found under the front cover available. The reference card has some valuable information on how to find and evaluate a good teacher and studio. The good teacher—the experienced teacher—has spent years preparing for your lessons.

Movement Memo

Digest this book a piece at a time. If you read it like a novel, the experience belongs to the characters in the book. You will be on the outside looking in! If you read this book too fast, it will be like eating a delicious steak in one bite—you will choke on it. Take it slowly and savor every bite!

As a pupil, your job is to let your teacher administer the lesson. Complaining about your lack of practice, your aches and pains, or what has gone wrong with your day is not going to weaken your teacher's resolve to teach you. But such complaints will divert your attention and prevent you from accomplishing what you came to do—to learn dance. The time spent under the careful tutelage of your teacher has a goal: to bring you to your highest level of dance performance. The pupil's goal should be to grow in dance experience and to learn what makes the body operate to music. This will ultimately benefit both partners.

During your lesson commit your body to the preparations, exercises, and choreography without fear or concern for your partner's look of approval. You and your partner are in the same boat! When there are tips or highlights given for a step, pay close attention to them. These tips or highlights are the result of my cumulative teaching experience and having observed all the common errors made by students. These tidbits are there to help you remove error or to focus your attention on an important point. I have always told my students if it were not for their mistakes, I would not have a job. As a pupil, you should recognize the difference between a teacher and a person who shows you dance steps! It takes a teacher to give you mental, physical, and even emotional ideas about what makes the journey between and through your feet work. Once you have found a real teacher of dance, a teacher who is a student of dance himself, then allow that person to tinker with your equipment.

It is only through physical change that you can go forward in your dance experience. Without physical change, improvement is next to impossible. If you continue at the same physical level and just keep adding more complex choreography, you may end up worse than when you started! Yes, it is possible to go backward in your dancing even as you learn more "steps." When this book—your teacher—makes you feel a difference, applaud yourself! Without the difference there is no change or growth. Feelings are subjective. I want my readers to know that very often the correct technique will feel wrong to you at first! Until any change has become an indelible part of your physicality, it may indeed feel foreign. This is not the time to start complaining about what feels right or wrong. If you were doing it *right* there would be no need to correct it.

I am reminded about the golfer who enlists the help of a PGA pro in order to eliminate a consistent and undesirable hook from his golf swing. The golfer's swing begins to improve and the hook begins to diminish. Only to have the golfer turn to his teacher and remark, "This doesn't feel right!" As the golfer returns to what *feels right* and is *more comfortable*, that hook swing comes right back. Each time you study, do not just read this book; allow it to take you to a higher level. Do not necessarily gauge your physical experiences by what comes easily to you—after all, these feelings already exist in your dancing. Gauge your lesson time by the number of changes you have to work for and then challenge yourself to become better by undergirding those changes with practice.

The Pupil's Practice

Practice is where you begin to make what is unfamiliar to your muscles part of your own physicality. This is only accomplished through repetition. Your attentiveness and cooperative learning during your time as a pupil is only supported by the quality moments of your rehearsal. This book is designed to direct your feelings away from error. Success depends on your preparation or homework. Practice will develop dependability and consistency into your dance movement. You must embrace and incorporate the changes to your feelings. Or you, like the golfer, will simply revert to bad form.

To achieve quality in your practice, you will need privacy as you study, especially if you are a beginner. It is never a good idea to attempt to execute in public what you have *not* practiced. More times than not, you will fail—and if you succeed, you just got lucky! Practice time is the time to build your confidence and not to weaken it. Cherish your privacy.

Set goals for each rehearsal session. Keep these goals short term, somewhat challenging, but definitely obtainable. Things you can achieve in short periods will become building blocks for dancing and boost your confidence to dance. It is unwise for people who are not professionals or high-level competitors to practice for extended periods of time. You can certainly become an accomplished dancer without an extended time commitment.

I would rather see you practice in two or three 5- to 10-minute intervals every day than to try to set aside one or two hours a week. Practice sessions defined in "hours" are daunting, and most students will never seem to "find" the time for one reason or another. The shorter, frequent intervals ensure minimal loss of the quality between one lesson and the next. Remember that your study of ballroom dancing uses a "building block" approach, and each new step is dependent on successfully learning and improving the previous material or technique. You may have initial success walking through a new dance step with book in hand. Then you will have to add music, and if you are like 99.99 percent of us, you will fail at first. So you will go back to walking through the step, using the proper technique, rhythm, and timing. You may do this a number of times, but you will get it. And once you get it, you will rehearse it over and over until you own it. Now it's yours!

In major league baseball, a great hitter fails 66.6 percent of the time, and a good hitter fails 72 percent of the time. That is why their batting average is .333 and .280, respectively! These batters learn to accept their failure as part of the process to succeed. They do not become mired in failure but use it as a catalyst to inspire themselves to practice and seek out advice. This is the only way to get up to the plate again and finally succeed! Unlike baseball, dancing is a life skill. Your timetable is the rest of your life. Approach practice as a way to give yourself the opportunity to enjoy success.

 Bet You Didn't Know

The expression "practice makes perfect" is only partially true and somewhat less than accurate. The reality is that quote says "It is not practice that makes perfect, it's perfect practice that makes perfect!"

Many sports enthusiasts have attributed this quotation to the premier professional football coach Vince Lombardi. Lombardi was a stickler for detail and precision. Above all else he demanded good *basics* from all his players. This approach to coaching taught the Green Bay Packers how a great work ethic eventually pays off. His teams won one championship after another.

Lombardi was a master in the study of leadership, inspiration, and practice. He also must have been aware of another master of his art. For it was not Lombardi that made this quotation, it was world-famous orchestra leader Guy Lombardo. The fabulous dance music of Lombardo and his Royal Canadians was termed "The sweetest sound this side of heaven!" Of course you now know it is precision timing and the ability to create perfect repetition that makes the best dance music.

Do not take your practicing lightly. Practice is the most important part of your dancing. Allen's Law of Dance states: Your "public" level of dance—including social, competitive, or performance—will never be better than your best average practice! Improving the quality of your practice and adding intensity to your practice will speed up your learning curve. You will be able to finally try that great dance step.

Increased practice intensity will also improve your "public dancing." Do not expect to be great at your wedding dance or at the nightclub if you cannot exceed that level alone or with your partner at home. To make this section complete and realistic, you must know these two things about practice. First, practice is where you find your errors and weaknesses both physically and mentally. Second, once you have identified these faults, you practice to eliminate them. The good news is that if you have never really set aside a genuine practice schedule with goals, imagine how much better and enjoyable your dancing will become when you do. As the expression goes, "Baby, you ain't seen nothin' yet!"

The Pupil's Performance

The performance level of your dance persona is different for everyone. This level is always your weakest and the one filled with the most demons. The performance level for you may be as simple as a wedding, the weekly social dance you attend, or a nightclub. On the other hand, it may be a shot at making the finals at Blackpool, England. Here is a reality that every athlete regardless of sport must face. Practice and conditioning have everything to do with your results publicly! Your performance level is also impacted by the quality of your source of information, including books, videos, teachers, and coaches. So if your teacher pushes you a bit to be better on a lesson or to practice with greater frequency, it is for your public level. I have written this book as a little push for you to do it! I want you to succeed. You will feel and look great out there with a partner. We will work together toward that end—but the onus is on you.

Let us get this right out in the open: There are pressures out on the public dance floor—both real and imagined—that do not or should not exist in practice. Public performance transforms any audience into a group of critics. The pressures of the social dance floor are in some ways much greater than that of the competitive dance floor. How is that, you say? The competitive dance floor is much more spatial in terms of congestion and more predictable as to the quality of dancer and the use of line of dance.

It is much easier for a beginner-level social dancer to navigate the floor during a competition than when out socially. After all, in a social setting, there are people out there just to gain experience in moving around a public dance floor or just for their own fun. Sometimes fun is very selfish and discourteous. The public dance floor is a microcosm of human existence. It is much the same as what you find on the highway. Vehicles can at times be life-threatening! You will find the same thing on a congested dance floor. The difference between the highway and the dance floor is that the human ego is greater and at the same time more fragile on the dance floor. This often brings out the best or the worst in people. When you first try out your dancing on a public floor, just remember when you were learning to drive. You will have to practice to gain control of your space out on the dance floor. You will have to get used to the movement of others and the congested space. Just like driving on the highway, you will learn to anticipate difficulties and avoid potential problems.

For these reasons and many more, the typical social dancer will lose as much as 75 percent of dance quality and choreography just by stepping out on a public floor. The percentage of loss is largely up to you. You will determine how much you lose by the type and content of your practice. Strive for and be happy with 70 percent of your best average practice. Imagine if you could achieve 70 percent of all the goals you have set in life—wow! I am sure that most competitors and performers would agree that if they could achieve in a public venue 80 percent of their very best

Movement Memo

From time to time during your practice sessions, it may be helpful to place moving or stationary obstacles in your path. Use your friends, practice mates, or dance partner, or even chairs and stools. You will find this an indispensable aid in your preparation for the social dance floor. You will find several dance figures throughout the choreography section (Chapters 15 to 25) that will actually help you avoid obstacles! I will prompt you when they suit this usage.

practice, they could put themselves in contention to be a winner. What? Only 80 percent? Yes, of their *best* practice. No one is perfect. We can come close to perfection and continually strive for it, but it never comes. We lift our performance level by focusing on becoming determined as a pupil, diligent in practice and empathetic as a human.

So there you have it: the indispensable interlocking physical, mental, spiritual, and almost magical trinity of the dancer—the pupil, the practitioner, and the performer.

Some Space to Dance

You really do not need a lot of space to dance, but that space needs to be clear. For my Quickstart to Social Dance Program© beginning in Part 3, "Two Become One: Creating the Dance Couple," you will need a space approximately the size of a full dining room table, including the surrounding chairs. Those general measurements would be approximately eight feet long and five feet wide. Any of the choreography that we cover in this book will fit in this space. Frankly, "the less is more" idea works well here. Do not learn to execute your figures taking up maximum space; take the minimal space route. You will dance in greater comfort socially if you take distance out of the equation of your practice time.

Movement Memo

I teach all my students that distance is the enemy of a dancer. Dancing is primarily a vertical art as opposed to a lateral one. When learning physical skills, human beings are prone to exaggeration. Beginner dancers are particularly guilty of too much exaggeration. A dance step is completed with a weight change from one foot to the next. There is no prerequisite for distance. There will be a standard stride, but you also must learn to move inside small spaces. After all, when you want to croon and swoon to songs by Sinatra and King Cole being sung by your local lounge lizard, you will not find big dance floors. Travel with finesse rather than trying to travel far!

Consider the Surface

A hardwood floor built on floor joists is best! Okay, actually I lied. A spring-loaded hardwood floor, which many studios have installed, is an even better surface, but they do not build houses or apartments with these. Many of you belong to health clubs or racquetball clubs. You might be surprised how receptive these clubs would be to letting you practice there in off-hours. Who knows? Your practicing and dancing may drum up some more interest, and you could make some more friends.

The tile floor is the next best choice, and hopefully, it is not laid over concrete. That makes it a very hard surface and tough on your feet, ankles, and knees. This is especially the case over prolonged periods of time. Practice in your sneakers if this is the case, or place protective inserts in your dance shoes. A low-pile carpet (you know—the indoor/outdoor or commercial type) will do fine. Practice in your socks or your dance shoes if you are going to "cut a rug."

If you live in an apartment complex, there may be a recreation room or common area that you can use. Get your neighbors together and take lessons together! Take turns being the designated reader. The directions and commands for your dance steps are easily understood, but it really helps if they are read aloud. Everyone will learn to dance, and then everyone shows up for the party! You will be the toast of the neighborhood.

Movement Memo

If it is nice outside, or you live in a warm climate, put your sneakers on and take your practice sessions out on the patio or driveway. Make sure you block the entrance to your driveway so there will be no uninvited vehicles in your dance space.

Give Yourself a Good Look

Working in front of a mirror will help you familiarize yourself with what the different dance positions look like. This will help reinforce the way they feel. In this way, no one will have to tell you how you look while you are dancing, performing, or competing. Some of you may not like to use the mirror initially, but make friends with your appearance.

If you do not like the way you look while dancing, it is likely that others will not like how you look, either. Our attitude and physical posture convey to others how we are feeling. If we are not feeling confident, it will show! As you become more familiar with your new "dance feelings," the usage and control of your muscles will cause your confidence level on the dance floor to soar!

By using a mirror and teaching your muscles the appropriate movements, you will exhibit greater control with respect to your torso, legs, and arms. As you become more physically controlled, your concentration will be focused toward where you are going on the dance floor, your partnering skills, and your transitional capabilities.

Suit Up and Hoofs On

Attire for practice and social dancing need only follow this general rule: Your threads must be comfortable and must not impede movement, particularly leg swing. Ladies—that means a skirt that limits the swing of your leg or blocks the gentleman from swinging his leg is unacceptable! Other than that, let fashion and the amount of sweating you plan to do dictate what to wear. I always change immediately after I practice or go out dancing to avoid a chill and catching a cold.

Shoes for dancing is a more complex issue. So let's talk about comfort first—your feet must be comfortable. At the beginning, wear anything that stays on your foot and that is flexible. Ladies, avoid wearing flip-flop sandals or shoes that allow the inside surface of the shoe to move away from the bottom of your foot. Gentlemen, do not wear "gunboats." Your shoes should also be flexible and lightweight. In all probability you will begin in sneakers.

Dance shoes: Okay, here is the scoop. You have probably figured out by now I am an advocate of just letting your feet remain "stupid" horizontal platforms. I do not want you to prioritize your feet while learning a dance pattern, and I do not want your feet to distract you. Another Allen's rule of dance: Let your feet break-in your shoes—never let your shoes break-in your feet! This means that you should protect with a bandage or insert the top of your toes, edge of your heels, and anywhere you may feel a little chafing.

Dance shoes are issues of growth and money. When you are ready for dance shoes, get a pair that is described as a ballroom dance shoe, not a character shoe! A good dance shoe is extremely flexible and becomes more flexible as you break it in. Therefore the first moment you wear new ones, they should be snug without pinching. Most dance shoes have a chrome leather or suede sole. These are for indoor surfaces only and are not meant to get wet on the bottom.

Attitude Is Food for Your Muscles

As long as you keep a great attitude, you will be feeding all the muscles in your body very positive information. Muscle usage begins with electrical impulses deep in the central nervous system. A chemical known as ATP (adenosine triphosphate) is released to the muscles by these impulses. Think of it as a commuter train that regularly delivers its passengers to their destination—sometimes comfortably, sometimes not. ATP acts upon the muscles with recorded information and experience. However, when you get tense, it heats up the muscles and overcooks them—just like a too-hot oven can overcook your food. The food can become too crisp, hard, or just plain overdone. When ATP becomes supercharged with heat, it causes the joints operated by certain muscle groups to stiffen and react differently than you planned.

When this happens, your muscles will not perform at anywhere near their capability. In other physical activities and sports, athletes refer to this as "choking." Once stress or anger has invaded your practice time, you and your partner must stop! The stress will cause your efforts to be very counterproductive.

A Fresh Step

Once you have mastered a dance step or pattern, it is, of course, time to learn another. Unfortunately, this can be tough on the ego. Just when you feel confident about the dance step you are doing, it is time to begin all over again with another. But if you do not learn several patterns, you will become bored very quickly. Let's say a dance step takes $1\frac{1}{2}$ measures to complete and the speed of your dance is 32 measures per minute. That means in one minute you can repeat that step just over 21 times. I would say that gets pretty boring.

Since the basic step of any dance contains virtually all of that dance's characteristics, you will expedite your learning if you maintain all the good qualities of balance and lifting your ribcage that we discussed in Chapter 6, "The Challenges of Ballroom Dancing." The more things you learn to keep the same, the easier it will be to learn what may be different.

To effectively learn new choreography, you must commit your entire body to the step as an approach to learning. Do this with a positive mental attitude as if you had been doing the new step, figure, or position for years! Never be afraid to make errors when you are learning something new; this is how we train our muscles. Errors in your dancing will only remain errors if you persist in repeating them. Once you have discovered the use of proper techniques from your practice or exercise patterns, make sure you apply them to any new dance figure or choreography.

Movement Memo

At the end of each specific dance chapter (Chapters 15 to 25) you will find a choreographed routine for that dance. That routine has been developed with good physical logic to tie together the elements presented within each dance figure as well as the series of five to seven figures presented in each dance. Make sure you master the basic box step and its development presented in the Quickstart Program© found in Part 3 to maximize your learning curve!

Gearing Up for Practice

It is important during the course of your practice to set realistic goals for that particular practice session. In that way, you will become success-oriented in achieving your designated goal. If you are able to surpass your goal, your practice time will also have become motivational. You will look forward to your next practice with great affirmation.

Part of goal setting should include bringing your dance figures, patterns, routines, and so on to the speed of the music. If you only attempt to perfect your dancing at a very slow, methodical pace, when you introduce music to the formula it will be very, very discouraging. A better idea is to add the music into your practice as soon as possible. The lack of physical perfection in your new dance amalgamation should not deter you from adding music. These two major entities—the physical and the musical—will merge quickly. You will find that there is a great disparity in performance with and without music. Music's mathematical perfection requires you to be "on time." Therefore, in spite of your love for the music, it is very unforgiving. You will find that your practice time without music will be easier. This is very normal!

To deal with the music in your practice session, I feel the following sequence will be helpful:

1. Give attention to each physical movement and transitional skill, along with the leads and follows.
2. Follow step 1 for a single figure or a short sequence of figures.

3. Add the music once this practice has been accomplished.

4. Connect any new choreography to a basic pattern or a preceding pattern, and continue to practice the patterns in succession.

The development of a routine will include using the "adding-on idea." Keep the new figure at the end and start your material from the beginning. Dance your existing material to the point of failure or weaknesses. Rework the weaker material and start from the beginning of the routine. You will be surprised at how many "mountain top" experiences you will have. The older material will be executed with greater confidence and familiarity. Therefore, your attention and concentration will be focused on the new material, and you will get through it sooner.

The Next Big Dance Step

In your goal setting, there is a reality you must understand. You will never dance better than the level of your best practice session! Never deceive yourself into believing that you will dance better when the pressure is on! The truth is your public performances, at whatever level, will include any and every mistake, weakness, or insecurity that exists in your practice sessions. Most highly skilled professionals are elated when their performances or competitive dancing achieves a level of 85 percent of their best practice. Your practice session must include achieving the 100 percent level of your physical capability as frequently as possible.

Movement Memo _____

Practicing in a nightclub is not practice unless you consider learning to drive in the midst of rush hour a good idea! Also, don't drink alcohol before your lesson time or practice session unless you also believe that you can drive effectively and safely under the influence. Alcohol impairs your capability to concentrate mentally and physically. When you are out publicly to dance, enjoy yourself, but please observe safe and smart social habits!

The 100 percent level of ballroom dancing is the level that you must improve. To achieve a higher level of dance in a public venue, competition, showcase, or performance, you will have to practice to increase your capacities. This must be done at the 100 percent level! Practice sessions held in a public venue such as a nightclub or social dance floor will not produce the desired results and may become discouraging. There are too many negative variables to contend with to use this public practice as your only form of practice. Do your homework at your own pace and in privacy. Remember that this privacy will always produce your best practice. If you do not have space at your residence for private practice, it is a good investment of time and money to lease space somewhere for an hour or two. Think about it and you will find some accessible public hall.

The Least You Need to Know

- Treat yourself and your partner kindly and patiently—be cooperative and encouraging.
- Eliminate negative emotion from your learning and practice time, and do not practice when you are exhausted or have just eaten.
- Once you have planned what you are going to practice, endeavor to practice at the 100 percent or "full tilt" level.
- Get your dancing up to the speed of the music as soon as possible.
- Set realistic goals for each practice session.

Part 3

Two Become One: Creating the Dance Couple

This part of *The Complete Idiot's Guide to Ballroom Dancing* may be the most important! It is about the technique. Technique is the base on which to build your ability to be successful on the dance floor with a partner—any dance floor. From master teachers I have learned that dancing is 90 percent technique and—contrary to what you may currently believe—only 10 percent choreography. To the extent that you abide by this ratio, its reflection will be in the quality and success of your future dancing.

Once upon a time when you learned how to drive a car, the engineering and building of the vehicle were done for you. Regardless of its style, age, model, or price tag, you and your teacher expected and depended on the fact that the vehicle performed with what could be described as theoretic perfection. You then learned to operate the vehicle in a condition that was somewhat forgiving, like an open parking lot. If you had a good teacher, you acquired many fundamental skills and became proficient at each before you were allowed to venture out into traffic from location to location. So it should be with ballroom dancing!

Many years ago I developed the Quickstart Program© to give individuals the building blocks of physical priorities and required skills to move with someone "attached to them." I will share the Quickstart Program© with you for the remainder of this section of the book. Return to it often and improve upon it; for in it, exists the life skills of ballroom dancing.

Chapter 10

The Quickstart Program© Progressive Movements

In This Chapter

- A new entity—the dance couple
- Walk your way to good dancing
- The body dances—not the feet
- Forward, back, or side—accuracy is key

Today we finally get at it: learning dance movements with our newly structured body! The following methods are exactly those that I have used to introduce dancing to countless numbers of students personally and many thousand others through my books. I have been calling it my Quickstart to Social Dance Method© since 1994. That was when I began writing about its creation and development, but I have been using these methods since I began teaching after concluding my competitive amateur career in 1984.

I had always thought it unfair to begin showing dance steps to new dancers by immediately joining together and beginning to move. As individuals they did not yet know the dance steps, but more important, they did not know how to move together as a couple—the latter being much more difficult! After you complete the work in this and the next two chapters, you will be physically ready and have a much better understanding of what a dance couple is: a new entity that moves to personify music!

Simple but Very Necessary

The Quickstart program is a very simple procedure that allows you to develop the geometric movement skills necessary to be successful at ballroom dancing. Yes, I am talking about the need to improve the way you walk. In the many years I have been teaching people to dance, seldom, if ever, did a prospective student walk into my studio or class who did not need to improve the way they walk. Walking correctly as an individual is the beginning of dancing with a partner.

If any of the words in the following list describe the way you walk, then take this chapter very seriously. It will be a means to accomplish the goal you set out to achieve. Scurry, scamper, lope, shuffle, drag your feet, scuff your feet, scuffle, hobble, trundle, lumber, plod, walk heavily, shamble, hobble, trudge, stager, tramp, traipse, toddle, sway, wobble, swing back and forth, waddle, bob, dip, amble, walk leisurely, or stroll!

If you are unable to find something in your gait that was described here, you are an extraordinary individual with impeccable movement and balance skills. Congratulations! However, developing a standard stride for you and your partner with accurate linear geometry is also required, so stay tuned. For the rest of us—who tend to generate energy from the top of our body, particularly the shoulders, and do not consider lift of body when walking—the Quickstart method is the way to go.

We have to learn to use Newton's third law of inertia: *For every action, there is an equal and opposite reaction.* Most of us ruin our feet and our lower spine by inclining our shoulders to create movement and using our feet as catcher's mitts. How we travel was never an issue when walking down the street, but now it is! The quality of your movement will allow you to keep time while you are dancing. We all love music, but music is mathematically perfect and its intervals are consistent. Our intervals of movement must have a degree of perfection in order to maintain a degree of compatibility with music. Another way of saying this is that when we dance, we are on someone else's timetable—not our own. Therefore, we must be responsive to the music and responsible to our partner.

Most of us have thought of walking as a means to go from point A to point B. That is probably why most people think that learning to dance is just a matter of placing the feet somewhere, like tracing footprints on the floor. Unfortunately many divisive or marketing-oriented dance instructors know this and have taught their students just foot patterns. It really takes no dance skills to teach or learn a foot pattern—it just takes memory! The problem is that the legs and feet really just accommodate the movement of the body. So in reality it is the body, the positioning of the body, and the carriage of the body that "dances." The footprint way of learning is intellectual; the body method of learning is physical. Dancing is a physical activity, and that is why the chapters leading up to this progressive movement chapter have taught you about body positioning and carriage of the solo dancer.

The good news is that there are only three dance steps: forward, backward, and sideways. There are only two types of rotations: clockwise and counterclockwise. We will learn about rotation a little later. For the time being, just know this: The quality of your forward or back movement will dictate how well you will be able to rotate!

By following my Quickstart program, you will overcome the fear of committing one of the major social faux pas of all time—stepping on your partner's feet! There is no way you can dance with someone while trying to avoid them at the same time. Yet the idea of avoiding another person is more natural than moving aggressively in and through your partner's space. To dance with a partner, you must stay and be with that partner. My Quickstart program will teach you how to move as a dancer and a dance couple, dispelling any concern with stepping on toes.

We will begin at the beginning, learning how to move together before trying to learn how to "go somewhere" together! I assume you learn to drive first before going out gallivanting in your father's automobile. So it is with ballroom dancing, at least from my perspective. Let's learn how to move together first, and then we will learn where to go. Many hundreds of dance instructors across this country are applying my Quickstart program and teaching their students how to move prior to dance steps or choreography. I am happy to report that the learning curve of the Quickstart students is about seven times faster than the learning curve of those who are simply trained to move their feet somewhere. Are you ready?

Forward

Everyone comes to dance class with the ability to walk or run forward. Sometimes that turns out to be a problem. We take this most common of all human movements for granted. Our style, good or bad, has always suited us while moving from point A to point B. Now you'll find out that your current mode of movement may not be good enough to dance with a partner. Let's find out why.

Straight Line, Due North, Twelve O'Clock

The first thing we must learn to do is walk together in a straight line. I want the gentleman to place all of his weight on his right foot, leaving his left foot free of weight. I want the lady to place all of her weight on her left foot, leaving her right foot free. We will always start in this manner throughout this book when beginning any of the choreography.

Tear the reference card out from the front of this book and notice at its center where it says "Start Here" there's an arrow pointing due north or "down line of dance." Assume your best dance posture learned from the previous chapters and begin to walk down line of dance. You may do this alone or with a partner, and to add some spice you may hold hands. Make sure you hold the reference card so that line of dance is perpendicular to the wall you are facing. Imagine stretching a tightrope between your body and the wall. You must walk on the imaginary tightrope as your line of dance. To be a good partner and a successful dancer, when you walk either forward or backward you must attempt to be this accurate. Unless you are a trained circus performer, the use of a real tightrope is unnecessary. Accuracy in the directional movement of your body is the key to good partnering skills. Please do not take this section lightly.

Now I want both of you to walk forward, taking four steps down line of dance or more if you have room. However, I want you both to walk at exactly the same cadence or speed.

As you begin to walk forward, please notice that your knees flex slightly. Every single movement of your body will definitely include a slight flex in the knee. This flex will occur regardless of the direction—forward, backward, or sideways—in which the dance couple will travel. Removing your foot from the floor should be a product of flexing your knee and lifting your thigh. This type of release is the key to balance while walking. Please notice that when you lift your thigh to release your foot from the floor prior to your stride forward, your body does not rock, sway, lurch, or falter. This action replaces the use of your shoulders to remove your foot from the floor and therefore eliminates 99 percent of unwanted movement. Walking forward also includes another very ordinary occurrence. The bottom of the heel of your shoes strikes the floor first.

This place of contact on the lady's or gentleman's shoe is approximately $1/2$ inch from the back edge of the heel of the shoe. Do not attempt to walk on the very back edge of the heel where the flat of the heel meets the rise of the heel. There is no support for the body on this edge. It is better if you feel your natural heel inside the shoe as you apply weight to your foot. Learning to walk forward in the Foxtrot and the Waltz will include the use of this natural heel placement first. You will be directed when a different foot placement is required. Until then, just walk normally with your best dance posture.

In Chapter 8, "Timing and Rhythm for the Layperson," we learned how to keep time and the difference between a quick unit of timing and a slow unit of timing. We will proceed with this Quickstart program as if we were dancing the normal rhythm of a Foxtrot. Each forward and backward walk we use will be to the slow unit of timing, which is two beats of music.

The cadence or Count I referred to previously will be: Slow (Count 1, 2) for the first step, Slow (Count 3, 4) for the second step, Slow (Count 5, 6) for the third step, and Slow (Count 7, 8) for the fourth step. These four steps take eight beats of music. This might be a good time to practice a series of forward walks with your partner to the Foxtrot music that came with your book. Repeat this process until you move accurately down line of dance as if on your tightrope to the music. Remember, each walk forward takes two beats of music, and we call that a *Slow* count.

Forward Man's Left, Lady's Right.   *Forward Man's Right, Lady's Left.*

Forward by the Book

All of the choreography we will use throughout this book has a degree of standardization with other syllabi. It therefore will allow you to dance with anyone who knows it. Most of the choreography I have interpreted for you exists in the syllabi of a major dance organization: Dance Vision International Dancers Association (DVIDA), for which I am a regional examiner. The National Dance Council of America (NDCA) recognizes DVIDA as a member organization. I want you to read and then begin to memorize the DVIDA description of a forward walk. It would be difficult to improve upon it, and the following description will help you immensely!

DVIDA's description follows:

> Stand in an upright position with the feet together and the weight held slightly forward, toward the balls of the feet. Swing the leg forward from the hip with the ball of the foot in contact with the floor, then with the heel lightly skimming the floor with the toe slightly raised. As soon as the front heel moves past the back toe, the back heel will be released from the floor so that at the fullest extent of the stride, the weight will be equally divided between the heel of the front foot and the ball of the back foot with the front knee straight and the back knee slightly flexed. The front toe will then lower as the weight of the body moves forward. The back foot commences to move forward first with the toe, then the ball of the foot, skimming the floor until the feet are level. The back foot then continues forward into the next step.

Backward as If You Were Blindfolded

What, no eyes in the back of your head? Regardless, someone in the dance couple must be able to move backward to reciprocate their partner's forward movement. I will teach you how to use your big toe to act like "eyes in the back of your head!"

Straight Line, Due South, Six O'Clock

Now I want both of you to repeat this walking procedure backward, which would be due south. Make sure both of you retain the same cadence, so count aloud, and please do not fall off your imaginary tightrope! Your count for the backward walks will be "Slow-Slow-Slow-Slow." The four walks backward equal the same eight beats of music in the Foxtrot.

I want to give you a little hint about walking backward. Okay, it's a big hint! Since you cannot turn your head around and look where you are going, you are indeed blind when traveling backward. A moment before your body begins to move backward, lift your thigh lightly and swiftly swing your thigh backward so that the big toe of your foot touches the floor behind you. Even though the swing of your thigh is swift, it should never cause movement or sway in your upper body. The leg will move before your body moves.

In this way you will be like a blind man with his cane. Knowing that you are in contact with the dance floor is a confidence builder, so you can proceed without fear. Even if you were to bang into anything, including the wall behind you, it would only be with the bottom of your foot. You do not have to bang the wall to test this point!

This light, swift leg swing will not cause damage to anyone or anything because the leg is quite loose at this point. When you put your weight on the foot, naturally you will apply much more pressure than this.

The accurate placement of your feet and continuing to count aloud using this cadence of slows is increasing your learning curve.

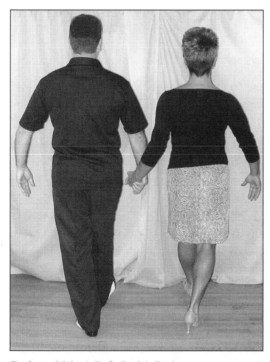

Backward Man's Left, Lady's Right.

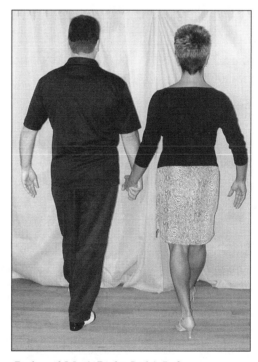

Backward Man's Right, Lady's Left.

Backward by the Book

Now I want to quote the definition of the backward walk from the DVIDA syllabus:

> Stand in an upright position with the feet together and the weight held forward over the balls of the feet. Move the foot back with the ball of the foot, and then the toe skimming the floor, then lower again onto the ball of the foot. As soon as the back foot moves past the front heel, the front toe will be released from the floor so that, at the fullest extent of the stride, the weight will be equally divided between the ball of the back foot and the heel of the front foot. The back knee will be slightly flexed and the front knee straight. The front foot then commences to move back, first with the heel and then with the ball of the foot skimming the floor until the feet are level. The back heel should then lower. It should be noted that the back heel lowers slowly and with control.

"Perfect Practice Makes Perfect"

One last item regarding forward and backward. There should not be daylight or space between your thighs. If there is space between your thighs, you will fall off your imaginary tightrope. To correct this problem, be sure that when you walk forward or backward swing your left leg rightward and your right leg leftward toward your center. This will help to fine-tune the forward or backward walk.

You are doing a great job! You are learning the life skills of ballroom dancing. The development of these skills takes time. Attention to detail, accuracy, body position, balance, and timing in your forward and backward movement will ensure that you are on the road to success.

Practice moving forward taking four steps for eight counts of music. Allow your thigh to swing as you come to the end of the eighth count and then change directions with your partner at your side and begin moving backward. Always visualize a mirror image of yourself moving in opposition. Ask yourself this question: *Am I moving well enough to accommodate my mirror image?* Do this counting aloud with and without music. This is your foundation, so do not take it lightly. Use this procedure to warm up even as you continue into the choreography sections of this book.

Sideways: The Third and Last Linear Direction

Now we are going to work on side steps and closing the feet with a weight change. In dancing, the action of moving the foot to the side and then following that action with closing the free foot to it is commonly called a Chassé. It is a French word that means to *chase*. The idea here is that the closing foot chases the foot moving to the side. We will use the Chassé as a predominant dance step in several of the upcoming dances, including Merengue, Swing, and Cha-Cha.

Remember, to begin any action that includes movement of the body in partner dancing, a very slight flex of the knee is necessary. This flex brings you or your partner into the music and keeps you from looking like a robot. You will also notice as a result of bending your knee while swinging a leg that the first part of the foot that touches the floor is the inside edge of the foot. The average sidestep in the Smooth dances equals the distance from your sternum (at the center of your chest) to your elbow if your arms are raised out to the side. Stepping to the side for a distance any greater than this will cause you to lose balance, produce a lurching movement, and start the weight change prematurely.

The use of the inside edge of the foot helps create a smooth, soft action that cannot be obtained if the whole sole of the foot is placed down at once. The use of this foot placement and action is very important. We will cover more of it under the heading of "knee veer." Try both ways, and you will see and feel the difference. This technique will be particularly beneficial for the Latin rhythms you will learn.

At this beginner level of partner dancing, your side steps are generally quicker than your forward or backward steps. Use this quicker idea to relate to the timing of Quick, Quick. We have already discussed that a Quick will take just one beat of music.

I want the gentleman and the lady to face each other with your bodies parallel in solo or apart position. Sorry, no contact yet, but you will be in contact very soon! You should be on the proper standing foot, and each partner should have the correct foot available for its swing action to the side.

I want you to begin moving to the side about 8 to 10 inches wide using the cadence of 1-2-3-4-5-6-7-8. This equals the total of eight Quicks, and do not forget to count aloud. You will use four combined sets of side together movements. Try this with and without your Foxtrot music.

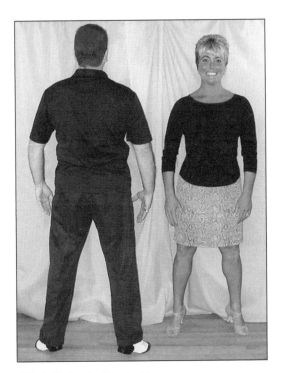 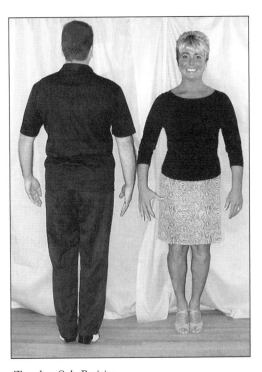

Side Mid-Stride Solo Position. *Together Solo Position.*

Choreographed Routine

Now try this practice routine in the following sequence:

♦ Face each other in solo position, the gentleman moving forward on his left foot and the lady moving backward on her right foot for one Slow count.

♦ After this step is taken, move sideways to the right (lady's left) and close the feet four times, for eight counts of music.

♦ At the conclusion of the last close, the gentleman's right foot should be free, and the lady's left foot should be free. The man should then walk backward on his right and the lady forward on her left.

♦ At the conclusion of this slow walk, move sideways to the left (lady's right) and close the feet four times also for eight counts of music.

♦ This should bring you back to the beginning. Repeat this exercise frequently.

The second exercise is exactly the same, with one major exception. You will use only two side and closing steps rather than four. Do both exercises with and without counting aloud, adding music when you are ready.

Simple but very necessary—doing these two exercises alone in solo position develops your individual skills. Remember that you want to contribute balance and timing to the partnership and not take it away. The quality you develop here will be indicative of the progress you will make later!

The Least You Need to Know

- Geometric accuracy is the key to good partner dancing.
- Begin every movement with a slight flex of the knee.
- When walking forward or backward, there should be no visible space between your thighs.
- Develop good movement skills as an individual before attempting to move in dance position with a partner.

Chapter 11

The Quickstart Program© Nonprogressive Movements

In This Chapter

◆ The step that goes nowhere

◆ Make it instinctual

◆ The common denominator of ballroom dancing

◆ Side—together—release—say it loud

In Chapter 10, "The Quickstart Program© Progressive Movements," we developed the three progressive movements in ballroom dancing: forward, backward, and sideways. During the exercise at the end of that chapter, we touched on the closing action. Now we will pay great attention to the step called the *close*.

This closing step happens with such frequency that it is quite possibly the most important transitional movement that we cover in this text! Unlike progressive movements, we cannot call upon our natural instincts to unravel its mysteries. Yet to maintain the physical logic of ballroom dancing, which is the gentleman's left to the lady's right foot and the gentleman's right to the lady's left foot, we must quickly learn to master the closing step. Are you ready?

Your First Real Dance Step

The progressive movements are natural to your daily environment. The wonderful gyroscope in your brain senses the need to retain support for the protection of the brain as we walk or run. This gyroscope began operating in our infancy as soon as we possessed enough strength to stand up and move forward. The quality of this initial progressive movement was not particularly important. What was important was safety. As long as the platforms known as our feet provided competency for our body's balance, our brain allowed us to progress.

When I am asked to teach or train someone in the art of ballroom dancing, I do not have to teach walking in any of the three progressive directions. As you have already learned, I do have to help new dancers improve their quality. And then add rhythm and dance characteristics to the movements.

But when it comes to the closing steps, I almost ask my students' forgiveness because I know of the impending difficulty they will face in mastering the first dance step. You see, no signal is given from your brain to the closing foot. The other foot is already acting as a platform for support so your brain is safe. The closing step is not within your environmental or daily instincts. The closing step is something we must endeavor to develop and make part of your dancer's instincts!

To see what I mean, please take a step to the side. No great mystery here; you are now standing on the foot that you just moved. Now close the other foot to the one you are standing on. Was any instinct triggered to cause you to change weight or seek support from the closing foot? No. If you are like most of us, you closed the foot but did not place any body weight on it. Therein lies the problem. As a dancer you will have to learn to place your body weight on that closing foot immediately if not sooner!

I just want to give you an admonition of kind caution: Do not become frustrated! Always remember that people just like you have learned to do this effectively but not necessarily quickly. This is about instinct, in the same way that any athlete develops instincts in their particular sport. This is not about intellect, and if you treat learning to perfect the closing movement as an intellectual idea, it will make the proverbial monkey out of you. Even if you are an exceptional athlete, you are not born with the instinct to close your foot and instantaneously use it as your next platform. The only people who possess this instinct are those who have trained, studied, and practiced the art of ballroom dancing! So this is your first dance step.

Be prepared to make the error of not changing weight 100 times more than all your other errors combined. It will be like learning to ride a bicycle—you fell down every time until the moment you "got it" and rode the bicycle. From that moment on, you seldom, if ever, fell off that bicycle. It is my job to provide advice on how to overcome any problems you might have closing your feet and your job to practice, practice, and practice.

I provide this groundwork for you so you will not become emotionally frustrated and quit. Good teaching technique will see you through, and you will dance enjoyably for the rest of your life!

The Common Denominator of Ballroom Dancing

If you have investigated any of the choreography in the later chapters, you will note one consistent occurrence: Virtually each and every time a side step is called for, it is followed immediately by a closing step. For my new dancers, I put this together in a triplet and call it the common denominator of ballroom dancing! As you might suspect, this triplet consists of three distinct movements:

- The first of the three is your side step.
- The second of the three is your closing step.
- The third of the three, and the most important, is releasing the foot that was formally used for your side step from the floor.

The triplet is first developed intellectually by verbalizing the following: side—together—release! The next phase will be to do what you have just said. So let's do it! The choice of beginning the side step with either the right or left foot has no particular importance because you will be able to do it—in fact, you must do it—in both directions.

1. Move your right foot to the side.
2. Close your left foot to your right foot.
3. Release your right foot from the floor immediately, if not sooner!

Now you have the physical logic of right, left, right. Repeat this process to the left using the physical logic of left, right, left. Repeat this process many times!

As a new dancer, what you can anticipate is whenever a side step is taken, you will close your free foot to the standing foot and release that standing foot from the floor. This will become the common denominator to your early development in ballroom dancing. When and if you make the error, laugh at yourself and then repeat the process through any dance figure that you might study. As I suggested earlier, the error will occur and practice will eradicate it.

Closing Actions in the Smooth Dances

The two most common Smooth dances are Foxtrot and Waltz. So let's take a few minutes and practice how *side—together—release* works for these two dances. After you have taken either a forward or backward step during the box step, which we will discuss in a few moments, you will be using the common denominator of ballroom dancing. Again, that is moving your free foot to the side then closing the next foot to it, releasing the former supporting foot from the floor.

For both the Waltz and Foxtrot, the side step will be taken using the ball of the foot, including the toe (we describe this as just "toe"). The closing foot will also strike first with the ball of the foot including the toe, and the dancer will then shift their body weight onto this closing foot. The net effect of this shift of body weight will be the release of the other foot from the floor while the body is up in what we call *rise*. To assist the release from the floor, I suggest that you slightly flex your ankle and remove the toe of the former supporting foot from the floor. Once you have done that, the leg that is to move next in any desired direction is free to begin its swing. Typically when this happens the body begins to lower in a controlled way through the leg and foot that have just done the closing movement.

> **Dancing Definition**
>
> **Rise and fall** is the process of either elevating or lowering through the feet, legs, and body. You will notice that *rise* is the natural and the greatest when your legs are under your hips. Additionally, rise is achieved by lifting the heels from the floor. I have never liked the term "fall" because its connotation suggests a loss of control. Nothing of the sort happens in good dancing! Fall, or the lower elevation of the body, is greatest at your full stride with absolutely no loss of body lift or control of your ribcage. I would prefer to rename *fall* as your normal elevation found while dancing in stride or the middle of a walk. It is an elevation of the body suitable for movement with nominal flex or compression of the knees. Fall is simply an older term and easier to say!

Stay in Time

Since your body moves to the side with the moving foot, the weight change begins to occur at virtually the same moment. This is not the case on the closing action. As we just stated, a conscious effort must be made to shift the body weight and release the former foot from the floor. As a practical matter, this takes a longer period of time. In the case of both the Foxtrot and the Waltz, you only have one beat to accomplish this. Therefore the following is extremely important! You must close the foot at a much faster rate or pace than the former side step. If you do not, you will simply fall behind the timing and either have to rush the lowering action into the next progressive movement or remain behind or later than the timing of the music. Simply stated, the closing actions should happen as quickly as you can do them, allowing for good preparation toward the next movement.

When using the practice position as shown in the following picture (or when you have achieved closed dance position, as covered in Chapter 12, "Dance Positions with Your Partner"), review the practice exercises given at the end of the last chapter. Practice closing your feet with more pace to stay in time with the music of your choice.

Practice Position.

The Box Step Is Your Trailblazer

We are now going to study the piece of choreography that becomes your foundational pattern for movement in the following dances: Waltz, Foxtrot, Viennese Waltz, Rumba, and frequently Merengue. The other dances share the same common denominator that we have previously discussed, but not in the same "foundational" way.

The following is a physical lesson—including the use of your own voice. I reiterate, the more senses that you bring into the development of any physical skill, the faster your development. Please do not let the remedial nature of what we are about to do offend you. This is the remedial portion of your dance education and it is all about thinking, saying, and then doing. Concentrate on what you are doing and do not let your ego play games with you. The adult ego often gets in the way of learning new skills. The following steps are to be done and not just read.

Movement Memo

Review all the exercises given in Chapter 10 and this chapter in the practice position shown in the nearby figure.

This will be the intermediate stage between solo position and your closed ballroom position. Remember: Balance comes from your legs, body, and the dance floor, not your partner!

The Forward Half Box Step—Development Exercise

Start out in side-by-side position with both partners participating the same way.

Step 1. Repeat aloud: "My body moves forward." Now you do it. Move away from your right foot and finish on top of your left foot. Your right foot is now free of any body weight, and, therefore, it has to be the next foot!

Step 2. Repeat aloud: "My body moves sideways." Now you do it. Your body moves away from your left foot and finishes on top of your right foot. Your left foot is now free of any body weight, and, therefore, the left foot has to be next! Review the dynamics of taking a side step if necessary.

Step 3. Repeat aloud: "Now I close my feet" and close the left foot to the right foot until the heel of each foot is only one-quarter inch apart from each other. Then instantly take the right foot off the floor no more than one-half inch. Your right foot is now free of all body weight and, therefore, is the next foot.

Do you see how simple this process is? My words repeat themselves, you repeat the words, and then you are empowered to move dynamically and confidently. This completes the Forward Half Box Step.

The Backward Half Box Step—Development Exercise

Start out in side-by-side position with both partners participating the same way.

Step 1. Repeat aloud: "My body moves backward." Now you do it. Your body moves away from the left foot until it is over the right foot. Your left foot is free of body weight and, therefore, is the next foot that will move. Review the dynamics of taking a backward step if necessary.

Step 2. Repeat aloud: "My body moves sideways." Now you do it. Your body moves away from your supporting foot—that is, your right foot—until the weight of your body is completely over the left foot.

Step 3. Repeat aloud: "Now I close my feet." Now you do it. Close your right foot to your left foot until the heels are only one-quarter inch apart from each other and take your left foot off the floor no more than one-half inch. Your left foot is now free of all your body weight and, therefore, is the next foot.

Congratulations—you just completed both the Forward Half Box and the Backward Half Box. When these two figures are done together, they comprise the foundation of the most fundamental dance figure done in social dancing.

Now apply the music and timing of Foxtrot, and we will dance the six full steps of the box step. Your timing will be Slow for two beats on either the forward or backward steps. The side step and the closing step each take one beat apiece and are Quick, Quick. The box step will take a total of eight beats of music. You will count it aloud saying, "Slow, Quick Quick, Slow, Quick Quick." Review and repeat as often as you wish.

Now apply the music and timing of Waltz, and we will dance the same six full steps of the box step. Your timing will be one beat for each of the six steps, for a total of six beats of music. Review and repeat as often as you wish.

You will learn to rotate these box steps both clockwise and counterclockwise once you begin the choreography of each dance. In the next chapter, you will learn how to form the Closed Ballroom Position. I recommend that you review and practice all the progressive and nonprogressive exercises in this chapter and Chapter 10 in Closed Ballroom Position.

The closing actions in the various Latin dances and the East Coast Swing will be essentially the same, with some differences occurring due to the characteristic of the dance itself. The speed of the closing action will always be necessary. It will be faster than a side action. The difference in physical movement will accommodate the dance style and will be fully explained in the choreography of each dance.

The Least You Need to Know

- There is no physical reason to change weight when we close our feet, so we must make it a natural instinct.
- The closing action will always be faster than the actual step to the side.
- The common denominator in social ballroom dancing is the closing action and subsequent weight change.
- Use the Box Step exercise to hone your skills with the closing step.

Chapter 12

Dance Positions with Your Partner

In This Chapter

- ◆ Do not look at those toes!
- ◆ Close together but not cheek to cheek
- ◆ The ultimate contact sport
- ◆ Ladies—keep your eyes above the horizon

By now you have gone through the development and moving exercises of the Quickstart to Social Dancing Program© and are getting ready to repeat any and all of those in Closed Ballroom Position. Remember, the key is to allow for and accept each other willingly and also aggressively through each other's space without any evasive maneuvers.

You have worked hard to develop good body position and movement skills—do not spoil them by looking at the floor! Doing so will certainly create a chain reaction of misplaced body positions! Your error will be amplified in your partner's response. You are trying to bring something to the table here and not take your partner's balance from them. Gain all of your support from the dance floor using your muscles. The overall idea is to move with someone attached to you as if they were not there. This is not magic, nor is it particularly easy—so give yourselves time. Remember and believe: Others have done it, and so you will, too!

Closed Position is the most popular and effective means for traveling around the dance floor. In the Smooth dances, you will dance closer and attempt to retain body contact. In the Latin dances, Swing, and Hustle, there is more space between your bodies, giving you the ability to express rhythmic body movements.

Movement Memo

In the closed basic ballroom stance, the partners' bodies are essentially parallel to each other. Please note that in any of the following descriptions, the dance couple must make allowances for size and shape differentials. Please use the best approximations while maintaining the comfort of your partner. In the dance frame, you each have a quadrant in which to operate. This quadrant is left and forward of each other. "Sorry, Mr. or Ms., allow me my space—it is only here that you are not welcome. Let's be very comfortable so our movement is fluid and balance is impeccable!" Please note that a large disparity in height will create an obstructed view for the shorter partner.

Let's Get Close and Physical

First, each of the partners will stand with feet together. The balance of weight exists over the area around the balls of the feet. The feet of each partner will be facing the other's. The point that is formed by the toe of the right shoe will face the space equidistant between the partner's feet. Please note that you do not line up face to face! The toes of the partner's feet will be no less than three inches and no more than six inches from your own.

Please observe strong compression in the area of the abdominal wall. The contraction of the abdominal muscles will result in control of the upper body and a lengthening of the spinal column. This abdominal contraction can be created by a strong exhale from the diaphragm. Breathing out or exhaling at rhythmic intervals will maintain this strong abdominal alignment while you are dancing. This abdominal control is essential to all forms of partner dancing, including all styles of ballroom dancing.

Movement Memo

Owing to the flex in the knees, the skill, and experience of each of the partners, the bodies may indeed create contact from the upper thighs and continue all the way up to the middle of the torso. As you become better, this contact is preferable, because the couple becomes one entity sharing one common center of gravity and, therefore, accepts the impact of the laws of physics favorably.

You are looking for the following lineup:

◆ The right foot of each partner is pointing dead in line at the center point between the other partner's feet.

◆ The vertical center of the right thigh of each partner is directly opposite the other.

◆ The right side of the gentleman's ribcage is opposite the sternum or vertical center of the woman's ribcage.

◆ The right side of the woman's ribcage is approximately opposite the gentleman's sternum. Two partners would have to be exactly the same size for these reference points to be perfect, and that is unlikely.

◆ The chin of the gentleman is in line with or pointing over the woman's right shoulder. This would be approximately between the edge of her deltoid and the center of her neck.

◆ The chin of the woman is in line with or pointing toward the gentleman's right shoulder. This would be approximately between the edge of his deltoid and the center of his neck.

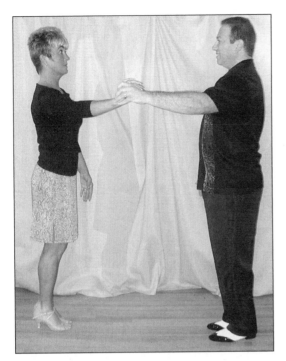

Invitation.

Closed Position Front.

Closed Position Back.

Closed Position Side.

The elevation of the head must be maintained in any dance. The center of the ears should be over the dancer's shoulders. The jawbone of the dancer's head should remain parallel to the dance floor and/or the dancer's shoulders. The gentleman's jaw should be level (parallel) with the dance floor with his gaze at his eye level. The woman's jaw is held at a comfortable level (according to her ability) slightly above the parallel plane of the dance floor. Her gaze is above her eye level. If you were standing at one end of the room facing the other, this would be at the level where the ceiling meets the wall.

Contact Points for the Hands and Arms

Consider the following as a sequence of events to best collect each other into the closed dance position. Closed position should always feel relaxed and not intrusive to your partner—there is never pushing or pulling!

1. **Man's left hand to lady's right hand.** The butt (the part of the palm opposite the wrist) of the lady's palm is in contact with the center of the man's palm in an upper-hand clasp, with fingers and thumbs closed but not squeezed around the partner's hand. The thumbs are relaxed and side-by-side touching the outside of the lady's index finger. There are many varieties to the hold, and the hold will actually change for reason of size and body positions. The most important aspect is comfort and uniform pressure.

2. **Man's right hand on lady's back.** The right hand is loosely cupped with fingers and thumb together (not spread apart). His hand connects to her back on her shoulder blade. His forearm makes contact with her triceps.

3. **Lady's left arm and hand to man's right arm and shoulder.** She may connect on top of his arm or slightly around the deltoid.

One Last Word

Congratulations! You are now ready to begin your walking and development exercises as described in Chapters 10, "The Quickstart Program© Progressive Movements," and 11, "The Quickstart Program© Nonprogressive Movements," using Closed Dance Position. As you work on your rhythm together, take note of and begin to appreciate the spatial requirements that each of you need at the inside contact points (between your bodies) and the outside periphery of the dance couple's frame. Keeping it simple at first is the best idea! Do not sacrifice the vertical alignment and carriage of your bodies nor the geometric accuracy of your stride. These qualities make your partner's job much easier!

Remember that you should always strive to move comfortably with your partner rather than move in strife. Your partner is neither your means for support nor your handrail. Rather, your partner is your traveling companion. For support use the dance floor and your own muscles.

When you bring your exercises to the level of rehearsing the box step in Closed Dance Position, the gentleman will begin with the Forward Half of the Box Step, and the lady will begin with the Backward Half. Good luck!

Promenade Position

Promenade position is a V-shaped dance position with the man's left side and lady's right side slightly open. The direction of travel is toward the open side. It might be wise to become comfortable with movement in Closed Position before delving into Promenade Position.

Promenade Position Front.   *Promenade Position Back.*

Positioning

The gentleman and lady stand in front of each other in body contact, slightly offset to the left, with the lady's middle connected to the man's right front. The lady's left hip and foot should be positioned slightly behind the man's. In promenade position, the man's head should be turned to the left to view the line of dance between his left shoulder and elbow. The lady's head should be to the right to view the line of dance between her right shoulder and elbow.

Contact Points

Consider the following as a sequence of events to best collect each other into promenade position (PP). Promenade position should always feel relaxed and not intrusive to your partner—like the Closed Position there is never pushing or pulling!

1. **Body contact.** The right side of the man's torso is in contact with the middle of the lady's torso. The connection begins at the lower hips and should continue all the way up to the middle of the torso.

2. **Handholds.** The left-to-right handholds are essentially the same as in the closed position.

3. **Arms and hands.** The use of the man's right and his partner's left arms and hands is the same as in the closed position.

4. **Sustained elevations of couples' ribcages.** Pay particular attention to this detail. A feeling of stretch is preferable to the man's right side, and the lady's left side does not drop. Additionally, as the couple travels, a feeling of moving up a grade rather than downhill is a continuous idea that will serve you both well!

The Wedding Dip

As promised, here is a very comfortable and attractive ending to your first wedding dance. (Refer to Chapter 4, "Dancing Through Your Big Day.") The gentleman's and lady's movements are described together using the sequence below.

The Wedding Dip is a final "one time only" movement to attract attention and applause at the end of the wedding dance. The directions to a happy ending—the Wedding Dip:

1. The groom starts in the closed position with his left foot free. Sway to the left, slightly changing weight and release your right foot from the floor. This releases your bride's left foot from the floor.

2. Allow the released foot to skim to the gentleman's right for a wide step. From there, the couple flexes their knees and braces against the floor in the lunge position, as shown. Ladies, when you practice this movement, make sure that if your partner moves away from you, there is *no* loss of balance. Never give up your balance on the social dance floor! The lunge and dip is not intended to be solely supported by the strength of the groom.

3. From the lunge position, the bride rotates a quarter turn clockwise on her left foot so that she is perpendicular to the groom's right side. She continues to lower through her knee by releasing her right foot from the floor, as shown. The groom places both hands behind the bride's shoulder blades for additional security and moves his body slightly upward in opposition to his partner. Hold the position for a few moments because it is picture time, and then kiss your bride!

4. The exit from this picture line should not be abrupt. The bride should not try to get up all at once. Instead, move forward and then up through your knees by planting both feet securely on the dance floor. The groom assists the bride gallantly with a sweeping action from his right to left side and then upward until she is comfortably up on her feet. Now the groom presents the bride to the guests. Take your bows!

Entry Movement to Man's Left.

The Lunge.

The Dip's Final Position.

The Exit from Dip.

The Least You Need to Know

- In basic Closed Ballroom Position, the partners line up slightly left of each other.
- In basic Closed Ballroom Position, partners often have body contact from the upper thigh to mid-torso.
- Promenade position is a V shape in which the lady's left hip and foot are slightly behind that of the man.
- The Wedding Dip is a picture-perfect ending for any special dance.

13

The Interactions
of the Dance Couple

In This Chapter

◆ Invite him in

◆ Put your shoulders on the shelf

◆ Step, then turn

◆ Torque a little, turn a lot

So far in the third part of this book we have been working to cumulatively develop the dance couple for successful movement together in each of the three directions—forward, backward, and sideways. In this chapter, I outline the life skills of ballroom dancing: leading and following, hands and arms, and the essential elements of rotation. Return to this chapter frequently to reinforce your choreographic experiences.

Leading and Following

It all starts with the leader's mind as he quickly assembles and coordinates his most comfortable moment to begin. The leader must survey the floor for open space, hear the first beat of a measure, feel the connection and poise of his partner, and then transmit all this information right to his knees to activate the movement and carriage of his body into what we call *body flight*. His body transmits directional and/or rotational lead through to his arms and hands and then to his feet. This quantitative lead must be transmitted responsibly to his partner so as not to negatively challenge the follower's balance. The leader's body creates a desired degree of rotation or linear progression with either acceleration or deceleration. The follower's body must be prepared to reciprocate. The follower has prestructured her body within the couple's frame and waits with fluid buoyancy, "all systems go," for just the right impulse and pressure to activate the knee of her supporting foot, sending her body into flight. The follower then, in essence, becomes the leader. As she creates space for her partner to fill, she allows him to start this process again and again. Therefore countless leads and follows occur through the course of a dance. As more of this activity occurs, the lead becomes subtler and is done with more finesse. The ultimate result is a highly skilled and very smooth dance couple.

Once the dance couple is in frame, the leader depends on the partner to travel backward using a slow rhythm as a standard. As the follower walks backward, an "invitation" is created. This invitation says *pass into my space, visit me here, and speak to me!* Her continued commitment to walking backward then becomes the progressive movement of a back walk, and her physical commitment to it makes the leader's job in changing directions much easier.

Use of the Hands and Arms

The usage of the hands and arms are fundamental to the ability to interact as a couple and decorate the dance by changing directions. Their correct usage is as important to you as the steering components of the vehicle that brought you to the bookstore for this text! Let's begin with these important concepts.

Shoulders Relate to Your Ribcage

Here are two items you must remember. First, the shoulders are always relaxed and positioned with downward pressure toward the ribcage. The muscles around the front and back of the ribcage will flex and provide a shelf for the arms. And second, do not try to sustain the necessary lift in the upper arms with the shoulders.

I stress these two points because when 999 out of 1,000 people are told to lift their arms into dance position, they will use the top of their shoulders, as in a shrug. This is wrong and can cause some painful cramping if allowed to continue for any length of time. This incorrect use of the shoulders is the reason why new dancers often produce such a poor dance frame. The instinctive attempt to avoid pain in the shoulders results in the constant need to adjust the dropping arms and elbows. The new dancer must make these constant adjustments because he lacks the knowledge of the muscular creation of a good frame. A better idea is to learn how to position the arms and back into a solid position, like a shelf, that breathes or is still as necessary. I want to teach you the correct procedure to lift your arms and maintain a workable, comfortable dance position for any of the ballroom dances.

Stand with your arms hanging freely and relaxed by your sides. Then press down from your shoulders. This should feel as if you are wedging your fingers up into your underarm. With your good vertical forward poise and your arms loosely held from the shoulders, your palms will hang in front of your upper legs facing the thighs. While flexing your abdominal wall, as well as your pectoral muscles, swing your upper arms from the shoulders forward and up until your elbows reach the elevation of your bust line or sternum. This should create a flexing of the muscle group known as the *latissimus dorsi*, commonly called the *lats*. Once your arms are lifted, rotate the area between the elbow and shoulder (which includes the biceps and triceps) until that part of the arm creates a 45-degree angle from the arm's hanging position to the dance floor. Your elbows are then moved back, but only far enough to match the normal contour of your shoulders. This rotation will diminish the elevation of the trapezius muscles, also commonly called the *traps*, and will produce a long, smooth shoulder line that is parallel to the dance floor.

As you assume the dance position, you will both feel and see the result of the "opening" or expanding of the underarm area. As the underarms expand, you will feel a firming of the upper back muscles. This procedure will complete the shelf for your upper body framing. One major result of this new framing technique is increased flexibility and rotation of the upper arms, because the "firmness" of the frame is in your torso rather than in your arms. Your arm and hand gestures will begin from your shoulder, as they should. It is very important to your dancing, regardless of style or type, that you maintain the feeling of openness in the underarm area. This posture will dramatically increase your arm speed and flexibility.

It is critical for a dancer to allow the arms to "breathe," as this will help prevent any inadvertent movement of the body. Inadvertent body movement that results from arm movements must always be avoided. "Breathing the arms" is a description that I use in my teaching to denote the condition of flexibility, connection, flexing, and response within the frame of the dance couple. When done correctly, "breathing the arms" ensures that the transmission of leads and follows from within the couple is fluid. Fluidity will be felt within the joints and firmness within the muscles. In addition to leading and following, "breathing the arms" will signify to each partner when their counterpart has completed a dance step. Practice this new concept using very simple figures like the box step. Keeping your muscles firm and your joints fluid will allow you to dance without the loss of balance or elevation of frame. It will also help you overcome the undesired need to look at the feet! Once you are secure with simple figures, move on to additional or more challenging figures.

Movement Memo

Maintaining your dancer's frame throughout your normal lifestyle can do wonderful things for you. Notice that your neck looks longer and more elegant. In addition to being very important to the appearance of a dancer, the longer appearance of the neck displays confidence. You have changed your body language. You should find this new position to be relaxed through the shoulders and very firm through and across the upper back, thus providing you with the ability to sustain your upper frame comfortably for several minutes at a time. Together with the tone of your abdominal wall, your back may feel better than usual by the end of the workday; you may not get that headache that can be caused by compression on your vertebrae. As a result, you will have more energy and vitality to go out dancing!

Check to see if you can swing your forearms from your elbows like a windshield wiper without dropping the elbows or the upper arms. How did you do? This is the physical demonstration of "breathing arms." Correct arm positioning is the freedom to let the arms "breathe" or move when desired without creating inadvertent movement of the body. When your arms are positioned so as to be part of your standard closed position, they will be securely integrated into your back muscles, and your leading and following applications will transmit the correct messages.

Comfort in Holding Hands

I want the lady to give the gentleman her right hand by placing the base of her palm (the area just above the wrist) into the center of his left palm. This way, as she closes her fingers gently, they will reach over to the back of his hand. The area of the gentleman's hand where the lady will fold her fingers is between his thumb and index finger. This handhold is comfortable, and when he gets nervous or is concentrating intensely, the woman's fingers cannot be squeezed to the point of turning purple. Please note that experienced dancers never clamp down tightly on their partner's fingers with their thumb or fingers. This clamping is more restrictive than useful. We need to create accessibility to all interior points of our partner's palm and fingers. The joining of our hands is always designed for both interlocking and for quick release. Hand positions are never static, nor do they continue in the same position throughout a dance. The leader will use both sides of his fingers in addition to his palm in a multitude of positions painting directional information on the canvas of his partner's interior hand and fingers. The trick to doing this is to always have the availability of the basic handhold at your disposal. As you practice, see to it that no matter what position you find your hands in (owing to the particular dance figure), you can instantly return to the basic closed position!

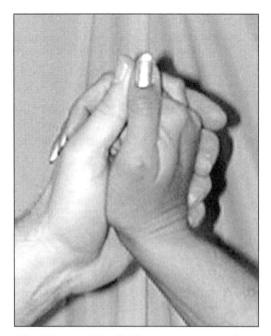

Closed Position Handhold.

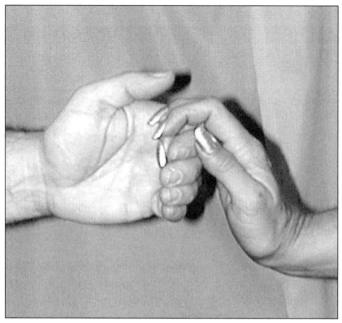

Open Facing Handhold.

Leading Rotation

The man possesses various devices to lead rotation while he himself continues to move—completing his present direction and weight change. These are like the blinker arm and lights on your automobile. They operate both independently and coincidentally with the couple's movement. It might sound complex, but it really isn't. Let's explore your steering mechanisms.

Body Torque and Contrary Body Movement (CBM)

When the twisting effort initiated by the muscles of the body, predominantly around the ribcage and abdominal wall, are applied to the various lateral assemblies, the body turns about its axis of rotation. The time to best experience and use body torque is after the impact and correction, and just as compression ensues, as described as part of the "Dynamic Duo" in Chapter 6, "The Challenges of Ballroom Dancing." This axis of rotation can be thought of as an imaginary laser beam passing through the skull, the entirety of the spinal column, and continuing through the standing or supporting leg to the focal contact point of the foot on the floor. In the vast majority of cases, this contact point will be the ball of the foot. This action where the plane of the upper torso begins to rotate creating rotation in the hips is called contrary body movement, or CBM. It is the opposite or contrary side of the body that rotates toward the moving foot.

Movement Memo _____

To best illustrate the action of body torque, I want you to fold a bath towel to approximately three feet in length and begin twisting each end of the towel until it becomes quite firm. The center of the towel can be likened to the main part of your torso. Release the towel by holding either the bottom or the top of the twisted portion, and you will see the remainder of the towel explode into rotation. You have now seen how a soft, inanimate object can produce powerful torque and rotation. Now let's liken this to your dancing. If you concentrate your energies on your center rather than on your extremities (hands, legs and feet, shoulders), you will see rotation flourish in your dancing.

Body Torque Influences Your Direction

When the leader is moving forward on his left foot, he will create the torque for left or counterclockwise rotation. Once the establishment of the new vertical axis has been created over his left foot, the dancer can either rotate or lead the counterclockwise rotation. The exact opposite is true when moving toward his right foot and leg. In this case, the rotation will be right or clockwise. The rule continues with backward movements and dance steps. The right foot back produces left torque and the left foot back produces right torque in the dancer's body. With respect to his partner, the reciprocal is true. Therefore the couple's connected dance frame works harmoniously with the rule of body torque. Once you have experimented with, as well as mentally digested, this rule of torque, the leader will make better choices on the dance floor.

"Step, Then Turn"

Once a dance step has commenced with the objective of rotation or leading rotation, the rule of "step, then turn" must be applied. This technique is very simple to understand. However it requires good form throughout your dancing. We have already discussed what components make up a good dance step. The first portion of the "step, then turn" rule is taking a technically good dance step!

In the case of leading and following, the follower must achieve a position of a new vertical axis on which to rotate before the rotation should be led or even attempted. The optimum time for this to occur is just as the dancer's knees are passing each other. At this moment, the body is centered perfectly. When we stand normally, our knees are together and all the weight of our body is vertically in line. When moving, the body turns best when all, or the great majority, of our weight (including our legs) is in line vertically. Achieving this position of inline verticality is the key to the "step, then turn" rule. When you begin to apply both of these rules, you will find that making up to one-half a rotation in your dancing will become effortless.

No Overpowering the Turn

I know that record turntables are becoming scarce, but here is a helpful illustration for leading. Place your middle finger right next to the spindle at the center of the turntable. Attempt to rotate the turntable, and you will find there is a good amount of resistance. Now move the same finger to the outside edge of the turntable and attempt to rotate it. If you anticipated and applied the same force, I bet it spun right out of your control. The effort to turn it is many times less at the outer edge than at the center. The farther we move from the center, the less force required. What we learn here is that with a good vertical center (spindle), the outer circumference of a balanced object will rotate with great ease.

The application of this knowledge to our ballroom dancing will work something like this: Create a wide dance frame with the upper arms away from the ribcage, and control your vertical center. Notice that the periphery of the body becomes responsive to the lightest pressure from your partner. Therefore, it will only be a matter of speed and timing to generate a change of direction or a spot rotation. A breeze is enough pressure to turn your partner or to turn with your partner. Reserve your strength to create your own vertical elevation and internal muscular control! You do not need to use extremity force to lead your partner. Such force only challenges the partner's balance and center. If you need to generate greater amounts of rotation or sharpness in rotation, do so by increasing the amount of CBM in preparation. CBM is definitely an internal application of power for rotation rather than an external one.

The Time to Lead Rotation—"As the Knees Pass"

"As the knees pass" is an expression that I use with great frequency. I often joke with my beginner students (of one to three years) when answering many of the questions I pose that to receive a grade of 90 percent, they simply should answer "as the knees pass." It is a key moment in the dancer's movement!

At this moment the dancer's weight is about to change. It is the moment best suited for rotation, because the dancer has achieved their best vertical alignment and balance. To lead a partner into a rotation even just a moment before this position is achieved can be hazardous to her balance and jeopardize the completion of the desired rotation. Work on your walks with your partner. Pay close attention to when the knees pass and exactly how you feel at that moment. Then work on your rotation. For example, walk and then walk into the Waltz's Left Box Turn (refer to Chapter 15, "Waltz"). As the follower's knees converge, the leader begins CBM, so at the moment of the knees' passage, the couple is into their turn. Each and every progressive dance movement experiences knee passage. Therefore, there is an appropriate time to lead and follow any rotation. You will find when practicing this technique that you may have to slow down or speed up various aspects of your dance movements and configurations. Recognizing the moment the knees pass is vital to smooth transition and to greater clarity in the understanding of timing.

Ladies, Just for You—When to Follow

Ladies, just for a moment lift one or both of your arms in the air. Did any of you feel that you wanted to turn as a result of doing this? Of course not! Lifting your elbows will also have no bearing on the time to rotate. I mention these two examples because for some reason that I have yet to figure out, there is a great misconception about whether the vertical lift of the arm actually causes turn. It doesn't! Yet unskilled beginners or followers who are not properly trained seem sure that it does. They are so certain of this that they will lift their own elbow and upper arm and lurch through their self-designed entrance arch in an effort to create an imaginary moment to turn. Clearly they are off balance, the shoulders are very uneven, and the outcome of the turn is so unpredictable that it is usually necessary to stop dancing. There is a term that is used to describe this mess: *twirling!* I define twirling as a nondescript, uncontrolled rotation! So what is the alternative?

This sequence will help you and the leader perfect the timing of any rotation, whether in open or closed position.

Here is a hint: Wait until you feel rotation through your clavicle.

Technique

Technique (General for Ladies): In a good closed position frame, the lady will first feel the lead in her hand, then up to her elbow, on to her upper arm, and finally at her clavicle or collar bone. These body parts are moving in CBM. Please note that in closed position you are attached to your partner on both sides. As a result, there must be reciprocity—as you feel pressure to move away from your partner on one side (the lead), you must try to move your other side closer. This will indicate any turn including the lead to promenade position.

In an open-facing position, it is the movement of your wrist first, followed by your elbow, upper arm, and clavicle that indicates lead for a rotation.

When your wrist moves upward, your elbow bends—do not straighten your arm above your head! Keep your elbow bent at a 45-degree angle, which I call "waitress position." As the leader applies slight pressure outward and toward the wall behind you, wait until you feel your clavicle begin to turn before you start your clockwise rotation.

When your wrist moves forward and across your ribcage, be sure to maintain slight resistance toward your partner. Again you must wait until you feel your clavicle begin to turn before you attempt a counterclockwise rotation.

Remember, we must allow our arms to "breathe" freely. So the best time to follow a rotation is once the signal gets to your body and your clavicle changes direction.

Foot Position in CBMP

This is a very useful and aesthetically pleasing position for the foot and leg. It is frequently used in Tango and in the Basic Twinkle figures in both Waltz and Foxtrot when stepping in promenade position. Holding the foot in CBMP accents the partner's rotation.

One of the important characteristics of quality dancing is controlling the movement of both feet at all times.

Now that we have clarified the differences of foot movement and placement, I want to discuss once again a use of the foot and leg position that is common to both styles. We will call these positions placing and/or holding the foot in CBMP. CBMP stands for an important dance term critical to all forms of dancing: contra-body movement position of the feet. This is not as complex as it sounds. When we move with CBMP, the free or traveling foot crosses the plane or line of the dancer's body in the direction he is moving. For instance, the second step in promenade position (PP) requires a movement of the foot with CBMP technique. In this case, the free foot of the dancer will be released sufficiently from the dance floor to travel just slightly above and across the standing or supporting foot. If you omit this important technique from a second step moving in promenade, the couple will be forced farther away from each other and create a loss of balance and connection.

To place or hold your foot in CBMP, it is best to make the first contact on the floor with the outside edge of the foot. That is the portion of the foot that is farthest from your body's center—the little toe side. There should be a good amount of tone and pressure between the sole of the shoe and the dance floor. This pressure however, is not to be construed as a weight change or even the beginning of a weight change. It should be thought of as a strong and beautiful leg line. Additionally, this tone between the foot and the dance floor will secure the partner who is leading a rotation. The lady who has completed a rotation will often finish her figure's movement in CBMP. This will then match the position of the gentleman's leg line and create a very pretty picture!

Inside and Outside of a Turn

Any time a couple turns in ballroom dancing, both an inside and outside of that rotation exists. The inside of the turn generally occurs for the partner stepping backward. At the inside of the turn, the body and feet of the dancer will generate more rotation at a faster rate than the partner who is at the outside of the turn. The partner who is at the outside of the turn will have to travel farther. The earlier rotation on the inside of the turn creates and/or permits accessibility for the partner passing on the outside of the turn.

A simple example of this concept is your car. When your automobile is turning right, the left wheels travel farther and seemingly catch up to the right wheels as the turn completes.

Magic Part of the Foot

This particular use of the dancer's feet during the Swing Rock and the Hustle's first step backward will contribute greatly to your success. The appropriate footwork on any back step should produce poise, rhythm, and stability, particularly in the upper body. The uses of the various sections of the dancer's feet are not arbitrary. Without a high-quality platform, good dancing is impossible.

When students are learning to dance, they place choreography above all else in an attempt to get to the dance floor in a hurry. Much that is learned during the process of this very casual approach includes inadvertent error. One such error is found in how the foot is placed on the dance floor during a back step. When the center of the ball of the foot or any point behind it, including the heel, is placed down first, the body's tendency is to roll off or go backward. Imagine how difficult it must be to try to balance yourself on a ball like a circus performer, especially if you were moving backward. Let's fix this common annoyance right now!

I want to introduce you to a platform I call "the magic part of the foot." The area of the foot where coincidental contact exists on the dance floor between the front of the ball of the foot and the center of the big toe is the magic part of the foot. This position is achieved when the arch and heel of the foot are almost perpendicular to the dance floor. This application of the foot should be used as the first point of contact when taking any backward step. This is true in the Latin dances that use turnout to make the contact on the inside edge of the toe and ball, and in the Smooth dances where just toe is felt, followed by the magic part of the foot. This area of the foot puts on the breaks of backward momentum while the torso has the opportunity to restructure to the new vertical axis by using the plié action of the knee. From this point, the heel of the foot can lower according to the speed of the music (lower if slower) without the feeling of falling back "head over heels." As the dancer prepares to exit from that same foot, they then elevate their heel to feel maximum foot pressure and use that pressure to push their body forward to the replacement position. The strength of the foot is at a maximum here, and this technique, as much as any single item I can tell you, will change the quality of your dancing.

"Magic Part of the Foot."

Knee Veer

Knee veer is an important technique to the development of the ballroom dancer's center. Once a dancer finds that theoretical center point (the belly button is as good as any), he or she discovers how to balance and control their center. Knee veer accommodates the usage of two other important skills. The first usage is elevation adjustments to eliminate rise and fall. Increased knee veer can actually eliminate rise as the legs pass each other during progressive movement. The second usage allows the dancer to roll through his or her feet on progressive sideways movements.

I often instruct new Tango and Swing dancers to develop leg veer by placing a small throw pillow between their upper thighs very close to, if not in contact with, their crotch. Moving in promenade, sideways, or in small steps forward or backward with the pillow between the thighs will help the dancer develop greater strength, balance, and control. Many experts feel that without knee veer there is a missing link in the character of Tango.

Dancing Definition

Knee veer can be described as a feeling of compression. The thighs and knees of the dancer slightly compress toward each other while the dancer's body is directly over the final contact point—his foot. Both the knees and ankles will be closer together to the body's center than the dancer's feet. Knee veer gives the dancer a feeling of strength enabling greater control.

This is particularly true in the American style of Tango. Knee veer will keep the toes pointing slightly at each other and the feet just apart. Another important application of knee veer is in the elimination of rise and fall—not just in Tango, but the Latin dances as well. To test this concept, dance alone with random rhythmic movements for a few moments with the knees turned out from your center, then pointed absolutely forward. Now, dance alone using knee veer and observe how smoothly and rhythmically you can roll side-to-side between your feet. You decide!

Knee veer is sustained by creating leg swing from the hip and upper thigh rather than below the knee. This technique is very prevalent in the Latin dances, where knee veer is used to retain a very small portion of shoe contact with the floor toward the inside edge of either the ball or big toe of the moving foot.

Bet You Didn't Know

Elvis was a master of knee veer, it was his secret for hip movement. Perhaps he should have been called Elvis "the Knees" rather than Elvis the Pelvis. As you continue into the Latin dances, it is the use of the knees that moves the hips. If you think you just move your hips to move your hips, you'll quickly find all you do is loose control of your ribcage and shoulders adversely affecting your balance!

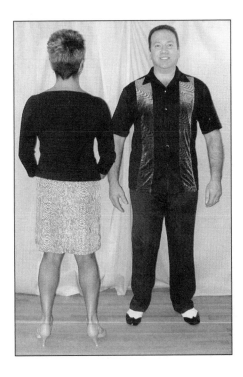

Knee veer shown in Solo side-by-side.

Sway

Sway is the inclination of the body away from the moving foot and toward the inside of the turn. Inclining the body to the left or right from the knees and not the waist will create the correct sway. Broken sway from the waist should be avoided. Turns in the Smooth dances begin with *contrary body movement* (*CBM*) with sway beginning immediately following the step with CBM. This usually occurs on the following two steps. Even a slight inclination in the opposing direction of the moving foot will help balance the beginner dance couple. Sway can be very attractive when used properly, while the total absence of sway produces a mechanical appearance. Allow sway to happen; do not force it. The more experienced you become, the more automatic the sway. You will note that sway occurs on side steps and closing steps. Sway generally increases gradually while the dancers rise. Sway is then lost immediately when the lowering action occurs. The feeling of sway is one of stretch rather than inclination. That means the area between both sides of the ribcage is increased, not diminished!

The Least You Need to Know

- In a good dance frame, there is firmness and structure in the torso while the arms are allowed to "breathe."

- Improve your ability to rotate by concentrating your energy in your center, not in your extremities.

- Applying the concept of inside and outside of the turn will improve the ability to turn the dance couple.

- When used properly, sway helps the couple to stay balanced and improves the appearance of dance figures.

Part  4

Fred and Ginger Here We Come: The Smooth Dances

Dancing is about movement and direction in relationship to the dance floor and, most important, to your partner. I have included an easy-to-use diagram of *Line of Dance.* Referencing this frequently will help you greatly as you begin the choreography sections of the book.

Waltz and Foxtrot are your two foundational dances. They are also the two most popular wedding dances among the generic ballroom rhythms. You will find routines designed perfectly for your wedding dance—even if you are very late in your preparations.

Tango is definitely the most theatrical dance covered in *The Complete Idiot's Guide to Ballroom Dancing.* Ladies, a special note to you: Men love Tango! This dance has a dominant masculine rhythm and is not very difficult. The last dance in this section is the mother of all ballroom dancing and has its roots firmly in classical music. That dance is the Viennese Waltz, and it is the dance of which dreams and fairy tales are made.

Chapter 14

Your Best Directions

In This Chapter

- ◆ Angles create more space
- ◆ Look where you are going
- ◆ Allow space enough for two
- ◆ Mind your manners

Just as there are rules of the road while you are driving, there are rules for effective travel on the dance floor. Imagine a baseball field or tennis court without its stripes to determine inbound or legal play—the sport would be reduced to chaos and anarchy. It would be impossible to determine whether there is legitimate scoring or play.

This chapter is a brief but effective way to help you, the new dancer, reduce what looks like chaos out on the dance floor to a fairly simple road map. An understanding of the following diagram will also assist you in understanding the development of the dance figures and the way they travel. You will be able to visualize, practice, and then dance publicly using the choreographed routines at the end of each of the following chapters.

Diagram of Line of Dance

The illustration you are now looking at is a road map that relates to you and your partner and the directions in which you will travel on the ballroom dance floor. You will also find a diagram of the line of dance on the reference card at the beginning of this book. Be sure to tear out the card and use it to learn and practice each dance. Take it with you on your visits to the ballroom where you will dance socially or to your practice space—I promise it will be of great help to your mind's eye to visualize what you are about to do or study!

Your diagram of line of dance.

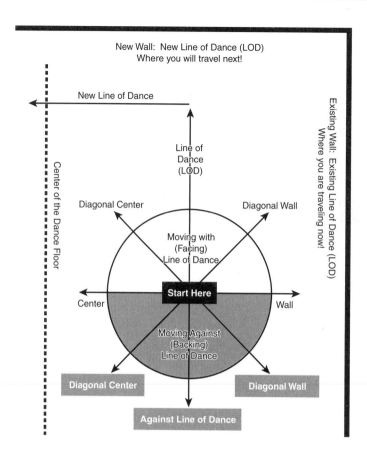

Description of Line of Dance

Obviously we do not draw lines or patterns or footprints on the public dance floor or our practice space. The line of dance is a series of imaginary lines and directions that you visualize or even feel by reducing them to your dancer's instincts.

In a very simplistic sense, the line of dance (often abbreviated as LOD) travels around the dance floor in a counterclockwise direction. The dancers keep to the right of an imaginary center line, regardless of the wall they are traveling along. Dance floors are generally centered in a room, with the tables and chairs, onlookers, etc. outside their perimeter. Anything outside the perimeter of the floor we refer to as a *wall*. Experienced couples do their best to keep the center of the dance floor to their left and the perimeter or wall of the dance floor to their right.

Why We Use Line of Dance

Line of dance is used primarily to avoid collisions on the dance floor by standardizing the direction of traveling and to maximize the available space for dance couples. We have already stated that the general direction of line of dance is counterclockwise around the floor. That is only part of the story.

To maximize space on the dance floor, dance couples usually take advantage of diagonal directions. Using directions such as diagonal to the wall or diagonal to the center helps us maximize the space on a given dance floor. It simply allows more bodies to use the same space. A herringbone pattern or zigzag line provides more linear direction than a straight line. By traveling on diagonals, a couple has the opportunity to travel or keep dancing in the midst of congestion on the dance floor.

From time to time in this text, you will read "this dance figure may travel in other alignments." This means if there is no room to go forward down LOD, then perhaps there is an opportunity to travel on a diagonal rather than waiting for a dance couple to move out of your space or line. As you become more experienced and in control of your dance figures, you will become more adept at adding or diminishing the amounts of turn to facilitate movement on the dance floor. Remember one very important thing: Nothing is carved in stone! Never collide into another couple for the sake of a written direction for any dance figure or combination of figures.

How We Use Line of Dance

The progressive dances in this book are the Waltz, Foxtrot, Tango, Viennese Waltz, and Samba.

These dances consist of figures that travel around the dance floor, as well as figures that are localized to one area of the floor. When a couple is dancing a progressive dance, the direction of travel is not necessarily predicated on the direction of the leader or follower. What is much more important is that the couple cumulatively moves counterclockwise around the dance floor, regardless of who is facing the direction of travel.

In the descriptions of the dance steps, I frequently first give the final direction in which a particular step travels. Think of that direction as your line of sight. Then using the physical descriptions and amounts of turn given in that step, you will ultimately achieve that direction. During my teaching, I'm a great advocate of both knowing and looking where you are going!

The nonprogressive dances in this book are the Rumba, Merengue, Cha-Cha, Mambo, East Coast Swing, and Hustle.

These dances are generally done in a very localized area on the dance floor. Frequently, the greatest amount of traveling is accomplished when the lady and the man trade places with each other. This is accomplished by using a circle with a common center or a slot similar to parallel lines like railroad tracks.

Where directions are given in these figures, they refer to positions relative to the leader. These directions are accomplished from starting positions and are developed through rotation.

You will find that the instructional commands given are perpendicular, parallel, or in the case of diagonal, 45 degrees to the direction described.

Movement Memo _____

An example would be: Move, start, or face the direction of the diagonal wall—from a position that faces (looking forward) down Line of Dance or 12 o'clock, you would turn clockwise 45 degrees where you are standing to face the wall creating a diagonal tangent line that would be also be 45 degrees to that wall. If you are told to face (looking forward) "diagonal center" then you would turn counterclockwise 45 degrees from where you are standing.

Another important direction given during the course of this text is pointing. Pointing simply means that the feet are advanced to the final direction while the body remains between the former position and the final direction. Another way of saying this is: The feet will get there first and on the next step complete the direction. You will note that on the following step you may read "Body completes the turn," this would be the time the center of your body actually catches up with the pointing or facing position of your moving foot. This happens for the partner who is on the inside of a curving figure. Typically pointing occurs on the step that follows a backward movement.

Common Courtesies on the Dance Floor

In a ballroom dance competition, the only forgivable collision takes place when the gentlemen of two couples collide with each other back-to-back. It is understood that we do not have eyes in the back of our head, and although these collisions are infrequent occurrences, they are forgivable. Other than that, the leader has the responsibility of avoiding all collisions on the dance floor and keeping his partner safe by selecting figure types that avoid collisions. If a collision occurs, please acknowledge the collision and ask for a pardon or forgiveness. Be sincere and not gratuitous about apologizing. In the midst of the social dance floor with many unskilled, untrained, and inexperienced dance couples, collisions will surely happen—especially in a nightclub where alcohol consumption may add to the unpredictability!

Use dance figures in the same way that you drive—move to open areas. If you cannot see it, then don't do it! Again the concept is a brilliant one: Look where you are going!

Gentlemen, when you are practicing, learn to leave several feet of space between your partner and the edge of the floor, tables and chairs, or onlookers. Remember that your spatial considerations are greater for you as a couple and distances seem to close in on you much sooner than expected.

Avoid dancing into a corner. Often inexperienced couples become trapped in a corner and wait unhappily while the other dancers circle by. I have always felt that dancing kitty-corner or across the corner to the next line of dance is a much better idea.

Learn to dance in small spaces! We humans are prone to physical exaggeration when learning a new physical skill. This is amplified in the dance couple. With each figure, you learn to develop finesse in your dancing as quickly as possible. In this way you will be able to taper the size of each new figure learned.

Do not teach on the dance floor. Please move off the floor and preferably to a far-off corner of the room. Stopping to instruct your partner can obstruct the flow of couples moving around the line of dance and can be embarrassing to your partner.

Believe it or not, the very center of the dance floor is a good place for beginners, who may not yet possess the floor craft and traveling finesse to stay. This is especially true during the progressive dances. In this way, those who can travel are not restricted and everyone is happy.

Dealing With a Congested Floor

Here are some helpful hints on how to deal with a congested floor:

- The leader must be allowed to lead, and the follower must be prepared to respond immediately. This strategy allows the leader to get the couple out of trouble.
- Both partners must maintain strong vertical alignment.
- Increase the floor pressure of your feet.
- During progressive dances, softer knees and ankles will accommodate more rise and fall, which will keep the figures or steps smaller.

The Least You Need to Know

- Observing line of dance (LOD) will help avoid collisions and maximize the space on the dance floor.
- Dances described as progressive are generally reserved for the larger ballroom or banquet hall where there is room to travel with the other couples as they travel around Line of Dance. They do not work well in the nightclub environment.
- Dances described as nonprogressive work well in both the ballroom and nightclub environments because they restrict themselves to a localized area on any dance floor.
- The direction of any dance figure or step described should be viewed as the eventual ending direction of the couple.
- The gentleman must always consider the space required for the whole couple when leading any dance figure.
- Please be careful to observe good dance etiquette at all times in all venues.

Chapter 15

Waltz

In This Chapter

- The foundation of the "ballroom" house
- Easy as 1-2-3
- Rise and fall
- Don't trap those feet

You are about to begin the study of the most classical of all ballroom dances. The Waltz is considered by many to be the most foundational experience of ballroom dancing. The type of figures that we use, the dance positions, the line of travel around the dance floor, and the choreography have changed very little in the last 100 years.

No other dance can provide the dreamy Cinderella feelings of pure romance in the way that a Waltz can. That is one of the reasons why many couples select a Waltz for the first dance on their wedding day. In my opinion, there is no dance that better portrays the beginning of married life on the wedding day than the dance that began it all! The light but distinct ¾ timing and tempo are intoxicating and very easy to follow.

I have placed the Waltz first in your book because it will help you develop the skills necessary to become a successful ballroom dancer. After all, the Waltz was and is the model for dance structure and technique.

Box with Underarm Turn

This dance figure begins in the closed position. The alignment of the box with underarm turn is the ending position of the previous figure. Please maintain the normal ¾ timing of the Waltz throughout this figure. There is no CBM.

Gentleman's Part: Box with Underarm Turn

Details forthe gentleman's Box with Underarm Turn:

Step 1. Walking forward on your left foot, start to rise using your normal footwork of heel, then the toe of the left foot.

Step 2. The right foot moves to the side while you continue to rise on both the second and third steps. The footwork on the second beat of music is the toe, including the ball of your right foot. There is sway to the left.

Step 3. The left foot will close to your right foot. Use the technique you have learned for lowering at the end of the close. The footwork is toe and then the heel as you lower. All of this occurs on the third beat of music using sway to the left.

Step 4. Walking backward on your right foot, make sure that you first make contact with your toe and then finish over your heel. Commence to rise through your body without lifting your foot. This is what we call a *no-foot rise.* This step takes place on the first beat of the second measure.

Step 5. The left foot moves to the side while you continue to rise on both the fifth and sixth steps. Your footwork on the second beat, or step 5, is toe with sway to your right.

Step 6. Your right foot closes to your left foot. Begin your lowering action using the footwork of toe, then heel. The leg swing must begin at the top of the rise prior to the lowering action! Your sway to the right diminishes once the lowering action is complete.

Step 7. Walking forward on your left foot, commence to rise using your normal footwork of heel, then the toe of the left foot.

Step 8. The right foot moves to the side while you continue to rise on both the eighth and ninth steps. The footwork on the second beat of music is the toe, including the ball of your right foot. You will sway left.

Step 9. The left foot will close to your right foot. The footwork for your left foot is toe, and then as you lower, the heel. All of this occurs on the third beat of the second measure of music. Retain your sway to the left.

Step 10. Walking backward on your right foot, make sure that you first make contact with your toe and then the ball; finishing on your heel, commence to rise through your body with no-foot rise (NFR). This step takes place on the first beat of the second measure.

Step 11. The left foot moves to the side while you continue to rise during this step and the next. Your footwork on the second beat is toe with sway to your right. Please remember that you will spend half the time on step 12 in rise and then lower on the latter portion of the step. This is generally consistent throughout the dance on the third beat of music.

Step 12. Your right foot closes to your left foot. Begin your lowering action using the footwork of toe, then the heel. Your sway to the right diminishes once the lowering action is complete.

You will end this figure in the closed position by allowing your partner to walk directly into you. Do not lurch forward attempting to grab her with your "mitts." Allow the frame of your couple to collect gracefully—there is no rush to close up the dance frame!

Technique

Technique (Step 4 Gentleman): You will lead your partner by releasing your right hand from her back in Step 4. Your left arm is up, allowing your partner to move forward under it by the beginning of step 5. This action of your arm will allow the lady to move forward, making a large circle clockwise and then returning to the closed position in steps 10 to 12. Remember that as you take any movement backward in ballroom dancing, you should accelerate your abdomen through to your spinal column while retaining your best physical alignment vertically.

Technique

Technique (General Waltz): The first six steps of this figure use what is known in ballroom dancing as the "normal rise and fall." To eliminate redundancy, I will state when a figure uses the normal rise and fall after the figure's title. For the remainder of this figure, we will continue to use the full description, but as we begin the lady's figure, we will preface the figure's description by stating, "Use the normal rise and fall with the normal footwork."

Here is the "how to" for using the body during rise and fall when walking forward. Once the first step forward is taken, the dancer commences to rise. The dancer continues to rise through the second and third step and then lowers at the end of the third step. The rise in the body is felt in this order: first, ribcage; second, hips; and third, knees.

The footwork that accompanies the normal rise and fall on the forward walk of the first of three steps is heel, toe; toe; toe, heel. I will state "Use the normal footwork" and describe the footwork only when there are differences.

The description for moving backward follows: Once the first step backward is taken, the dancer commences to rise through the body but with no-foot rise. The second and third steps following a backward walk include a foot rise as the dancer continues to rise on those steps. The dancer then lowers at the end of the third step.

The footwork that accompanies the normal rise and fall during the back walk is the first of three steps: toe, heel (no-foot rise), toe, and then toe, heel of the closing foot. It is very important that as you lower to the heel of this third step, you have the next foot ready and free of any body weight. Beginners often lose sight of this and trap that foot under their body, preventing it from moving freely.

For example, consider your backward step. You move back on the right foot and then side with the left, followed by closing the right to the left foot. Upon lowering to the heel of the right, the left foot must be free to move. As you lower to that right heel, allow that left foot to slip forward slightly without weight so you are ready to move to it. I will state to use the normal footwork and describe the footwork only when there are differences. You will also use this technique in the Foxtrot and Viennese Waltz.

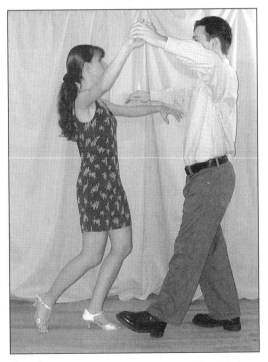

Step 4.

Step 5.

Step 8.

Step 11.

Lady's Part: Box with Underarm Turn

Details for the lady's Box with Underarm Turn:

Step 1. Walk back on your right foot.

Step 2. Move to the side on your left foot using sway to the right.

Step 3. The right foot closes to your left foot using sway to the right. Remember to lose your sway as you lower to your right heel.

Step 4. Move forward on your left foot.

Step 5. Walk forward on your right foot, moving under the man's raised left arm.

Step 6. Walk forward on your left foot.

Movement Memo

Use the normal rise and fall and normal footwork. Use CBM on steps 5 and 7.

Movement Memo

From steps 4 through 12, the lady will complete one full turn clockwise to end in a closed position with her partner.

Step 7. Walk forward on your right foot.

Step 8. Walk forward on your left foot.

Step 9. Walk forward on your right foot.

Step 10. Walk forward on your left foot.

Step 11. Move to the side on your right foot with sway left.

Step 12. Your left closes to your right foot with sway left.

Your last three steps, 10 to 12, are the forward half of your box step. Therefore, you need to have completed all amounts of turn prior to these steps. This means that on step 10, you walk directly forward with your left foot and finish in a closed position with your partner on the side steps (11 and 12).

Technique

Technique (General for Both): Be very careful, never drop into your heel when taking a backward walk. Instead, continually strive to use a controlled lowering. An illustration of controlled lowering I often use is to imagine that you have a tennis ball under your heel and have to flatten it gradually. Remember that as you take any back walk, you should accelerate your abdomen through to your spinal column while retaining your best physical alignment vertically. You will also use this technique in the Foxtrot and Viennese Waltz.

Balance Steps—Forward and Back, Side (Fifth-Position Breaks)

Use the normal rise and fall and footwork, while maintaining the ¾ timing of the Waltz. There is no CBM. This figure begins with the alignment of the previous figure. Steps 1 through 12 can also be danced with NFR (no-foot rise). Some dancers find this easier, but I find the normal rise more elegant and characteristic of the Waltz for these types of steps.

Gentleman's Part: Balance Steps

Details for the gentleman's Balance Steps:

Step 1. Move forward on your left foot.

Step 2. Your right foot closes to your left foot without weight.

Step 3. Hold your position.

Step 4. Move backward on your right foot.

Step 5. Your left foot closes to your right foot without weight.

Step 6. Hold your position.

Step 7. Move your left foot to the side.

Step 8. Your right foot closes to left foot without weight using sway to the right.

Step 9. Hold your position using sway to the right.

Step 10. Move side to your right.

Step 11. Your left foot closes to your right foot without weight using sway to the left.

Step 12. Hold your position using sway to the left.

Movement Memo

In steps 8 and 9, as well as 11 and 12, the sway counters the strong side movements in order to maintain the couple's balance. It is always important to sustain lift in the side of the ribcage that corresponds to the moving leg.

Movement Memo

Remember that turns generally occur over several steps.

Step 13. Move your left foot to the side using the footwork of toe, heel, with a rise at the end of this step. Use a slight turn counterclockwise between steps 13 and 15. Rise at the end of step 13 using the footwork of toe, heel, and then back to the toe to produce the actual rise.

Step 14. Place your right foot behind your left foot, moving up on the toe, using sway to the right.

Step 15. Replace your weight forward to your left foot, remaining up through half the beat and lowering at the end of that same beat.

Step 16. Move your right foot to the side using the footwork of toe, heel; and then finish on the toe of the same foot with rise. You will make a slight turn clockwise between steps 16 and 18.

Step 17. Place your left foot behind your right foot, rising up to the toe. Your sway is left.

Step 18. Replace your weight forward to the right foot, remaining up on your toe, and then lowering at the end of this figure to finish in the closed dance position.

Technique

Technique (General for Both): Steps 13 through 18 of the side balance steps are known as *fifth-position breaks*. Although they are not difficult, I would consider them optional for the absolute beginner. Fifth-position breaks are a lovely step, especially for a wedding couple. When executing fifth-position breaks, you will achieve your rise earlier and to a higher position. This means your legs will straighten more fully by comparison to the normal rise. To do this, move your body up away from your knees sooner. This will allow you to cross your foot behind with greater ease. Be careful not to lock your ankles. You can amplify your shape for a "good look" by exposing your ribcage while straightening your leg with sway when doing steps 14 and 17.

Step 1.

Step 4.

Step 7.

Step 10.

Step 14.

Step 17.

Ballroom Bloopers

Remember not to trap your feet under your body. This means do not finish a dance step with weight on both feet. Even with the relatively slow tempo of the Waltz, we simply do not want to have to think about which foot is free! Many beginners make that error on this step by not remembering to support their ribcage throughout all of the dancing. When the ribcage collapses by lowering on one side or the other, it invites the body to protect itself by using both feet for stability.

Lady's Part: Balance Steps

Details for the lady's Balance Steps:

Step 1. Move back to your right foot using the footwork of toe, heel.

Step 2. Your left foot closes to your right foot.

Step 3. Hold your position.

Step 4. Move forward to your left foot.

Step 5. Close your right foot to your left foot without weight.

Step 6. Hold your position.

Step 7. Move to the side on your right foot.

Step 8. Close your left foot to your right foot without weight, using sway to the left.

Step 9. Hold your position with sway to the left.

Step 10. Move to the side on your left foot.

Step 11. Close your right foot to your left foot without weight using sway to the right.

Step 12. Hold your position with sway to the right.

Movement Memo

To more fully understand rise and fall, see Chapter 6, "The Challenges of Ballroom Dancing," and review the exercise demonstrated. Remember that rise and fall are actions first of the body and then accommodated by support from the feet. As you become more proficient in ballroom dancing, push your torso weight against your knees so that rise and fall are also felt in your quadriceps.

Step 13. Move to the side on your right foot with full rise at the end of this step using the footwork of toe, heel and then finishing on the toe. There should be a slight turn counterclockwise between steps 13 and 15.

Step 14. Place your left foot behind your right foot and, using full rise, place your weight on your toe. There is sway to the left.

Step 15. Replace your weight forward to the right foot, remaining up and then lowering at the end of the step using the footwork of toe, heel with sway to the left.

Step 16. Move to the side on your left foot using the footwork of toe, heel and then returning to the toe while rising at the end of this step. There is a slight turn clockwise between steps 16 and 18.

Step 17. Place your right foot behind your left foot using full rise on the toe. There is sway to the right.

Step 18. Replace your weight forward to the left foot up on your toe, and then lower at the end of the step and finish in the closed position.

Simple Twinkle

Use the normal rise and fall and footwork. This figure begins with the alignment of facing diagonal to the wall. Please maintain the normal ¾ timing of the Waltz throughout this figure. This figure uses promenade position, CBM, and CBMP. There is CBM in steps 1 and 4. The simple twinkle can begin in different alignments.

Movement Memo

There is CBM in steps 1 and 4.

Movement Memo

Reminder that CBM creates the beginning or commencement to turn. Nothing, dance or movement in general or in life, begins without commencement from static to moving.

Gentleman's Part: Simple Twinkle

Details for the gentleman's Simple Twinkle follow:

Step 1. Move forward on your left foot facing the diagonal wall.

Step 2. Move to the side on your right foot, retaining the diagonal wall alignment with a slight $\frac{1}{8}$ turn counterclockwise between the first and second steps. There is sway to the left.

Step 3. Close your left foot to your right foot, finishing in promenade position. Your alignment remains facing the diagonal wall. There is sway to the left.

Step 4. Place your right foot forward and across in CBMP and promenade position. Your alignment remains facing the diagonal wall as you move along LOD. You will commence to turn clockwise.

Step 5. Move your left foot to the side, facing the wall and completing the $\frac{1}{8}$ turn clockwise. You will use sway to the right.

Step 6. Close your right foot to your left foot, facing the wall with sway to the right, finishing in the closed position.

Technique

Technique (Step 2 Gentleman): The lead-to-promenade position is more about finesse than strength or amount of turn. It can be mystifying to the beginner, but with some practice, it becomes easy. The ability to leave your hips and feet facing the diagonal wall while using a slight twist from the waist clockwise will cause your partner to open to promenade position without overturning her body. Make sure that your arms move in relation to your body and not in opposition—do not spoil that good frame! What you will accomplish is a slight turn to the left to retain the proper alignment on the dance floor while using the body twist to the right to lead your partner to promenade position. Make sure you amplify the feeling of lift on your right side!

Step 4 Front View.   *Step 4 Back View.*

Lady's Part: Simple Twinkle

Details for the lady's Simple Twinkle follow:

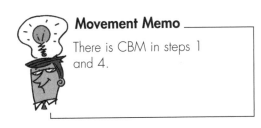

Movement Memo

There is CBM in steps 1 and 4.

Step 1. Move back to your right foot using the alignment of backing diagonal to the wall. You will commence to turn clockwise.

Step 2. Move to the side on your left foot, pointing your foot diagonal center while your body turns clockwise ¼ turn between steps 1 and 2. At this moment, your body will respond to your partner's lead by turning less through the torso than through the legs.

Step 3. Your right foot closes to your left foot in promenade position while your alignment is facing diagonal center. There is sway right.

Step 4. Move your left foot forward and across in CBMP and promenade position. As this happens, you will have a tricky alignment, but as you try this using good technique, you will understand it. You begin facing center while you are moving diagonal center. You will commence to turn counterclockwise finishing a quarter of a turn by the end of the next step.

Step 5. Move to the side on your right foot with the alignment of backing diagonal to the wall. There is sway to the left.

Step 6. Close your left foot to your right foot with the alignment of backing diagonal wall. There is sway to the left as you finish in the closed position.

Movement Memo

Promenade position produces a streamline appearance for the dance couple. The effect should be to travel in the same direction together through a narrower space. Too often ladies and gentlemen move to an open promenade position in contrast to a closed promenade position. Please see the photos for closed promenade position. Another very important feature of promenade position is that the lady's hips are not even with her partner's hips. The lady's left hip is slightly behind the hip of the gentleman. This allows you to easily step forward in promenade position with your partner. The left leg of the lady is slightly behind that of her partner so that she is following his right leg.

Progressive

This dance figure serves some important functions on the dance floor. The first is obvious. Its name is *progressive*, and it helps you travel on the dance floor. The second function of the progressive is less obvious to the beginner. It helps the dancer change from one leading foot to another. The leading foot is simply the foot that begins any dance figure. This is accomplished when either half of the progressive is done.

The normal footwork as well as the normal *rise* and *fall* is used.

This dance figure quickly answers the question that beginners seem to ask regarding the direction that any foot can take. The answer is forward, back, or side. The progressive can travel straight down the line of dance, diagonal to the wall, or diagonal to the center.

Gentleman's Part: Progressive

Details of the gentleman's Progressive follow:

Step 1. Walk forward on your left foot.

Step 2. Move to the side and slightly forward on your right foot using sway to the left.

Movement Memo

There is slight CBM in steps 1 and 4.

Step 3. Close your left foot to your right foot using sway to the left.

Step 4. Move forward on your right foot.

Step 5. Move your left foot to the side and slightly forward using sway to the right.

Step 6. Close your right foot to your left foot using sway to the right.

Technique

Technique (General for Both Steps 1 to 3): Complete the first half of the Progressive. Notice that your right foot is now available to begin any other dance figure. You have in effect prepared yourself for any dance figure that begins with your right foot free. Of course, the opposite is true for your partner.

In step 2 you read the description "side and slightly forward." This means that during a side step that follows a progressive movement forward, your body generates what we call *body swing*, causing the free side to move slightly forward in the direction of the progressive. This will also be true for a backward movement, which would be described as "side and slightly back."

This is why there is slight CBM in the description of the step indicating a slight amount of turn. The amount of distance or degree of turn is equal to approximately one-half of the length of your foot. As a result of the CBM, the foot that you have placed to the side is slightly ahead of the plane of your former movement either forward or back.

Step 4.

Step 6.

Lady's Part: Progressive

Details for the lady's Progressive follow:

Step 1. Move backward on your right foot.

Step 2. Move your left foot to the side and slightly back using sway to the right.

Step 3. Close your right foot to your left foot using sway to the right.

Step 4. Move backward on your left foot.

Step 5. Move your right foot to the side and slightly back using sway to the left.

Step 6. Close your left foot to your right foot using sway to the left.

Movement Memo

There is slight CBM in steps 1 and 4.

Ballroom Bloopers

If necessary, please review the information pertaining to the closing action in Chapter 11, "The Quickstart Program© Nonprogressive Movements," if you are having trouble ending or beginning on the wrong foot.

Box Turn—¼ Turn to Left (Counterclockwise)

The Box Turn is the same box step we studied in "The Quickstart Program© Nonprogressive Movements" in Chapter 11; it rotates ¼ turn in a counterclockwise direction every three steps or weight changes. On the surface this may seem like a very easy dance step. However, it will test your ability to move forward or backward aggressively into each other's space while fully completing your weight changes. The success of this dance figure rests on your understanding and execution of what I call the *inside and outside of a rotation*. You use the normal rise and fall and footwork.

Gentleman's Part: Left-Turning Box

Follow these steps for the gentleman's Left-Turning Box:

Step 1. Move forward on your left foot facing LOD and commence to turn counterclockwise with no sway.

Step 2. Move your right foot to the side, backing to the wall and continuing to move ¼ turn counterclockwise, completing that turn by the beginning of the third step. You will use sway to the left.

Step 3. Close your left foot to your right foot, having completed your alignment of backing to the wall using sway to the left.

Step 4. Move back on your right foot in the alignment of backing to the wall. Commence to turn counterclockwise with no sway.

Step 5. Move your left foot to the side in the alignment of pointing against LOD. Use sway to the right. Your body will turn less than the pointing direction of your left foot.

Movement Memo

There is CBM in steps 1, 4, 7, and 10.

Step 6. Close your right foot to your left foot facing against the line of dance while your body completes the turn.

Option to continue to turn: Please note that while I have shown and described two 90-degree turns counterclockwise over six steps, you may at this point continue with steps 7 through 12 in exactly the same manner, producing a 360-degree or full rotation. This will give you the capability of turning to face any direction on the social dance floor. Therefore you may use the step to change directions, avoid other couples, or move from one line of dance to the next.

Step 1.

Step 4.

Lady's Part: Left-Turning Box

Follow these steps for the lady's Left-Turning Box:

Step 1. Move backward on your right foot using backing LOD as your alignment. Commence to turn counterclockwise.

Step 2. Moving your left foot to the side, your alignment is pointing to the wall. Continue to move ¼ turn counterclockwise, completing your rotation by the conclusion of this step. Use sway to the right. Your body will turn less than the pointing direction of your left foot.

Step 3. Closing your right foot to your left foot, your alignment is facing the wall. You will use sway to the right. Your body will complete the turn, realigning yourself to the closed position.

Movement Memo

There is CBM in steps 1, 4, 7, and 10.

Step 4. Move forward facing the wall and commencing to turn counterclockwise.

Step 5. Move your right foot to the side while backing LOD by completing ¼ turn counterclockwise. There is sway to the left.

Step 6. Close your left foot to your right foot while maintaining the alignment of backing against LOD. There is sway to the left. You will end this figure in the closed position.

Box Turn—¹/₄ to Right (Clockwise)

Apart from the direction in which this figure rotates, there is virtually no difference from the box that turns left.

Begin this figure by using the technique we described for the dance step called the progressive. This will allow you to begin with the normal left foot forward for the leader and right foot back for the follower and then change to a figure that begins with the leader's right foot and the follower's left foot.

Gentleman's Part: Right-Turning Box

Follow these steps for the gentleman's Right-Turning Box:

Steps 1 to 3. Use the first three steps of the progressive.

Step 4. Move forward on the right foot with the alignment of facing line of dance. Commence to turn clockwise.

Step 5. Moving your left foot to the side with the alignment of facing wall, complete a ¹/₄ rotation clockwise by the end of this step using sway to the right.

Step 6. Close your right foot to your left foot maintaining the alignment of facing the wall. You will use sway to the right.

Step 7. Move back on your left foot using the alignment of backing center. Commence to turn clockwise.

Step 8. Moving your right foot to the side while pointing against LOD, make a quarter turn clockwise with your body turning less. You will use sway to the left.

Step 9. Closing your left foot to your right foot maintaining the alignment of facing against LOD, complete your body turn. You will use sway to the left.

Option to continue to turn: Please note that while I have shown and described two 90-degree turns clockwise over six steps, you may at this point continue with steps 10 through 15 in exactly the same manner producing a 360-degree or full rotation. This will give you the capability of turning to face any direction on the social dance floor. Therefore you may use the step to change directions, avoid other couples, or move from one line of dance to the next.

Use steps 4 through 6 of the progressive to allow for any following figure using the leader's left foot. This is an ending for steps 1 through 9 or the second option.

Bet You Didn't Know

As a rule of thumb, figures in ballroom dancing that rotate clockwise tend to feel more comfortable if they are allowed to rotate toward the outside of the dance floor. Conversely, figures that rotate counterclockwise tend to be more comfortable if they are allowed to rotate toward the center of the dance floor.

Movement Memo

There is CBM in steps 1 (slight), 4, 7, 10, 13, and 16 (slight).

Step 4.

Step 5.

Lady's Part: Right-Turning Box

Follow these steps for the lady's Right-Turning Box:

Steps 1 to 3. Use the first three steps of the progressive.

Step 4. Move back on your left foot using the alignment of backing LOD. Commence to turn clockwise.

Step 5. Moving your right foot to the side, complete a ¼ turn clockwise while your body turns less. Your alignment is pointing to the center. Use sway to the left.

Step 6. Close your left foot to your right foot, allowing your body to complete the turn maintaining the alignment of facing center. Use sway to the left.

Movement Memo

There is CBM in steps 1 (slight), 4, 7, 10, 13, and 16 (slight).

Step 7. Move forward on your right foot, maintaining the alignment of facing center. Commence to turn clockwise.

Step 8. Move your left foot to the side using the alignment of backing against LOD. Make a ¼ turn clockwise with a sway to the right.

Step 9. Close your right foot to your left foot while maintaining the alignment of backing against LOD. You will sway to the right. See the preceding section, "Gentleman's Part: Right-Turning Box."

Choreographed Routine: Waltz Routine

This routine combines all of the figures you have worked and learned and is suitable for a lovely wedding dance or in general ballroom dancing. Try this beautiful Waltz routine by performing these steps:

♦ Box with Underarm Turn dance steps 1 through 12.

♦ Balance Steps 1 through 18 (steps 13 through 18 are optional).

- ◆ Box Step Turning Counterclockwise steps 1 through 12 to complete one full rotation.
- ◆ Simple Twinkle steps 1 through 6.
- ◆ Progressive steps 1 through 6.
- ◆ Box Step Turning Clockwise steps to 1 through 18 to complete one full rotation.
- ◆ Box Step Turning Counterclockwise steps 1 through 6 to complete one-half rotation.
- ◆ Repeat routine.

This routine is 78 beats of music, so dividing by 3 (remembering that the Waltz is 3 beats to the measure), this routine equals 26 measures of music. Your CD practice song is 31 measures of music per minute, so as a percentage, this routine will take 84 percent of a minute, or just over 50 seconds to repeat.

Movement Memo

The timing analysis is given at the conclusion of each dance studied. If you are planning to use this routine for your wedding dance, work out the time duration that you will spend out on the dance floor of your song with your DJ. Then, if necessary, edit your song accordingly. Remember, two minutes of dancing alone out on the dance floor is a long time!

The Least You Need to Know

- ◆ The technique used in the Waltz is the foundation for all other ballroom dances.
- ◆ The progressive step allows a change of the leading foot.
- ◆ Any figure that turns the couple's direction 180 degrees can be repeated to produce a full rotation.
- ◆ Repeating the Waltz routine twice would make it absolutely perfect for a bride and groom's wedding dance!

Chapter 16

Foxtrot

In This Chapter

◆ Romance set to music

◆ Brush your way to vertical

◆ Box or Key—the rhythm's great

◆ In a ballroom or on a postage stamp

The Foxtrot is the smoothest of the smooth! This light, lively, infatuating rhythm has been vocalized and harmonized by the best pipes that ever put their lips to a microphone! The music is timeless and will remain so, as long as lovers can drift through a park on a Sunday or swoon and spoon at the local watering hole on Saturday night. Some call it jazz, some call it swing, some call it standard, and some call it pop—I call it pure American. The Foxtrot speaks to every boy and girl or man and women about every facet of their relationship! Come join us out on the floor—top hat and tails no longer required, but dancing feet and a good crooner are a must.

In the Smooth dances, the alignment of the couple is based on the dance floor (LOD, facing center, diagonal wall, and so on). The reference card in the front of your book will serve as a road map around the dance floor while you practice or when you get into a bind. I will describe the rhythm of each individual figure, the footwork, and any additional techniques that will help you to enjoy the world's most popular Smooth dance.

Rise and Fall with Rhythm

Please maintain the normal ⁴/₄ timing of the Foxtrot using the two major rhythms: the *Key Rhythm* of Slow, Slow, Quick, Quick or the *Box Rhythm* of Slow, Quick, Quick. The beat value of a Slow is two beats of music and the beat value for a Quick is one beat. The counting for a figure in Key Rhythm is 1, 2 for the first step; 3, 4 for the second step; 5 for the third step; and 6 for the fourth. Repeat if necessary. The counting for Box Rhythm is 1, 2 for the first step; 3 for the second; and 4 for the third. Repeat if necessary.

Rise and *fall* and *footwork* in the Foxtrot have a lot to do with personal preference, the skill of the dancer, and the spatial considerations. *Rise* and *fall* always occur first throughout your body. Your footwork is a response to first amplify the lift in your body and then the lowering through your legs. The body itself never falls.

I have presented the footwork in this Foxtrot section according to my Quickstart to Social Dancing Program©. As you know from the technique found there, the side steps and closes are the common denominator for social dancing. The footwork for the side step is toe and the closing step is toe, heel. The small amount of rise that happens on the "toe only" side steps allows for a more distinguishable transfer of weight and subsequent release of the next foot from the floor at the top of the rise. Trapping both feet under your body is the most common error in all of ballroom dancing, and my Quickstart Program© method provides a solution to this error.

Movement Memo _____

Remember that the feet support the lift of the body and the lowering actions of your legs.

Another method, which I also endorse, favors the footwork of toe, heel for the side steps and then toe, heel for the closing steps. Providing you are not having any difficulty transferring weight from foot to foot between these steps, this alternative provides a nice rhythmic pulse particularly useful in congested situations.

I think you should eventually learn both methods, as you will certainly encounter varying spatial considerations. When my new students are concerned about having "enough room" to dance, I tell them if you have room to stand together with your partner and take a step or two, regardless of size, you should be able to dance. This *is* what it is all about!

The Basic: Key Timing

This figure characterizes the progressive nature of the Foxtrot. It is a very useful figure for beginners in that it can begin in a variety of directions. We will begin this at an easy starting point to get you used to the slow walking and the rhythm of the Foxtrot. Each walk forward or backward in the Foxtrot will use two beats of music, and their rhythm is Slow. Like the Waltz, the side steps and closing steps will take one beat each using the rhythm of Quick, Quick.

Movement Memo _____

Wedding couples, please take note. For whatever the reason, if you have waited until the last moment to prepare for your first wedding dance, please investigate the section "Choreographed Routine: Emergency Wedding Routine" at the end of this chapter. It is the simplest amalgamation of Foxtrot that I can put together to help you overcome the last-minute dilemma and still look great at your wedding!

There is no rise on the first step followed by the normal rise and fall on the latter three steps. You will use very slight CBM on the first step. Make sure you review my technique for the closing action in smooth dancing. This figure begins in the closed position.

Gentleman's Part: The Basic

Details for the gentleman's the Basic:

Step 1. Move forward on your left foot with no sway. Your footwork is heel. You will finish moving through the ball and the toe. The reason we do not describe the footwork as heel, toe is because you will experience no rise on the first of two slow walks taken in succession.

Step 2. Move forward on your right foot with no sway. Your footwork is heel, toe.

Step 3. Move your left foot to the side with sway to the right. Your footwork is toe.

Step 4. Close your right foot to your left foot with sway to the right. Your footwork is toe, heel, ending in the closed position.

Step 1.   *Step 2.*

Lady's Part: The Basic

Details for the lady's the Basic:

Step 1. Move backward on your right foot with no sway. Your footwork is toe, heel with no foot rise.

Step 2. Move backward on your left foot with no sway. Your footwork is toe, heel, toe. The latter toe will help you lift your body to the following side step.

Step 3. Move your right foot to the side using sway to the left. Your footwork is toe.

Step 4. Close your left foot to your right foot using sway to the left.

Left Box Turn (Counterclockwise)–Box Rhythm

This is the same box step that we studied in the Quickstart to Social Dance Program©. This is identical to the figure with the same name you danced in the Waltz with one major exception—the timing. In the Waltz, you danced this and every figure in ³/₄ timing (one beat per dance step); in the Foxtrot, we are using ⁴/₄ timing. This changes the beat value from one beat to two beats on the forward and backward steps. We have described these as *Slow Walks*.

The Box Turn rotates ¹/₄ turn in a counterclockwise direction every three steps or weight changes. Like the Waltz version of this step, you will need to move forward or backward aggressively into each other's space while fully completing your weight changes without sacrificing your posture or dance frame. For more information, please refer to the description of the inside and outside of a rotation in Chapter 13, "The Interactions of the Dance Couple."

Gentleman's Part: Left Box Turn

Details for the gentleman's Left Box Turn:

Step 1. Move forward on your left foot facing LOD. Commence to turn counterclockwise with no sway. Your footwork is heel, toe.

Movement Memo

There is CBM in steps 1, 4, 7, and 10.

Step 2. Move your right foot to the side, backing to the wall and continuing to turn ¼ counterclockwise, completing that turn by the beginning of the third step. You will use sway to the left. Your footwork is toe.

Step 3. Close your left foot to your right foot after completing your alignment of backing to the wall using sway to the left. Your footwork is toe, heel.

Step 4. Move backward on your right foot in the alignment of backing to the wall. Commence to turn counterclockwise with no sway. Your footwork is toe, heel with *no* foot rise. This means do not release your heel from the floor.

Step 5. Move your left foot to the side in the alignment of pointing against LOD. Use sway to the right. Continue to turn ¼ counterclockwise, completing your rotation by the conclusion of this step. Your body will turn less than the pointing direction of your left foot. Your footwork is toe.

Step 6. Close your right foot to your left foot facing against line of dance while your body completes the turn. Your footwork is toe, heel.

Option to continue to turn: Please note that while I have shown and described two 90-degree turns counterclockwise over six steps, you may at this point continue with steps that would be numbered 7 through 12 in exactly the same manner. This will produce a 360-degree or full rotation. This will give you the capability of turning to face any direction on the social dance floor. Therefore you may use the step to change directions, avoid other couples, or move from one line of dance to the next.

Step 1.

Step 2.

Lady's Part: Left Box Turn

Details for the lady's Left Box Turn:

Step 1. Move backward on your right foot using backing LOD as your alignment. Commence to turn counterclockwise. Your footwork is toe, heel with *no* foot rise. This means do not release the heel from the floor.

Step 2. Moving your left foot to the side, your alignment is pointing to the wall. Continue to turn ¼ counterclockwise, completing your rotation by the conclusion of this step. Use sway to the right. Your body will turn less than the pointing direction of your left foot. Your footwork is toe.

Step 3. Closing your right foot to your left foot, your alignment is facing the wall. You will use sway to the right. Your body will complete the turn realigning yourself to the closed position. Your footwork is toe, heel.

Step 4. Move forward facing the wall and commencing to turn counterclockwise. Your footwork is heel, toe.

Step 5. Move your right foot to the side while backing LOD by completing a ¼ turn counterclockwise. There is sway to the left. Your footwork is toe.

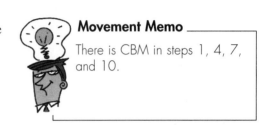

Movement Memo

There is CBM in steps 1, 4, 7, and 10.

Step 6. Close your left foot to your right foot while maintaining the alignment of backing against LOD. There is sway to the left. Your footwork is toe, heel. You will end this figure in the closed position.

Rock Turn to Left: Key Rhythm

This figure is particularly useful for changing directions at the corner of the room, avoiding other couples on the dance floor, or as a rhythm step in nightclub situations. It is not unlike the three-point turn you use when driving—moving toward a target and then quickly moving away changing directions. This figure may commence in many alignments.

There is slight rise on the first step, followed by the normal rise and fall on the latter three steps.

Gentleman's Part: Rock Turn to Left

Details for the gentleman's Rock Turn to Left:

Step 1. Move forward on your left foot using a brushing action toward your chosen alignment.

Step 2. Move backward on your right foot using a brushing action in your present alignment. Commence to turn counterclockwise with no sway. Your footwork is toe, heel with *no* foot rise. This means do not release the heel from the floor.

Step 3. Move your left foot to the side in the alignment of pointing against LOD. Turn ¼ counterclockwise between step 2 and this step. Your body will turn less than the pointing direction of your left foot. Your footwork is toe. Use sway to the right.

Movement Memo

There is CBM in step 2.

Step 4. Close your right foot to your left foot facing against the line of dance while your body completes the turn. Your footwork is toe, heel.

Technique

Technique (General for Both throughout Foxtrot and the other dances): A brushing action occurs when the thigh of the unsupported or moving leg swings under the corresponding pelvis and momentarily stops there. This is particularly useful because it creates a good vertical axis from which to change directions—especially during rotation. As the thigh swings under the corresponding pelvis and pauses, the dancer can easily finish the footwork and weight change and be better prepared to change direction. You will use the brushing action when moving forward to back or back to forward. The brushing action is absolutely necessary when beginning a rotation using CBM. At the beginner level, this happens frequently when taking a side step during rotation from either a forward or back step.

Both of these varieties occur during the Rock Turn to Left. A good practice exercise to develop the skill of brushing and the usefulness of Rock Turn to Left is to repeat this entire pattern four times. Begin facing any wall and end facing the next wall to the leader's left. If you are successful, you will end where you started. Do this with and without a partner!

Step 1.

Step 2.

Step 3.

Lady's Part: Rock Turn to Left

Details for the lady's Rock Turn to Left:

Step 1. Move backward on your right foot using a brushing action toward your partner's alignment.

Step 2. Move forward toward your partner's alignment using a brushing action, commencing to turn counterclockwise. Your footwork is heel, toe.

Step 3. Move your right foot to the side while backing LOD by completing a ¼ turn counterclockwise. There is sway to the left. Your footwork is toe.

Step 4. Close your left foot to your right foot while maintaining the alignment of backing against LOD. There is sway to the left. Your footwork is toe, heel. You will end this figure in the closed position.

Sway Step: Key Rhythm

Here is a very simple but effective step to keep you dancing in rhythm when there is virtually no room to move either forward or back. Because it can be done in a very compact space, this step is perfect for night-club dancing. You may use any alignment.

There is a slight rise on the first steps, followed by the normal rise and fall on the latter three steps.

Movement Memo

There is CBM in step 2.

Gentleman's Part: Sway Step

Details for the gentleman's Sway Step follow:

Step 1. Move your left foot to the side with strong sway right. Use a brushing action. Your footwork is toe, heel.

Step 2. Move your right foot to the side with strong sway left. Use a brushing action. Your footwork is toe, heel.

Step 3. Move your left foot to the side (normal side step). There is no sway. Your footwork is toe.

Step 4. Close your right foot to your left foot. There is no sway. Your footwork is toe, heel, ending in the closed position.

Movement Memo

Sway will occur as a result of the movement. With respect to footwork, *sway* is like a policeman saying "Stop!" because it is intended to happen immediately.

Step 1. *Step 2.* *Step 3.*

Lady's Part: Sway Step

Details for the lady's Sway Step follow:

Step 1. Move your right foot to the side with strong sway left. Use a brushing action. Your footwork is toe, heel.

Step 2. Move your left foot to the side with strong sway right. Use a brushing action. Your footwork is toe, heel.

Step 3. Move your right foot to the side (normal side step). There is no sway. Your footwork is toe.

Step 4. Close your left foot to your right foot. There is no sway. Your footwork is toe, heel, ending in the closed position.

Simple Twinkle: Box Rhythm

Please use the normal rise and fall and footwork described throughout the Waltz chapter. This figure begins with the alignment of facing diagonal to the wall. You will use the promenade position, CBM, and CBMP. The Simple Twinkle can begin in different alignments.

Gentleman's Part: Simple Twinkle

Details for the gentleman's Simple Twinkle follow:

Step 1. Move forward on your left foot facing diagonal wall. Your footwork is heel, toe.

Step 2. Move to the side on your right foot retaining the diagonal wall alignment with a slight turn $1/8$ counterclockwise between the first and second steps. There is sway to the left. Your footwork is toe.

Movement Memo

There is CBM in steps 1 and 4.

Step 3. Close your left foot to your right foot finishing in promenade position. Your alignment remains facing the diagonal wall. There is sway to the left. Your footwork is toe, heel.

Step 4. Place your right foot forward and across in CBMP and promenade position. Your alignment remains facing diagonal wall as you move along LOD. You will commence to turn clockwise. Your footwork is heel, toe.

Step 5. Move your left foot to the side facing the wall completing the $1/8$ turn clockwise. You will use sway to the right. Your footwork is toe.

Step 6. Close your right foot to your left foot facing the wall with sway to the right and finishing in the closed position. Your footwork is toe, heel.

Technique

Technique: The lead-to-promenade position is more about finesse than strength or amount of turn. It can be mystifying to the beginner, but with some practice it will become easy. The ability to leave your hips and feet facing the diagonal wall while using a slight twist from the waist clockwise will cause your partner to open to promenade position without overturning her body. Make sure that your arms move in relation to your body and not in opposition—do not spoil that good frame! What you will accomplish is a slight turn to the left to retain the proper alignment on the dance floor, while using the body twist to the right to lead your partner to promenade position. Make sure you amplify the feeling of lift on your right side!

Step 3. *Step 4 Front View.* *Step 4 Back View.*

Lady's Part: Simple Twinkle

Details for the lady's Simple Twinkle follow:

Step 1. Move back to your right foot using the alignment of backing diagonal to the wall. You will commence to turn clockwise. Your footwork is toe, heel with *no* foot rise.

Step 2. Move to the side on your left foot pointing your foot diagonal center while your body turns clockwise by ¼ turn between steps 1 and 2. At this moment your body will respond to your partner's lead by turning less through the torso than through the legs. Your footwork is toe.

Step 3. Your right foot closes to your left foot in promenade position while your alignment is facing diagonal center. There is sway right. Your footwork is toe, heel.

Step 4. Move your left foot forward and across in CBMP and promenade position. As this happens you will have a tricky alignment, but as you try this using good technique, you will understand it. You begin facing center while you are moving diagonal center. You will commence to turn counterclockwise finishing a ¼ turn by the end of the next step. Your footwork is heel, toe.

Step 5. Move to the side on your right foot with the alignment of backing diagonal to the wall. There is sway to the left. Your footwork is toe.

Step 6. Close your left foot to your right foot with the alignment of backing diagonal to the wall. There is sway to the left as you finish in the closed position. Your footwork is heel, toe.

Movement Memo

There is CBM in steps 1 and 4.

Technique
Technique (General for Both): Promenade position produces a streamline appearance for the dance couple. The effect should be to travel in the same direction together through a narrower space. Too often ladies and gentlemen move to an open promenade position in contrast to a closed promenade position. Please see the photos for closed promenade position. Another very important feature of promenade position is that the lady's hips are not even with her partner's hips. The lady's left hip is slightly behind the hip of the gentleman. This allows you to easily step forward in promenade position with your partner. The left leg of the lady is slightly behind that of her partner so that she is following his right leg.

Promenade: Key Rhythm

This figure begins in promenade position so you must lead your partner *to* promenade position by making a slight turn to the left to retain the proper alignment on the dance floor while using the body twist to the right to lead your partner to promenade position. Make sure you amplify the feeling of lift on your right side!

There is no rise on the first step, followed by the normal *rise* and *fall* on the latter three steps.

Gentleman's Part: Promenade

Details for the gentleman's Promenade:

Step 1. Move the left foot to the side in promenade position. Your alignment is facing diagonal wall while moving a long LOD. There is no sway, and your footwork is heel.

Step 2. Move forward and across on your right foot in CBMP and promenade position. You will commence to turn clockwise on this step using no sway with the footwork of heel, toe.

Movement Memo

There is CBM in step 2.

Step 3. Move your left foot to the side. Your alignment is facing the wall with $1/8$ turn clockwise between this step and step 2. Your footwork is toe with sway to the right.

Second option: If you want to finish this figure facing diagonal to the wall or the corner of the room, which happens quite frequently, your turn is a slight body rotation clockwise in place of the $1/8$ turn clockwise. You will use this option for the routine at the end of the chapter.

Step 4. Close your right foot to your left foot, maintaining your desired alignment in the room. There is sway to the right, and your footwork is toe, heel ending in the closed position.

This figure may commence in several alignments according to your (the leader's) desire and traffic on the dance floor.

Step 1.

Step 2.

Step 3.

Lady's Part: Promenade

Details for the lady's Promenade:

Step 1. Move your right foot to the side in promenade position while facing diagonal center moving along LOD. There is no sway, and your footwork is heel.

Step 2. Move your left foot forward and across in CBMP and promenade position while facing diagonal center moving along LOD. You will commence to turn counterclockwise on this step. Your footwork is heel, toe with no sway.

Step 3. Move your right foot to the side using the alignment of backing to the wall with a $^1/_8$ turn counterclockwise between this and step 2. Your footwork is toe with sway to the left.

Step 4. Close your left foot to your right foot while maintaining your alignment. Your footwork is toe, heel, with sway to the left, ending in the closed position.

Movement Memo

There is CBM in step 2.

Movement Memo

If your partner chooses the **Second option** (see "Gentleman's Part: Promenade" between steps 3 and 4), your turn is increased to $^1/_4$ counterclockwise.

Zig Zag in Line: Key Rhythm

The generic name for this dance figure is *quarter turns right and left.* The content of this figure is nothing more than progressing the basic forward, making a 90-degree turn clockwise, and then progressing backward making a 90-degree turn counterclockwise. Choreographically, it is one of the most effective dance figures in ballroom dancing. Since it follows itself (repeats) so readily, the dance couple can easily traverse a large ballroom. This figure can even become very compact and therefore useful on the small, congested dance floor.

There is no rise on the first step, followed by the normal rise and fall on the latter three steps.

Gentleman's Part: Zig Zag

Details for the gentleman's Zig Zag:

Step 1. Facing diagonal to the wall, move forward on your left foot. Your footwork is heel.

Step 2. Facing diagonal to the wall, move forward on your right foot, commencing to turn clockwise on this step using heel, toe as your footwork.

Step 3. Facing the wall, move your left foot to the side turning $^1/_8$ clockwise between steps 2 and 3 with right sway using toe as your footwork.

Step 4. Backing diagonal center, close your right foot to your left foot turning $^1/_8$ clockwise between this step and step 3 with right sway and using toe, heel as your footwork.

Step 5. Backing diagonal center, move backward on your left foot using toe, heel as your footwork.

Movement Memo

There is CBM in steps 1 (slight), 2, and 6. Use a brushing action between steps 2 and 3, as well as between steps 6 and 7.

Step 6. Backing diagonal center, move backward on your right foot, commencing to turn counterclockwise on this step using toe, heel as your footwork.

Step 7. Pointing diagonal to the wall, move your left foot to the side making a $^1/_4$ turn between steps 6 and 7 using less of a turn with your body. Your footwork is toe, heel with right sway.

Step 8. Facing diagonal to the wall, close your right foot to your left foot, completing the turn with your body using toe, heel as your footwork with right sway ending in the closed position.

Step 2.   *Step 3.*   *Step 6.*   *Step 7.*

Lady's Part: Zig Zag

Details for the lady's Zig Zag are as follows:

Step 1. Backing diagonal to the wall, move backward on your right foot using the footwork toe, heel.

Step 2. Backing diagonal to the wall, move backward on your left foot, commencing to turn clockwise on this step. Your footwork is toe, heel.

Step 3. Pointing diagonal center, move your right foot to the side and make a ¼ clockwise turn between steps 2 and 3. Your body will make less of a turn. Your footwork is toe with sway left.

Step 4. Facing diagonal center, close your left foot to your right foot completing your body turn. Your footwork is toe, heel with sway left.

Step 5. Facing diagonal center, move forward on your right foot. Your footwork is heel.

Step 6. Facing diagonal center, move forward on your left foot commencing to turn left on this step. Your footwork is heel, toe.

Step 7. Backing to the wall, move your right foot to the side turning ⅛ counterclockwise between steps 6 and 7. Your footwork is toe with left sway.

Step 8. Backing diagonal to the wall, close your left foot to your right foot turning ⅛ counterclockwise between steps 7 and 8. Your footwork is toe, heel with left sway ending in the closed position.

Movement Memo

There is CBM in steps 1 (slight), 2, and 6. Use a brushing action between steps 2 and 3, as well as between steps 6 and 7.

Choreographed Routine: Emergency Wedding Routine

Imagine this: Your wedding song is a Foxtrot, and just two weeks remain until your big day! The solution is right here on these pages—a simple routine that requires the use of only two Foxtrot figures. This is also a great practice routine to acquaint you with the functioning of LOD. This routine is designed only for practice or, like a wedding couple, if you are alone on the dance floor. The Emergency Wedding Routine moves from the corner to the center and then to the next corner repeatedly. To determine the next corner, follow a counterclockwise direction around the room.

Visualize a square with an X drawn from corner to corner where the two lines intersect in the middle of the square. This will be your traveling route. Begin facing the center of the room from any corner. You do not have to be at the corner of the dance floor. Actually you need to approximate the distance it will take to reach the center of the room with three forward steps. Choose your starting point, and let's begin!

Dance the Emergency Wedding Routine by using these steps:

◆ The Basic: steps 1 through 4, travel to the center.

◆ Left Box Turn: steps 1 to 12, two times at or near the center ending to face the next corner.

◆ The Basic: steps 1 to 4, travel to that corner.

◆ Left Box Turn: steps 1 through 6, turn to face the center.

◆ Repeat routine until the music ends (two minutes recommended)!

Choreographed Routine: Nightclub Pattern (or Nowhere to Go)

It is not uncommon to be trapped on the nightclub dance floor unable to travel anywhere. This seems to happen most often during a slow dance or Foxtrot. Here is a nightclub pattern using Foxtrot figures that will permit you to dance until space becomes available to move. Used as a practice routine, the interchangeability of these three steps will help you gain a clearer understanding of the previous and following figures. You will note that the side step and closing step conclude each pattern. These two movements are the common denominator of social dancing! Let's begin:

♦ Sway Step: steps 1 to 4, you may repeat this figure as often as you like or proceed to the next immediately.

♦ Rock Turn to Left: steps 1 to 4, you may also repeat this figure or proceed to the next.

♦ Left Box Turn: steps 1 to 6, again you may repeat this figure or proceed to the next pattern.

♦ Repeat in any sequence you desire.

Choreographed Routine: Foxtrot Routine

Like a romantic walk in busy Central Park, this Foxtrot routine is to be danced in the following sequence:

♦ Zig Zag: steps 1 to 8, two times, begin facing diagonal wall (option—if the room is longer, repeat as necessary).

♦ Rock Turn to Left: steps 1 to 4, the step takes place just prior to the corner of the room and turns you to the new LOD. Do not trap yourself in the corner!

♦ Simple Twinkle: steps 1 to 6, begin and end in the promenade position, travel along LOD.

♦ Promenade: steps 1 to 4, begin in the promenade position and end in the closed position to face diagonal to the corner (option—if the room is longer, repeat as necessary).

♦ Rock Turn to Left: steps 1 to 4, you will end this figure facing the new LOD.

♦ Repeat routine.

This routine is 50 beats of music, so dividing by Foxtrot's four beats per measure, this routine equals 12.5 measures of music. Your CD practice song is 31 measures of music per minute, so as a percentage, this routine will take slightly more than 40 percent of a minute or 24 seconds to repeat.

The Least You Need to Know

♦ Although all Foxtrots are in ¼ time, there are two major rhythms used to dance the Foxtrot: the Key Rhythm of Slow, Slow, Quick, Quick; and the Box Rhythm of Slow, Quick, Quick.

♦ *Rise* and *fall* is a body action first, and the feet follow the body.

♦ Ladies, make sure your footwork is first toe (not ball) and then finish with all your weight on the heel at the end of every backward walk!

♦ The brushing action creates a good vertical axis from which to change directions or rotate.

♦ All of the Foxtrot figures presented can be used on a large ballroom dance floor or on a small, congested nightclub dance floor.

Chapter 17

Tango

In This Chapter

◆ A man, a woman, and *the* dance

◆ A favorite of the silver screen

◆ T-A-N-G-O

◆ The closer you get, the better you Tango

As a social dance, Tango is a means of recreation, creativity, and enjoyment for a lifetime. There are no sociological, chronological, or economic boundaries in Tango. In reality, one would be hard-pressed to find another activity that depends so heavily on the synchronized physical, emotional, and intellectual cooperation between a man and a woman. Tango requires this togetherness and rewards us with so much more. Passion, excitement, love, anger, romance, and every other sensation between a man and a woman are portrayed in this wonderful dance—the Tango.

Tango dancing is both theatrical and eccentric. It is the chosen dance for many leading men and women of the theater and on the silver screen. Tango is not a difficult dance. Therefore these nondancing actors have actually produced rather good interpretations of Tango. One of my favorite quotations regarding the ease with which a Tango can be danced is Al Pacino speaking to Gabrielle Anwar in the movie *Scent of a Woman:* "Tango is not like life, my dear. There are no mistakes in Tango. If you get tangled up, you just Tango on." Even though the danced is structured beautifully, within that structure, every figure has the potential for its own interpretation. Once the Tango bug has bitten you, please consult my book *Quickstart to Tango* (QQS Publications, 1998) for more Tango history, technique, and patterns. In addition to the American style of Tango, *Quickstart to Tango* also includes the Argentine style of Tango which is different from the American style of Tango described in this book. Argentine style is not one of the recognized compliments of ballroom dances.

In the Smooth dances, the alignment of the couple is based on the dance floor (LOD, facing center, diagonal wall, and so on). The reference card in your book will serve as a road map around the dance floor while you practice or when you get "tangled up." My goal is to help you begin with ease, so the rhythm of each individual figure in this text will be the same, and everything else will be described. Now let's Tango-on!

Adding the Special Touches to Your Tango

The following techniques and descriptions will help you develop the "cat-like" or stalking feeling of Tango. The movements are somewhat delayed and compressed—like a great jungle cat that stalks its prey and speedily pounces to the attack. This section will also help you gain more insight into the meanings of the written step descriptions.

A Counting Pattern Just for Fun

I would like to illustrate a counting pattern just for beginners to use and have some fun while learning. It will work for every Tango pattern in this book.

I want you to count the basic Tango pattern aloud as follows: Slow, Slow, Quick, Quick, Slow. The sum total of that cadence of counting was equivalent to eight beats of music. When displayed numerically, we have 1 2, 3 4, 5, 6, 7 8. Repeat this numbered pattern aloud with a pause where you read the comma. Once you become used to verbalizing your cadence, you will replace the numbers with the following letters: T, A, N, G, O.

This is a way to remember basic timing in the American Tango. This alphabetical representation of the timing is measured in the following way:

◆ The letter T replaces the first slow.

◆ The letter A replaces the second slow.

◆ The letter N replaces the first quick.

◆ The letter G replaces the second quick.

◆ The letter O replaces the final slow.

Once again, you will speak each letter rhythmically. You will always remember that the basic pattern in American-style Tango will be counted as T-A-N-G-O. This always brings a chuckle from the students but never seems to be forgotten.

Good Habit, Good Posture

Although similar to the general body position and alignments we have already spelled out, there are some differences in the Tango. The Tango requires your vertical axis to be a bit farther back in your foot. All other dances required your axis to be over the balls of your feet, while the Tango is expressed best from the center of the foot. There should be a bit of twist counterclockwise through the center body to create internal pressure. This slight twist is continuous for every forward and backward walk. This perpetual form of CBM will assist you in the general curving action of the dance and figures that require sharp rotations or pivots.

Framing Snuggles Up a Bit Closer

From the Ballroom Closed Position, move all the vertical and lateral assemblies of your body slightly left. Additionally, the lady and the man should be slightly rotated counterclockwise. Because of this body position, the couple will fit a little closer together. The man's right arm will extend farther around the lady's left side, and his hand will be placed closer to her spine than in the other Smooth dances. If you remember the ballroom position, the man's hand was placed at the left shoulder blade of the lady; for the Tango his hand will be slightly lower and toward the center of her back. To accommodate all of this, the lady must keep her head weight over her left foot throughout the dance. Men, you must be careful *not* to pull the lady into you! She must be allowed to stand over the center of each foot that she uses. Your gaze should be slightly above the horizon. Throughout all the Tango figures presented, the head positions of each dancer will always remain in opposition to each other in a leftward direction.

Negotiating Curving Walks

I am sure by now that you realize the importance of controlling your body while moving with a partner. The human body does not move well if stability is not achieved. A good idea is to imagine your spinal column passing through the front of your ribcage as you begin to move forward. By contrast, please feel your abdominal wall moving toward your spinal column as you begin to move backward. Be sure to keep the vertical alignments of your shoulders, ribs, and hips intact. This will help!

The Tango has no *rise* and *fall*. To accommodate this, we allow the moving foot to be released an inch or two from the floor—this in addition to swinging the thighs upward to begin foot placement. The knees remain flexed with knee veer, and like the Latin dances, the free or nonsupported leg's knee is held higher and more forward than the supporting leg's knee! In the other ballroom dances, the legs extend more fully as the feet continually skim the dance floor.

Now I want you to visualize an imaginary circle around the dance floor. Gentlemen, with your imaginary circle in place, each left foot forward will find the left side of that foot placed just on the outside of the imaginary line. When the right foot moves forward, the left side of the right foot will contact the imaginary circumference line. Exactly the opposite occurs for the lady. Ladies, each right foot backward will find the right side of that foot placed just on the outside of the imaginary line. When the left foot moves backward, the left side of the left foot will contact the imaginary circumference line.

Gentlemen, when you stride forward with your right, you should feel a release from some of the torque produced by a left foot forward walk in CBMP. The right side of the body will remain advanced slightly forward of the left side of the body. The right shoulder, ribcage, and hip aligned and moving together are known as a *right shoulder lead*. This will keep the right body side of the gentleman slightly ahead of his left body side.

Ladies, once again the opposite is true for your Tango. Your left side will advance slightly ahead of your right side on all of your left walks backward. Therefore you have a left shoulder leading on a left backward walk. Control of your body torque increases sensitivity in the language of lead and follows.

Developing the Tango Atmosphere

Here is a fun exercise to develop the "atmosphere of Tango" with your partner. Standing together, hold a broom handle in place as if it were a maypole. The man should hold the pole in his left hand; the lady should hold the pole with her right. Arms are fully extended. Now begin circling the pole counterclockwise. The man moves forward and the lady backward. The maypole *must* stay in place, and your eyes remain at the same elevation gazing at your partner. You will notice that as you do this, the described footwork will become natural!

Demonstration of Tango exercise.

Foot Placement: Strange but True

This type of left foot placement will be known as *CBMP* (contra-body movement position of the foot). CBMP occurs when the moving foot crosses the plane of the standing foot without the body turning. CBMP occurs when the left side of the left foot is placed outside the circumference of our imaginary circle. This walking will produce the precedent for moving with CBM in CBMP.

Because there is *no rise* in Tango, the footwork forward will simply be stated as *heel*. For your backward steps, the footwork will be *ball, heel* because we lift the feet slightly from the floor. This will be your standard unless otherwise stated. Your feet will strike the floor with the *inside edge* (IE) first. That is the side of the sole of the shoe closest to your own center. Now we are ready to start the marvelous choreography of the Tango!

Basic Straight

To give perspective to Tango's movement, one might say it is danced progressively to the stop. You move somewhere and then stop—observing your surroundings and your partner. Then you move on to the next interlude or physical conversation!

This figure begins in closed position facing LOD. Use your Tango standard timing and footwork, and there is CBM on steps 1 and 3. Although this figure is described as being straight, do not forget our imaginary circle. Visualize yourself in a large room, and remain on the perimeter of the dance floor curving leftward. You will complete a distance of ⅛ (can be more) of the imaginary curve through each of these five steps.

Gentleman's Part: Basic Straight

Details for the gentleman's Basic Straight follow:

Step 1. Move forward on your left foot in CBMP.

Step 2. Move forward on your right foot.

Step 3. Move forward on your left foot in CBMP.

Step 4. Move your right foot to the side inside edge of ball, heel, and then your whole foot.

Step 5. Your left foot almost closes to your right foot without weight making contact with the inside edge of the ball of your left foot. End facing LOD.

Your alignments and amount of turn can vary. This figure can end in either closed or promenade position.

Technique

Technique (General for Both—The Tango Draw in Depth): The last segment of the basic step in the American Tango is known as the *Tango draw*. These are steps 3, 4, and 5. This step pattern will be repeated in each of the five figures you will learn. The Tango draw can be used either as a connecting (or linking) figure or as a concluding figure to the great majority of dance patterns in the American Tango.

The importance of step 3 is often overlooked in the Tango draw. In their attempts to do the side step that follows, beginners often rush and leave the gentleman's forward or the lady's backward steps unfinished. Because step 3 is done in one beat of music, counted as a Quick, they do not develop a full weight change. As a result, they do not create a good vertical axis on which to rotate or change direction. Both the partners will have time to step with either the forward Tango draw (man) or the backward Tango draw (lady), so help one another here (direction can vary).

Make sure that when you do this step, particularly when going forward or in promenade position, your knee is over your toes and your hips are over your knee. The control of the abdominal wall will ensure that your spinal column will remain completely vertical—that is, perpendicular—to the dance floor. And, as a result, your shoulders will remain over your hips. We dealt with these physical issues in the Tango exercises. Your ability to rotate, curve, and lead or follow additional figures will be stymied if this step 3 is not taken properly. This step may be taken with or without CBMP, depending on whether rotation is desired.

Step 4: This is a side step and therefore should be taken with contact on the inside edge of your foot. This will allow the body to roll smoothly and quickly over the foot. This side step can be improved by placing the foot slightly forward of the plane of step 3. Slightly forward (slightly back, if you are the lady) would be measured as a position of the foot in which the foot taking the side step advances two to three inches from the position of the standing leg and the side step taken. This will enhance your ability to rotate and especially to create the lead or follow to promenade position. You must take this step with the knee flexed and braced to prevent any inadvertent *rise* from occurring. Do this by actually swinging your thigh rather than your foot. Knee veer must be considered—that is, the knees will be closer together than the ankles.

Step 5: Now we will discuss the drawing action itself and positioning to either closed or promenade position. When the left foot for the man (right foot for the lady) is drawn toward the standing foot, the heel of the left leg is released from the dance floor, and the knee is slightly higher in its position of flex than that of the right foot. The opposite is true for the lady. The inside edge of the toe retains pressure on the dance floor while the heel's position is up from the floor.

To finish step 5 in the promenade position, the man must generate a body turn just under a $1/8$ turn clockwise by rotating his right arm, shoulder, ribcage, and hip in conjunction with his partner's to lead his partner to promenade position. The man then returns to his normal abdominal compression counterclockwise, finishing facing in promenade position. This lead is called a *right-shoulder lead*. The man must be careful not to pull the lady toward him but simply allow her to rotate on her left foot. The lady will complete a $1/4$ rotation clockwise to finish facing in promenade position, being careful to maintain the weight of her head over her left foot. Ladies, it is almost as if you are rotating slightly around your leader's right ribcage. The movement is swift but does not require force. It definitely takes practice to achieve the proper finesse.

Step 3.

Step 4.

Step 5.

Lady's Part: Basic Straight

Details for the lady's Basic Straight follow:

Step 1. Move backward on your right foot in CBMP.

Step 2. Move backward on your left foot.

Step 3. Move backward on your right foot in CBMP.

Step 4. Move your left foot to the side inside edge of ball, heel, and then your whole foot.

Step 5. Your right foot almost closes to your left foot, without weight making contact with the inside edge of the ball of your right foot.

Basic Circular

This figure begins in the closed position facing LOD. Use your standard Tango timing and footwork; there is CBM on steps 1, 3, and 5. Visualize yourself on a much smaller circle—similar to your "maypole technique"—curving leftward. Complete a ½ turn (can be less) of the imaginary circle through each of these five steps.

Gentleman's Part: Basic Circular

Details for the gentleman's Basic Circular follow:

Step 1. Facing LOD, move forward on your left foot in CBMP, commencing to turn counterclockwise.

Step 2. Facing diagonal center, move forward on your right foot, curving to the left completing ⅛ rotation counterclockwise between step 1 and this step.

Step 3. Facing center, move forward on your left foot in CBMP and complete ⅛ rotation counterclockwise between step 2 and this step.

Step 4. Facing diagonal center against LOD, move your right foot to the side, completing ⅛ turn counterclockwise between step 3 and this step. Your footwork is inside edge of ball, heel, and then your whole foot.

Step 5. Facing against LOD, your left foot almost closes to your right foot without weight. Complete a ⅛ turn counterclockwise between step 4 and this step. Your footwork is contact with the inside edge of the ball of your left foot.

Your alignments and amount of turn can vary. This figure can end in either closed or promenade position.

Step 1.

Step 2.

Step 3.

Lady's Part: Basic Circular

Details for the lady's Basic Circular follow:

Step 1. Backing LOD, move backward on your right foot in CBMP commencing to turn counterclockwise.

Step 2. Backing diagonal center, move backward on your left foot curving to the left and completing ⅛ rotation counterclockwise between step 1 and this step.

Step 3. Backing center, move backward on your right foot in CBMP and complete ⅛ rotation counterclockwise between step 2 and this step.

Step 4. Backing diagonal center against LOD, move your left foot to the side, completing ⅛ turn counterclockwise between step 3 and this step. Your footwork is inside edge of ball, heel, and then your whole foot.

Step 5. Backing against LOD, your left foot almost closes to your right foot without weight as you complete ⅛ turn counterclockwise between step 4 and this step. Your footwork is contact with the inside edge of the ball of your left foot.

Promenade Turning Left

This figure begins in promenade position facing diagonal wall moving along LOD. It uses the standard timing and footwork, and there is CBM on steps 2 and 3.

Gentleman's Part: Promenade Turning Left

Details for the gentleman's Promenade Turning Left follow:

Step 1. Facing diagonal wall moving along LOD, move your left foot to the side in promenade position.

Step 2. Facing LOD, move forward and across in CBMP on your right foot in promenade position. Use a strong body turn counterclockwise to lead your partner's pivot to closed position.

Step 3. Facing LOD, move forward on your left foot in CBMP and commence to turn counterclockwise.

Step 4. Move your right foot to the side inside edge of ball, flat and then your whole foot. Rotate ⅛ counterclockwise turn between step 3 and this step to finish facing diagonal center.

Step 5. Facing diagonal center, your left foot almost closes to your right foot without weight making contact with the inside edge of the ball of your left foot. End facing diagonal center.

Your alignments and amount of turn can vary in this figure and can end in either closed or promenade position.

Promenade Position for Tango.

Step 1.

Step 2 Walk in PP prior to pivot.

Step 2 Ending position after pivot.

Lady's Part: Promenade Turning Left

Details for the lady's Promenade Turning Left follow:

Step 1. Facing diagonal center moving along LOD, move your right foot to the side in promenade position.

Step 2. Move forward and across in CBMP on your left foot in promenade position. Then make a strong swivel ⅜ turn counterclockwise to end backing LOD. It is helpful to divide the swivel using the "step then turn" rule.

Step 3. Backing LOD, move backward on your right foot in CBMP commencing to turn counterclockwise.

Step 4. Move your left foot to the side inside edge of ball, flat, and then your whole foot. Rotate ⅛ counterclockwise between step 3 and this step to finish backing diagonal center.

Step 5. Backing diagonal center, your right foot almost closes to your right foot without weight making contact with the inside edge of the ball of your left foot. End facing diagonal center.

Movement Memo _____

Both the former Promenade Turning Left and the following Promenade Turning Right include sharp rotations of $^3/_8$ of a turn. It is common for beginners to have problems during these sharper rotations. Generally, the causes for these errors are found when the emphasis is placed on the rotations too early in the step number's development. Please consult Chapter 13, "The Interactions of the Dance Couple," its contents are among the most important in this book containing your "keys to success"!

Promenade Turning Right

This figure begins in promenade position facing diagonal wall and moving along LOD. It uses the standard timing and footwork, and there is CBM on steps 2 and 3. This figure can help you turn at a corner to face the *new* LOD.

Gentleman's Part: Promenade Turning Right

Details for the gentleman's Promenade Turning Right follow:

Step 1. Facing diagonal center moving along LOD, move your left foot to the side in promenade position.

Step 2. Facing diagonal center, move forward and across in CBMP on your right foot in promenade position. Rotate $^3/_8$ turn clockwise to end backing LOD.

Step 3. Backing LOD, move side on your left foot commencing to turn clockwise. Your footwork is ball, heel, ball.

Step 4. Move your right foot to the side inside edge of your foot and then the whole foot. Rotate $^1/_4$ clockwise between step 3 and this step to finish facing center.

Step 5. Facing center, your left foot almost closes to your right foot without weight making contact with the inside edge of the ball of your left foot. End facing center (or the new LOD).

Your alignments and amount of turn can vary. The following figure can end in either closed or promenade position.

Lady's Part: Promenade Turning Right

Details for the lady's Promenade Turning Right follow:

Step 1. Facing diagonal center moving along LOD, move your right foot to the side in promenade position.

Step 2. Facing LOD, move forward and across in CBMP on your left foot in promenade position. Rotate your body clockwise to end facing LOD.

Step 3. Facing LOD, move forward on your right foot commencing to turn clockwise. Your footwork is heel.

Step 4. Move your left foot to the side inside edge of your foot and then the whole foot. Rotate $^1/_4$ clockwise between step 3 and this step to finish backing center.

Step 5. Backing center, your right foot almost closes to your left foot without weight making contact with the inside edge of the ball of your right foot. End backing center.

Step 2 Walk in Promenade Position prior to pivot.

Step 2 Ending position after pivot.

Step 3 Continuing to turn.

Step 4 Ending position after turn.

Corté–Single

When Tango is portrayed theatrically, this is the figure that has always captured the imagination. Few dance figures can capture all that is masculine and all that is feminine at the same moment; here is one of them.

It uses the standard timing and footwork, and there is CBM on step 3. In addition to creating a strong image, this figure is particularly useful when the floor is congested. It serves as a *pause* until the crowd moves by!

Gentleman's Part: Corté—Single

Details for the gentleman's Corté—Single follow:

Step 1. Moving backing LOD, take a strong step backward on your left foot with your left side leading. To create a strong image, make sure you exaggerate the stretch in your left ribcage with a slight body turn counterclockwise. Your footwork will be ball, heel.

Step 2. Replace your weight forward to your right foot. Your footwork will be heel.

Step 3. Facing LOD, move forward on your left foot in CBMP commencing to turn counterclockwise.

Step 4. Move your right foot to the side inside edge of your foot and then the whole foot. Rotate ¼ clockwise between step 3 and this step to finish facing center.

Step 5. Facing diagonal center, your left foot almost closes to your right foot without weight making contact with the inside edge of the ball of your left foot, ending facing center (or the new LOD) in closed position.

Your alignments and amount of turn can vary. This figure can end in either closed or promenade position.

Technique

Technique (Gentleman's Corté Step 1): To be successful at this beautiful picture step, the leader must resist the urge to draw his partner in with his arms. Instead imagine you are attached to your partner with a rope tied around your waists. Draw on the rope with your midsection by first contracting your abdominal region.

I am never in favor of "pulling" or "yanking" on your partner from either the leader's or follower's perspective in any dance. Your first instinct to do anything backward in ballroom dancing should be to brace your feet into the dance floor and initiate retraction through the midsection rather than the arms or shoulders!

Step 1 The Corté.

Step 2 Replacing Forward Boldly.

Lady's Part: Corté—Single

Details for the lady's Corté—Single follow:

Step 1. Moving against LOD, take a strong step forward on your right with your right side leading. To create a strong image, make sure you exaggerate the stretch in your right ribcage with a slight body turn counterclockwise. Your footwork will be heel.

Step 2. Replace your weight backward to your left foot. Your footwork will be ball, heel.

Step 3. Backing LOD, move backward on your right foot in CBMP commencing to turn counterclockwise.

Step 4. Move your left foot to the side inside edge of your foot and then the whole foot. Rotate ¼ clockwise between step 3 and this step to finish facing backing center.

Step 5. Backing center, your right foot almost closes to your left foot—without weight making contact—with the inside edge of the ball of your left foot ending backing center in the closed position.

Choreographed Routine: Tango Routine

Feel the electric passion of this Tango routine to be danced in the following sequence:

- Basic Straight: steps 1 to 5, two times.
- Basic Circular: steps 1 to 5, two times, end in Promenade Position (PP) facing between DW and LOD on the repeat.
- Promenade Turning Left: steps 1 to 5.
- Basic Straight: steps 1 to 5 end in PP.
- Promenade Turning Right: steps 1 to 5.
- Corté—Single: steps 1 to 5.
- Repeat routine.

This routine can vary according to the size of the dance floor. You may add or subtract basic movements to adjust for the length of the floor. You may increase or diminish the amount of curve of any figure to improve your position in relation to the line of dance.

This routine is 64 beats of music, so dividing by the Tango's four beats per measure, this routine equals 16 measures of music. Your CIG CD practice song is 32 measures of music per minute, so as a percentage, this routine will take 50 percent of a minute or 30 seconds to the repeat.

The Least You Need to Know

- Tango frame is closer, and the couple is more left of each other than in the standard ballroom position.
- There is no *rise* and *fall* in Tango. This usage is the proper noun.
- The "maypole technique" will help develop the shoulder lead needed in Tango.
- Do not rush your steps! Complete every weight change, particularly in step 3 of the *basic* movements.

Chapter 18

Viennese Waltz

In This Chapter

- ◆ A scandalous beginning
- ◆ The elegance of Waltz at twice the speed
- ◆ Distance is the enemy
- ◆ More energy than a four-minute mile

The Viennese Waltz is the dance that was depicted in the first chapter of this book. It certainly is not an exaggeration to state that this dance created one of the greatest "social scandals" ever experienced in the history of Western civilization! It was the very first dance in which a man embraced a woman in public. The couples danced in a closed position without the custom of having that woman's chaperon present.

Viennese Waltz developed out of the court dances, where it was considered a social impropriety to turn a lady to the left or counterclockwise. As the dance developed, counterclockwise rotation became a necessity. It was common knowledge that left-handedness and those things moving or operating to the left were discriminated against. In many ways, this has never changed! To appease these ancient conventions, a right turn was called a "natural turn," and a left turn was called a "reverse turn." The international style of dancing still uses these descriptions.

The images of dance on the silver screen depicting the periods from the Victorian era through the Civil War most frequently use the Viennese Waltz as their backdrop. Images of this beautiful dance evoke feelings of love's innocence and elegance, and occasionally society's decadence, but hardly seem scandalous.

I have placed the Viennese Waltz last among the complement of Smooth dances in this book. Due to its speed, or quick tempo, the Viennese Waltz is definitely not a beginner's dance! To be successful at this dance, it is important to first develop a good quality of consistency and competence at the Waltz. Use the Waltz as your model for this dance's structure and technique. Return to the overlapping figures in the Waltz frequently for descriptions of their coincidental technique.

Details, Details—or Dealing with Speed

There are many illusions and misconceptions in dance. Moving the feet faster to dance faster combines illusion and misconception into one wrong idea! You have learned from my Quickstart

Program© that it is the body that moves first, creating the necessity of proportionate leg swing and coincidental support. Therefore, in contrast to the Waltz or Foxtrot, you must move your body almost twice as fast to accomplish the speed necessary to do this dance. Let your feet and legs always complement the body's movement in any dance!

Gentlemen, you must think quickly to lead with competence. Then you must respond in proportion to allow for your partner's response. Ladies, your competence in a back walk is paramount during this dance. Start with and continue to hold your energies in your abdominal wall. The ability to skim the floor with your toe first on any back walk is vital to the smooth flow of this dance. Lifting your heel from the dance floor while exiting from a foot on any back walk will cause an immediate loss of balance! As learned earlier, this practice is called the no-foot rise (NFR) in your Foxtrot and Waltz.

Each partner must dance with pliable ankles to allow for a quick softness when entering the foot from a previous step. If you were to quantify the amount of rise or elevation the dance couple achieves during the Viennese Waltz (VW) versus the Waltz, the rise would be less because of the speed. However, the third beat of each measure, or the third and sixth step of the moving figures, will be described as "up." As a result of the speed, we achieve the last position of rise faster than in the Waltz! So when we say the "normal rise and fall" when talking about the VW, it means "up" on these steps.

On many of the closing steps, your footwork remains the same—toe, heel. However, the time it takes to lower to your heel is almost indistinguishable. This will feel and look as if you are putting your foot down flat. I will describe this toe, heel action as *foot flat*. To accomplish this you must dance with consistent and perfect balance as described through the technique of this text! Therefore when your knee bends, you must be over it with your body in good vertical alignment.

The last important idea to keep in mind is what I describe as "distance is the enemy." Attempting to gain distance on a forward or backward step in this dance can be deadly. Your movement will lurch and smoothness and balance will be lost! Because the VW is essentially a circular dance, you are spending much of the time of the forward or backward steps turning or starting a turn. For this reason, if there is distance to be gained, it is most appropriately done on side steps.

Balance Steps—Forward and Back, Side

Please use the normal rise and while maintaining the ¾ timing of the VW. There is no CBM. This figure begins with the alignment of the previous figure. Steps 1 to 12 can also be danced with *no-foot rise* (NFR). Some dancers find this easier, but I find the normal rise more elegant and characteristic of the Waltz for these types of steps.

Gentleman's Part: Balance Steps

Details for the gentleman's Balance Steps follow:

Step 1. Move forward on your left foot heel, toe.

Step 2. Your right foot closes to your left foot without weight. Continue to rise through your body.

Step 3. Hold your position. Lower at the end of the beat toe, heel.

Step 4. Move backward on your right foot toe, heel.

Step 5. Close your left foot to your right foot without weight. Continue to rise through your body.

Step 6. Hold your position. Lower at the end of the beat toe, heel.

Step 7. Move your left foot to the side toe, heel.

Step 8. Close your right foot to your left foot without weight using sway to the right. Continue to rise through your body.

Step 9. Hold your position using sway to the right. Lower at the end of the beat toe, heel.

Step 10. Move side to your right toe, heel.

Step 11. Close your left foot to your right foot without weight using sway to the left. Continue to rise through your body.

Step 12. Hold your position using sway to the left. You will lower at the end of the beat toe, heel. Finish in the closed dance position prepared for any following figure beginning with your left foot.

Forward Balance.

Back Balance.

Left Balance.

Right Balance.

Movement Memo _____

You will find these balance steps an indispensable aid in "catching your breath" or regaining control during this fast-paced and vigorous dance. Since balance steps hesitate in position, they are also useful in avoiding collisions on the dance floor! Another major feature of these steps is that you may break the directional components into their own individual figures and use them as required. When holding your position maintain pressure on the foot *without* weight!

Technique

Technique (General for Both): Be very careful to never drop into your heel when taking a backward walk. You must continually strive to use a controlled lowering action. An illustration of controlled lowering I often use is to imagine that you have a tennis ball under your heel and have to flatten it gradually. Please remember that as you take any back walk, you should accelerate your abdomen through to your spinal column while retaining your best physical alignment vertically.

Lady's Part: Balance Steps

Details for the lady's Balance Steps follow:

Step 1. Move back to your right foot using the footwork of toe, heel.

Step 2. Close your left foot to your right foot. Continue to rise through your body.

Step 3. Hold your position. Lower at the end of the beat toe, heel.

Step 4. Move forward to your left foot heel, toe.

Step 5. Close your right foot to your left foot without weight. Continue to rise through your body.

Step 6. Hold your position. Lower at the end of the beat toe, heel.

Step 7. Move to the side on your right foot toe, heel.

Step 8. Close your left foot to your right foot without weight, using sway to the left. Continue to rise through your body.

Movement Memo _____

Review the techniques for normal rise and fall located in the section "Box with Underarm Turn" in Chapter 15, "Waltz."

Step 9. Hold your position with sway to the left. Lower at the end of the beat toe, heel.

Step 10. Move to the side on your left foot.

Step 11. Close your right foot to your left foot without weight using sway to the right. Continue to rise through your body.

Step 12. Hold your position with sway to the right. Lower at the end of the beat toe, heel.

Left Turn—Your Hardest Step!

This dance step is definitely your final exam; it contains all the important components you have studied so far. You will be turning counterclockwise as a couple down LOD in virtually a straight line. The left turn in the Viennese Waltz is used repeatedly as a means of progression around the dance floor. As you continue ballroom dancing, it will be often used as an entree to many other dance figures.

The step begins and ends in closed position using the normal rise and fall while maintaining the ¾ timing of the VW. There is CBM on steps 1 and 4. Your partner's last three steps will duplicate your first three steps.

Gentleman's Part: Left Turn

Details for the gentleman's Left Turn follow:

Step 1. Facing LOD, move forward on your left foot having already made a body commitment to a counter-clockwise turn on your previous step. This step is heel, toe.

Step 2. Backing wall, move your right foot to the side and slightly back, turning ¼ counterclockwise between step 1 and this step. You will use the footwork of toe with left sway.

Step 3. Backing LOD, cross your left foot in front of your right foot, turning ¼ counterclockwise between step 2 and this step. You will use the footwork of toe, heel with left sway.

Step 4. Backing LOD with your toe pointed in toward that direction (this produces a turned in position of the toe), move backward and slightly side on your right foot, turning ⅛ counterclockwise between steps 3 and this step. There is no foot rise using the footwork of toe, heel.

Step 5. Pointing between diagonal wall and LOD, move your left foot to the side, turning almost ⅜ counterclockwise between step 4 and this step with less of a body rotation. Use the footwork of toe with right sway.

Step 6. Almost facing LOD, close your right foot to your left foot, completing your body turn at this time. Your footwork is foot flat with right sway.

Technique

Technique (General for Both): A good physical analogy of the left turn is something we have all done at one time or another. Hold a towel vertically. Twist the towel counterclockwise at the upper half, holding the lower portion still until the center portion is snug. Release the lower portion, and it spins counterclockwise. Pay close attention to the sequence of these events. The upper portion affects the center, and the center affects the lower portion.

To begin a turn as focused as the left turn, you must begin rotation with your ribcage creating a strong, firm twist in your abdominal wall. The resulting rotation will be expressed through your legs and foot positions. Okay, this takes care of the rotation. Let's move on to other elements.

We must observe inside and outside of the rotation. The partner taking the backward movement first is on the inside of the turn. Therefore, the degree of rotation is greater through the legs and hips than that of their partner. In addition, the backward-moving partner must perceive their partner as being the one traveling in the straight line. As a result, they must provide accessibility to continue through that tangent. How is this accomplished? On step 4 in the gentleman's part, you will read "move backward and slightly side on your right foot." The "slightly side" movement provides just enough room to clear an accessible space for his partner. Also on step 4 you read "toe turned in." This is a natural result of the continuing rotation of the body throughout this dance step, as well as a means of maintaining good foot pressure—in this case, the right toe at the end of this particular step.

Another example of good foot pressure is on the closing actions of the gentleman's step 6 and the lady's step 3. The foot is drawn in, remaining close to the floor with pressure. This assists in maintaining the dancers' alignment, the same way a rudder keeps the sailboat in a vertical position while the wind blows strongly through the sail. Believe me, your partner generates a great deal of momentum on this step, and this foot pressure will be of invaluable help to the couple.

The last item to emphasize on this step is that the distance down LOD is gained when each of the partners is taking the side steps. In this way the couple is allowed to travel easily, rather than either member of the couple forcing the issue individually with either forward or back steps.

Step 1.

Step 2.

Step 3.

Step 4.

Step 5.

Step 6.

Lady's Part: Left Turn

Details for the lady's Left Turn follow:

Step 1. Backing LOD having already made a body commitment to a counterclockwise turn on your previous step, take a backward step on your right foot. There is no-foot rise using the footwork of toe, heel.

Step 2. Pointing between diagonal wall and LOD, move your left foot to the side, turning almost ⅜ counterclockwise between step 1 and this step with less of a body rotation. Use the footwork of toe with right sway.

Step 3. Almost facing LOD, close your right foot to your left foot, completing your body turn at this time. Your footwork is foot flat with right sway.

Step 4. Facing LOD, move forward on your left foot, turning ⅛ counterclockwise on step 3 and this step. Use the footwork of heel, toe.

Step 5. Backing wall, move your right foot to the side and slightly back, turning ¼ counterclockwise between step 4 and this step. Use the footwork of toe with left sway.

Step 6. Almost backing LOD, cross your left foot in front of your right foot, turning ¼ counterclockwise between step 5 and this step. Use the footwork of toe, heel with left sway.

Forward Progressive Changes

This dance figure serves some important functions on the dance floor. The first is obvious! Its name is *Progressive*, and it helps you to travel around the dance floor. The second function of the Progressive is less obvious to the beginner. This figure helps the dancer change from one leading foot to another. The leading foot is simply the foot that begins any dance figure. This is accomplished when either half of the Progressive is done.

The normal footwork as well as the normal rise and fall will be used while maintaining the ¾ timing of the VW.

Gentleman's Part: Progressive

Details for the gentleman's Progressive follow:

Step 1. Walk forward on your left foot.

Step 2. Move to the side and slightly forward on your right foot using sway to the left.

Step 3. Close your left foot to your right foot using sway to the left.

Step 4. Move forward on your right foot.

Step 5. Move your left foot to the side and slightly forward using sway to the right.

Step 6. Close your right foot to your left foot using sway to the right.

Movement Memo

There is slight CBM on steps 1 and 4.

Technique

Technique (General for Both Steps 1 to 3): Complete the first half of the Progressive. Notice that your right foot is now available to begin any other dance figure. You have in effect prepared yourself for any dance figure that begins with your right foot free. Of course the opposite is true for your partner.

In step 2 you read the description "side and slightly forward." This means that during a side step that follows a progressive movement forward, your body generates what we call *body swing*, causing the free side to move slightly forward in the direction of the Progressive. This will also be true for a backward movement, which would be described as "side and slightly back."

This is why there is slight CBM in the description of the step indicating a slight amount of turn. The amount of distance or degree of turn is equal to approximately one-half of the length of your foot. As a result of the CBM, the foot that you have placed to the side is slightly ahead of the plane of your former movement either forward or back.

Step 4.   *Step 5.*

Lady's Part: Progressive

Details for the lady's Progressive follow:

Step 1. Move backward on your right foot.

Step 2. Move your left foot to the side and slightly back using sway to the right.

Step 3. Close your right foot to your left foot using sway to the right.

Step 4. Move backward on your left foot.

Movement Memo

There is slight CBM on steps 1 and 4.

Step 5. Move your right foot to the side and slightly back using sway to the left.

Step 6. Close your left foot to your right foot using sway to the left.

The Progressive can travel straight down the line of dance, diagonal to the wall, or diagonal to the center.

Right Turn

Think of this figure as a box step that is overturned by adding another quarter turn clockwise over each three steps. There is CBM on steps 1 and 4. On their last three steps, your partner will duplicate your first three steps. You will use the normal rise and fall and footwork for this figure while maintaining the ¾ timing of the VW. This step begins and ends in closed position.

Gentleman's Part: Right Turn

Details for the gentleman's Right Turn follow:

Step 1. Facing diagonal center and moving along LOD, move forward on your right foot turning ⅛ clockwise.

Step 2. Backing center, move your left foot to the side, turning ¼ clockwise with right sway.

Step 3. Backing diagonal center, close your right foot to your left foot, turning ⅛ clockwise with right sway.

Step 4. Backing diagonal center and moving along LOD, move backward on your left foot, turning ⅛ clockwise. No foot rise.

Step 5. Pointing diagonal center, move your right foot to the side, turning ⅜ clockwise with less body turn using left sway.

Step 6. Facing diagonal center, your left foot closes to your right foot as your body completes the turn using the foot flat technique with left sway.

Step 1.

Step 2.

Step 3.

Lady's Part: Right Turn

Details for the lady's Right Turn follow:

Step 1. Backing diagonal center and moving along LOD, move backward on your left foot turning ⅛ clockwise. No-foot rise.

Step 2. Pointing diagonal center, move your right foot to the side, turning ⅜ clockwise with less body turn using left sway.

Step 3. Facing diagonal center, your left foot closes to your right foot as your body completes the turn using the foot flat technique with left sway.

Step 4. Facing diagonal center and moving along LOD, move forward on your right foot, turning ⅛ clockwise.

Step 5. Backing center, move your left foot to the side turning ¼ clockwise with right sway.

Step 6. Backing diagonal center, close your right foot to your left foot, turning ⅛ clockwise with right sway.

Curtsey and Bow (Used Only to Start the Dance)

This figure commences in right side-by-side position with the couple facing LOD.

Gentleman's Part: Curtsy and Bow

Details for the gentleman's Curtsy and Bow follow:

Step 1. Backing against LOD, move backward on your left foot. Your footwork is toe, heel.

Step 2. Backing against LOD, close your right foot to your left foot without weight. Maintain pressure on the toe of your right foot.

Step 3. Hold your position.

Step 4 to 6. Hold your position while bowing from the waist, bringing your right arm across your body, and then stand upright. This takes one full measure of music.

Step 7. Facing LOD, move forward on your right foot to assume the closed position.

Step 8. Facing LOD, close your left foot to your right foot without weight with total pressure on your left foot. You will consummate closed position at this time.

Step 9. Hold your position with your left foot free.

Step 1 Opening Position.

Step 1 Ending Position.

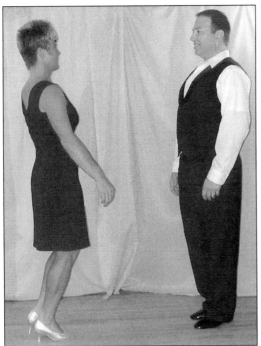

Step 2 and 3.

Step 4.

Lady's Part: Curtsy and Bow

Details for the lady's Curtsy and Bow follow:

Step 1. Facing LOD, move forward on your left foot. Curving to the left, commence to turn counterclockwise. Your footwork is heel. Yes ladies, you do begin this figure using your *left* foot!

Step 2. Facing against LOD (including the remaining steps), move your right foot to the side ¹/₂ counterclockwise between steps 1 and 2. Your footwork is toe, heel.

Step 3. Hold your position on your right foot, and cross your left foot behind your right without weight but with toe pressure. Your footwork is toe.

Step 4. Lower into both knees with pressure on the toe of the left foot and the majority of your weight still on your right foot.

Steps 5 and 6. Rise to your normal position with pressure on the toe of your left foot.

Step 7. Move forward on your left foot. Your footwork is heel. Offer your right hand to the gentleman.

Step 8. Close your right foot to your left foot without weight, consummating closed position.

Step 9. Hold your position with your right foot free.

Choreographed Routine: Viennese Waltz Routine

This is a formal and elegant Viennese Waltz routine to be danced in the following sequence:

◆ Curtsy and Bow: steps 1 to 9 (done once to start).

◆ Left Turn: steps 1 to 6 (may be repeated if room permits).

◆ Forward Progressive: steps 1 to 3.

- Right Turn: steps 1 to 6 (may be repeated if room permits).
- Forward Progressive Changes: steps 4 to 6.
- Balance Steps: steps 1 to 12 if desired (may be inserted elsewhere if necessary or desired).
- Repeat routine.

This routine is 39 beats of music, so dividing by 3 (remembering that VW is three beats to the measure), this routine equals 13 measures of music. Your CD practice song is 54 measures of music per minute, so as a percentage, this routine will take 24 percent of a minute or just above 14 seconds to the repeat. Do not forget that your balance steps can be used as frequently as you like to buffer between time and space, as well as stamina!

The Least You Need to Know

- Competence and quality in the technique used in the Waltz will lead to success in the Viennese Waltz.
- The Progressive step allows a change of the leading foot.
- Speed is achieved by accelerating the body—not by moving the feet faster.
- Do not attempt to gain distance on the forward or backward steps, as these are essentially turning steps.

This Stuff's Hot and Spicy and Real Cool, "Daddy-O"

The Mambo and Rumba are the choreographical foundations to the Cha-Cha and Salsa—the later two being the youngest on the present dance scene. The figure elements of all four dances, including underarm turns, have actually been taken in large from the various styles of American Swing.

These Latin American dances were all first danced as solo dances (no partnered positions) by groups of men or women or both. We return once again to the European form of the Waltz to find the developments of all partnered dances and how they were influenced into becoming part of the family of ballroom dances. The Latin American dances are like a great family recipe— a little of this, some of that, mix well, and serve *hot!* Africa, South America, Europe, the Islands—all cultures contributed in some aspect to create what is known today as Latin American dancing.

In addition to the Latin American dances of Rumba, Merengue, Cha-Cha, Mambo, and Samba, we are going to stay right here in the good old USA and learn to dance two more immensely popular rhythms—East Coast Swing and Hustle. East Coast Swing and its varieties are among the most popular dances in the world and are certainly the most versatile.

The Hustle has its roots in both Swing and Latin dancing and contributed greatly to the rebirth of ballroom dancing. It is an exciting dance that continues to grow in popularity among those in their teens to those in their 40s!

Rumba

In This Chapter

- ◆ A three-minute trip to the tropics
- ◆ A bicycle built for Rumba
- ◆ It's all in the knees
- ◆ The dance step turned out great

The Rumba is undeniably the music of love. The sound is a treat to our senses, and its alluring rhythm transports us to a tropical locale, if only for a moment. We can feel the power of the surf and the hot wind in our face, while the breeze plays melodies with the palms. We are seduced by this titillating music and virtually driven to dance. Do I have your attention? Let's begin!

In the Smooth dances, the alignment of the couple is based on the dance floor (facing center, diagonal wall, etc.). In the Rumba, as with most Latin dances, alignment is based on the couple's position relative to each other rather than some spot in the room. Please maintain the normal 4/4 timing of the Rumba using the rhythm of Slow, Quick, Quick. The beat value of a Slow is two beats of music, and the beat value for a Quick is one beat. Your timing or beat value for each measure of music will be one two (Slow), three (Quick), four (Quick). You will maintain this rhythm throughout all of the Rumba figures presented in this book. The footwork throughout each Rumba figure will be ball, flat. I will describe any additional techniques concerning footwork as we proceed.

Side Basic

This dance figure will begin in closed position. Please use the standard footwork and rhythm.

Gentleman's Part: Side Basic

Details for the gentleman's Side Basic follow:

Step 1. Move your left foot to the side.

Step 2. Close your right foot to your left foot.

Step 3. Transfer your weight to the left foot, leaving it in place.

Step 4. Move your right foot to the side.

Step 5. Close your left foot to your right foot.

Step 6. Transfer your weight to the right foot, leaving it in place. This figure ends in closed position.

Technique

Technique (General for Both): The technique used for this step will be the same for all figures in the Rumba that contain a side movement. As you take a side step, endeavor to touch the inside edge of your foot to the floor first. As you take weight into the ball of the foot, you will feel a rolling action beginning at that outside edge and moving across the bottom of your foot. Be careful not to roll to the outside edge of the foot. Stop "rolling" when your foot is flat and all your body weight covers all of the foot. This action will allow for rhythmic body movement, particularly through the hips. Stepping too quickly on the whole foot during a side step will cause your body to finish the weight change too quickly and too abruptly.

The closing action and weight transfer feel very much like peddling a bicycle. While maintaining good carriage of the body and support from the foot that contains your weight, pressurize the standing leg as you release the free leg upward in the same way that you peddle a bicycle. As your thighs move while you are "peddling," it is easy to feel the action of your hips and pelvis. As you take the downward stroke of your peddle, feel your quadriceps flex and the back of your knee stretch. At the same time, or with coincidence, the other thigh raises, releasing its energy and allowing the knee to bend. Even though you are releasing energy here, the good cyclists do not take their feet off the pedals. Some part of the foot must remain on the floor through all the steps of the Rumba. Draw the feet toward and under the body with slight pressure on the floor. The peddling action of the knees and thighs is what actually creates Cuban motion or hip action—not the hips! This sequence of events is vital for Latin American dancing. Another helpful device for perfecting hip action is to divide your timing. In place of "Quick," "Quick"; use "Quick *and*," "Quick *and*." The "Quick" represents ¹/₂ of a beat. Use this to complete the leg action and weight change. The "and" represents ¹/₂ a beat to allow your hip to settle while releasing the former foot from the floor. Imagine yourself standing outside an elevator impatiently settling your hip from one leg to another. Now try it. This often works as a physical analogy.

Latin American Closed Position.

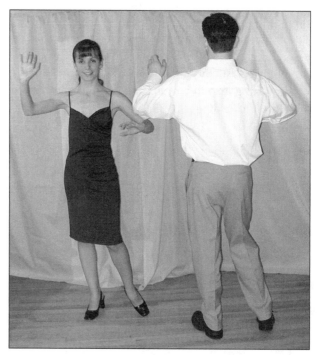

Step 1.

Step 2.

Step 3.

Lady's Part: Side Basic

Details for the lady's Side Basic follow:

Step 1. Move your right foot to the side.

Step 2. Close your left foot to your right foot.

Step 3. Transfer your weight to the right foot, leaving it in place.

Step 4. Move your left foot to the side.

Step 5. Close your right foot to your left foot.

Step 6. Transfer your weight to the left foot, leaving it in place. This figure ends in closed position.

Fifth Position

Begin this figure in closed position using the standard footwork and rhythm. Fifth Position occurs when the couple steps backward while standing in "Right Side-by-Side Position" or "Left Side-by-Side Positions."

Gentleman's Part: Fifth Position

Details for the gentleman's Fifth Position follow:

Steps 1 to 3. Dance steps 1 to 3 of the Side Basic.

Step 4. Move your right foot to the side while you complete up to ¼ turn counterclockwise between this step and step 5.

Step 5. Place your left foot behind your right foot.

Step 6. Replace your weight forward into your right foot.

Movement Memo

Steps 4 to 9 are the Fifth Position. You may repeat this section if desired. Then you would simply continue with step 10.

Step 7. Move your left foot to the side while releasing your right hand from your partner's back. Complete a ½ turn clockwise between this step and step 8.

Step 8. Place your right foot behind your left foot.

Step 9. Replace your weight forward to your left foot.

Steps 10 to 12. Dance steps 4 to 6 of the Side Basic, making up to ¼ turn counterclockwise to regain closed position.

Step 4 Notice Hand Position for Lead.

Step 5.

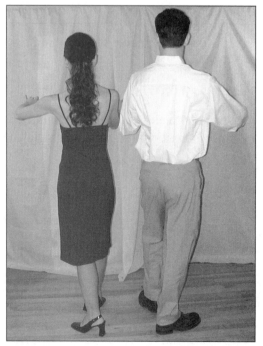

Step 8.

Step 9.

Technique

Technique (General for Both): Always observe my rule of "step then turn" that you will find explained in Chapter 13 about ballroom dance technique and partnering called "The Interactions of the Dance Couple." This rule must be observed each time either you or your partner commences to rotate or turn!

Lady's Part: Fifth Position

The lady's details for Fifth Position follow:

Steps 1 to 3. Dance steps 1 to 3 of the Side Basic in closed position.

Step 4. Move your left foot to the side, making up to $\frac{1}{4}$ turn clockwise between this step and step 5.

Step 5. Place your right foot behind your left foot.

Step 6. Replace your weight forward to your left foot.

Step 7. Move your right foot to the side while releasing your left hand from your partner's right arm. Rotate up to $\frac{1}{2}$ turn counterclockwise between this and step 8.

Step 8. Place your left foot behind your right foot.

Step 9. Replace your weight forward to your right foot.

Steps 10 to 12. Dance steps 4 to 6 of the Side Basic, regaining closed position while you turn $\frac{1}{4}$ clockwise between these steps.

Box Step Turning

This step uses the same box step that you learned during the Quickstart to Social Dance Program©. Please use the standard rhythm and footwork. The step is danced in closed position.

Gentleman's Part: Box Step Turning

Details for the gentleman's Box Step Turning follow:

Step 1. Move forward on your left foot, completing up to $\frac{1}{4}$ turn counterclockwise between this step and step 3.

Step 2. Move your right foot to the side.

Step 3. Close your left foot to your right foot.

Step 4. Take a small step back on your right foot, turning up to $\frac{1}{4}$ turn counterclockwise between this step and step 6.

Step 5. Move your left foot to the side.

Step 6. Close your right foot to your left foot, ending in closed position. This figure may be repeated as often as you desire.

Technique

Technique (General for Both): In Latin American dancing, you should use a position of turnout with your feet and legs. Turnout is created by rotating your upper thighs approximately $\frac{1}{8}$ of a turn away from your center (the middle of your body). This position opens up your pelvis and creates greater flexibility. Because of the turnout, when you step back in a Latin American dance, the inside edge of the big toe should strike the floor before the inside edge of the ball of the foot. This will give you, the dancer, much greater control with your timing on any back step.

Step 1 Forward movement is completed prior to rotation.

Step 1 concludes with lead from his body, i.e., "Step then Turn."

Step 4 Man leads from inside of turn.

Lady's Part: Box Step Turning

Details for the lady's Box Step Turning follow:

Step 1. Take a small step back on your right foot, completing up to ¼ turn counterclockwise between this and step 3.

Step 2. Move your left foot to the side.

Step 3. Close your right foot to your left foot.

Step 4. Move forward to your left foot, completing up to ¼ turn counterclockwise between this step and step 6.

Step 5. Move your right foot to the side.

Step 6. Close your left foot to your right foot, finishing in closed position.

Cross Body Lead

In addition to being a beautiful figure, the Cross Body Lead is one of the most functional and important dance figures in Latin American dancing. This figure is common to several dances and serves as a wonderful transitional movement connecting many other figure types. Please dance this in your standard rhythm using your standard footwork.

Gentleman's Part: Cross Body Lead

Details for the gentleman's Cross Body Lead follow:

Step 1. Move forward to your left foot.

Step 2. Move your right foot to the side.

Step 3. Close your left foot to your right foot.

Step 4. Move backward to your right foot, completing up to ¼ turn counterclockwise between this step and step 6. On step 4, begin to lead your partner to walk forward in front of your body while you are completing your rotation through step 6.

Step 5. Move your left foot to the side.

Step 6. Close your right foot to your left foot to finish in closed position. You must lead the lady to pivot on this step and take care to complete the pivot prior to any following step.

As an option, you may turn the first three steps of any Cross Body Lead up to ¼ counterclockwise.

Step 4.

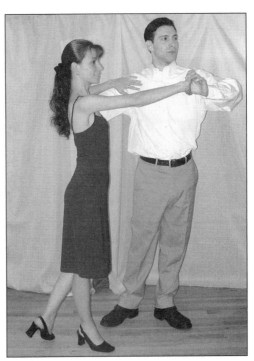

Step 5.

Step 6 Lady completes forward step.

Step 6 Lady pivots ½ turn at step's conclusion.

Technique
Technique (General for Both): Again, I must emphasize to please observe the rule of "step, then turn"! There are many foot swivels in this and subsequent figures. You may find the following advice helpful. Footwork for the Rumba begins with the ball of the foot (the metatarsal). While the weight remains on the ball, the rest of the foot is lowered in a very controlled manner. Be careful not to just drop into the heel. The action of swiveling on your foot occurs as your heel is lowering, and just to the point of grazing the floor, but before weight is taken into the whole foot. Virtually all rotation and dance begins with weight on the ball of the foot.

Lady's Part: Cross Body Lead

Details for the lady's Cross Body Lead follow:

Step 1. Move backward on your right foot.

Step 2. Move your left foot to the side.

Step 3. Close your right foot to your left foot.

Step 4. Move forward on your left foot.

Step 5. Move forward on your right foot.

Step 6. Move forward on your left foot pivoting counterclockwise up to $\frac{1}{2}$ rotation on this step. It is important that you are lead to and then complete the pivot prior to any following weight changes.

Outside Partner

Outside Partner position is a closed position, except the dancers are no longer in the standard position, or "in line." The leader's right foot moves forward to the outside of their partner's right foot. This is called "right outside partner." The reciprocal on the left is called "left outside partner." Please use the standard rhythm and footwork.

Gentleman's Part: Outside Partner

Details for the gentleman's Outside Partner follow:

Steps 1 to 6. Dance steps 1 to 6 of the Cross Body Lead, using up to $\frac{1}{4}$ rotation counterclockwise between step 1 and step 6.

Step 7. Step to the side, with your left foot making a $\frac{1}{8}$ turn counterclockwise between this step and step 8.

Step 8. Move forward on your right foot to right outside partner position (OP).

Step 9. Replace your weight back to your left foot while turning $\frac{1}{4}$ clockwise between this step and step 10.

Step 10. Move your right foot to the side.

Step 11. Move forward on your left foot to left outside partner position.

Step 12. Replace your weight back to your right foot, turning $\frac{1}{4}$ counterclockwise between this step and step 13.

Step 13. Move your left foot to the side.

Step 14. Move forward on your right foot to right OP.

Step 15. Replace your weight back to the left foot.

Step 16. Move backward to your right foot, turning ⅛ counterclockwise between this step and step 17.

Step 17. Move your left foot to the side.

Step 18. Close your right foot to your left foot, ending in closed position.

Step 7.

Step 8.

Step 10.

Step 11.

Lady's Part: Outside Partner

Details for the lady's Outside Partner follow:

Steps 1 to 6. Dance steps 1 to 6 of the Cross Body Lead, using up to $\frac{1}{4}$ rotation counterclockwise on step 6.

Step 7. Move your right foot to the side, using up to $\frac{1}{8}$ turn counterclockwise between this step and step 8.

Step 8. Move back to your left foot.

Step 9. Replace your weight forward to your right foot, turning up to $\frac{1}{4}$ clockwise on this step and step 10.

Step 10. Move your left foot to the side.

Step 11. Move back to your right foot.

Step 12. Replace your weight forward to your left foot, turning $\frac{1}{4}$ counterclockwise between this step and step 13.

Step 13. Move your right foot to the side.

Step 14. Move back to your left foot.

Step 15. Replace your weight forward to your right foot.

Step 16. Move forward to your left foot, turning $\frac{1}{8}$ counterclockwise between this step and step 17.

Step 17. Move your right foot to the side.

Step 18. Close your left foot to your right foot, ending in closed position.

Choreographed Routine: Rumba Routine

Try this beautifully sensual Rumba routine to be danced in the following sequence:

- ◆ Side Basic: steps 1 to 6.
- ◆ Fifth Position: steps 1 to 12.
- ◆ Box Step Turning: steps 1 to 6.
- ◆ Cross Body Lead: steps 1 to 6, two times (repeat).
- ◆ Outside Partner: steps 1 to 18.
- ◆ Repeat routine.

This routine is 72 beats of music, so dividing by Rumba's 4 beats per measure, this routine equals 18 measures of music. Your CD practice song is 32 measures of music per minute, so as a percentage, this routine will take 56 percent of a minute, or just around 34 seconds to the repeat.

The Least You Need to Know

- ◆ All the figures represented in this book use standard Rumba rhythm and footwork.
- ◆ The bending and straightening of the knees, not wiggling the hips, is what creates "hip action."
- ◆ Swiveling your feet happens after all your weight is on the ball of the foot, and before the foot is flat on the floor.
- ◆ You may extend the duration of your routine by repeating any of the figures in a row prior to the repeat.

Chapter 20

Merengue

In This Chapter

◆ Everyone loves Merengue

◆ The cruiseship dance

◆ Eight beats, eight steps, and you're dancin'

◆ Keep it small

The Merengue is a very important and essential Latin American dance. The technique used in its sideways movement is the basic form for most other Latin dances. It is the national dance and music of the Dominican Republic. It is quite possible that at any given moment on a Friday or Saturday evening, there are more people dancing Merengue in any Latin American country or community throughout the world than any other dance! The Dominicans like their Merengue hot and fast. Their neighbors in Haiti like their Merengue much slower, reflecting the Haitian reggae sound in their music. Both tempos are extremely popular in North America.

If you plan to travel by cruiseship or visit a tropical paradise in the Caribbean, you need to learn Merengue! Many refer to the Merengue as "the cruise dance," because on a ship it is taught by day and danced by night. If you ever plan to frequent a Latino nightspot in the USA, you need to learn Merengue! This will guarantee that you can spend most of the night on the dance floor rather than on the sidelines. The good news is that the Merengue is the easiest of the Latin American dances and uses very simple patterns. If you have completed Chapter 19, "Rumba," you are only minutes away from enjoying this island dance.

Like the Rumba, the alignment of Merengue is based on the couple's position relative to each other rather than some spot in the room. You must learn to execute this dance in the smallest of spaces, because the dance floor will be packed like sardines! Please maintain the normal $^4/_4$ timing of the Merengue using the rhythm of all Quicks. The beat value of a Quick is one beat. A typical figure in Merengue is eight steps—this matches the eight-beat phrasing of the dance. Each step equals one beat of music. You will maintain this rhythm throughout all of the Merengue figures presented in this book. The footwork throughout each figure is ball, flat.

Basic to Side

This dance figure will begin in closed position. Please use the standard footwork and rhythm. Accent beats 1 and 5.

Gentleman's Part: Basic to Side

Details for the gentleman's Basic to Side follow:

Step 1. Move your left foot to the side, medium-size step.

Step 2. Close your right foot to your left foot.

Step 3. Move your left foot to the side, small step.

Step 4. Close your right foot to your left foot.

Steps 5 to 8. Repeat steps 1 to 4, ending in closed position.

This figure may curve clockwise or counterclockwise in a circle or semicircle.

Technique

Technique (General for Both): This is used for any sidestep and will be the same for all figures in the Merengue. As you take a side step, endeavor to touch the inside edge of your foot to the floor first. As you take weight into the ball of the foot, you will feel a rolling action beginning at the outside edge and moving across the bottom of your foot. Be careful not to roll to the outside edge of the foot. Stop "rolling" when your foot is flat and all your body weight covers all of the foot. This action will allow for rhythmic body movement, particularly through the hips. Stepping too quickly on the whole foot during a side step will cause your body to finish the weight change too quickly and too abruptly.

Draw your feet toward and under your body with slight pressure on the floor. Use your thigh to draw in your foot, not just your knee. Another helpful device for perfecting hip action is to divide your timing. In place of Quick, Quick; use "Quick and," "Quick and." The Quick represents $1/2$ of a beat. Use this to complete the leg action and weight change. The "and" represents $1/2$ a beat to allow your hip to settle while releasing the former foot from the floor. Imagine yourself standing outside an elevator impatiently settling your hip from one leg to another. Now try it. This physical analogy usually works well to help you get the feeling.

The body and leg action of the Merengue between any side and closing step is as follows: Place your heels and ankles closer together than your toes to form a V. As you release your heels from the floor, the inside of your big toes will remain in contact with the dance floor. As you lift your thigh, your knee bends, and the heel of your foot will come off the floor, allowing your hip to settle backward. The knee of your lifted foot will cross slightly in front of the knee of your standing foot. This resulting action is called "knee veer." Once again, I use the analogy of standing in place impatiently while shifting weight from one foot to the other. Or—think Elvis! Using this technique, you will find it quite easy to accomplish the speed necessary for approaching the next count. Remember that on each step, your knees veer in and then straighten to normal position.

Step 1 Beginning Position.

Step 1 Ending Position.

Step 2.

Lady's Part: Basic to Side

Details for the lady's Basic to Side follow:

Step 1. Move your right foot to the side, medium size.

Step 2. Close your left foot to your right foot.

Step 3. Move your right foot to the side, small size.

Step 4. Close your left foot to your right foot.

Steps 5 to 8. Repeat steps 1 to 4, ending in closed position.

Nightclub Basic Left Turn

This dance figure will begin in closed position. Please use the standard footwork and rhythm. Accent beats 1 and 5.

This figure is particularly useful on congested dance floors or when the couple needs to turn very sharply.

Gentleman's Part: Nightclub Basic Left Turn

Details for the gentleman's Nightclub Basic Left Turn follow:

Step 1. Move your left foot to the side, small step.

Step 2. Close your right foot to your left foot.

Step 3. Dance with your left foot turned out, turning ¼ counterclockwise by crossing the left behind the right.

Step 4. Dance your right foot in place with body turn.

Steps 5 to 8. Repeat steps 1 to 4, ending in closed position.

Step 3.

Step 4.

Lady's Part: Nightclub Basic Left Turn

Details for the lady's Nightclub Basic Left Turn follow:

Step 1. Move your right foot to the side, small step.

Step 2. Close your left foot to your right foot.

Step 3. Move your right foot to the side, turning ¼ counterclockwise. Use turn out.

Step 4. Dance your left foot in place with body turn.

Steps 5 to 8. Repeat steps 3 and 4 twice, ending in closed position.

> **Bet You Didn't Know**
>
> Throughout this Latin and Rhythm section of the book I will prefix a step title with "Nightclub." It is very important for beginners or novices to learn that in a nightclub you are often faced with "sardine can"–like surroundings. The ability to dance "tall and small" is vital to your comfort and movement. "Tall and small" simply means that you will work extra hard to create lift in the area of the ribcage and below the hips. Lift (the carriage of the dancer's body) will always result in an increase of foot pressure on the dance floor. Greater foot pressure from both partners makes step recognition, rhythm, and direction all much more apparent to each other! Additionally, keeping it "small" means greater comfort for both you and your partner, as well as your neighboring dancers. In this case, "less is much more"!

Merengue Box Step

Many who have studied or grown up with Latin American dancing are unaware of the terrific step pattern in the Merengue! The Merengue Box Step is a wonderful addition to your repertoire in place of the monotony of repeated side steps. I find this step terrific and full of "attitude," when the turns are sharp and the size of the steps are small!

Gentleman's Part: Merengue Box Step

Details for the gentleman's Merengue Box Step follow:

Steps 1 to 6. Refer to the "Box Step Turning" section in Chapter 19. These six steps may or may not turn.

Step 7. Dance your left foot in place. This step may also turn ¼ counterclockwise by crossing the left behind the right, toe to heel.

Step 8. Dance your right foot in place, finishing in closed position.

Step 7.

Step 8.

Lady's Part: Merengue Box Step

Details for the lady's Merengue Box Step follow:

Steps 1 to 6. Refer to the "Box Step Turning" section in Chapter 19. These six steps may or may not turn.

Step 7. Dance your right foot in place. This step may also turn ¼ counterclockwise by crossing your right in front of the left.

Step 8. Dance your left foot in place, finishing in closed position.

Side Breaks

This dance figure will begin in closed position. Please use the standard rhythm and footwork. Use the similar technique found in the former Merengue figures.

Gentleman's Part: Side Breaks

Details for the gentleman's Side Breaks follow:

Step 1. Take a step side with your left foot.

Step 2. Replace your weight side on your right foot.

Step 3. Close your left foot to your right foot.

Step 4. Take a step side with your right foot.

Step 5. Replace your weight side on your left foot.

Step 6. Close your right foot to your left foot.

Step 7. Take a small step side with your left foot.

Step 8. Replace your weight side on your right foot, ending in closed position. This is more likely to be danced in-place.

Step 1.

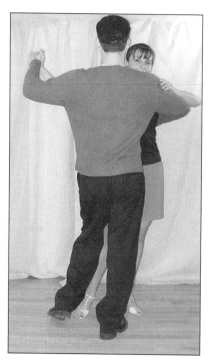

Step 2.

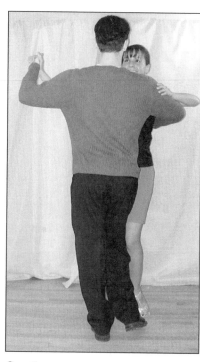

Step 3.

Bet You Didn't Know

Steps 1 to 6 of the Side Breaks are among the most popular dance figures in Latin American dancing. They are also termed Second Position Breaks because the dancer achieves Second Position on steps 1 and 4. Please see the interpretation of the five dance positions presented in the style of a Dance Master drawing in Chapter 1, "Past Ballroom Dancing Expressions: From the Renaissance to the Age of Reform." A more affectionate name for this pattern is the Spanish word for cockroaches: Cucarachas. I'll leave to your imagination as to why! Steps 1 to 6 are danced in the Salsa, Mambo, and Rumba to the rhythm of Quick, Quick, Slow in Merengue is danced with all Quicks.

Lady's Part: Side Breaks

Details for the lady's Side Breaks follow:

Step 1. Take a step side on your right foot.

Step 2. Replace your weight side on your left foot.

Step 3. Close your right foot to your left foot.

Step 4. Take a step side on your left foot.

Step 5. Replace your weight side on your right foot.

Step 6. Close your left foot to your right foot.

Step 7. Take a small step side on your right foot.

Step 8. Replace your weight side on your left foot, ending in closed position. This is more likely to be danced in place.

Arm Slide

This dance figure will begin in closed position. Please use the standard rhythm and footwork. The partners separate from each other according to the space they have available.

Technique
Technique (Gentleman Step 2): On step 2, you change to double handholds by placing your hands under her arms and sliding down from the shoulders to hands while stepping away from each other to step 4. The arms will be extended by this point and begin to lower at the conclusion of step 4. Regain closed position by step 8 unless repeating. If space permits, the arms may be circled from your sides up and down. This figure may be further divided by taking even smaller steps using eight back and eight forward.

Gentleman's Part: Arm Slide

Details for the gentleman's Arm Slide follow:

Step 1. Step back on your left with a small step.

Step 2. Step back on your right with a small step.

Steps 3 and 4. Repeat steps 1 and 2.

Step 5. Step forward on your left with a small step.

Step 6. Step forward on your right with a small step.

Steps 7 and 8. Repeat steps 5 and 6.

Step 1.

Step 2.

Step 3.

Lady's Part: Arm Slide

Details for the lady's Arm Slide follow:

Step 1. Step back on your right with a small step.

Step 2. Step back on your left with a small step.

Steps 3 and 4. Repeat steps 1 and 2.

Step 5. Step forward on your right with a small step.

Step 6. Step forward on your left with a small step.

Steps 7 and 8. Repeat steps 5 and 6.

You will retain arm and hand contact with slight pressure.

Practice Routine: Merengue Routine

Many of the most popular Merengues include two popular phrases in their introductory lyrics. First, "Merengue, Merengue," which is a call to the dance itself and second "baile, baile," which means to dance in Spanish or affectionately "get up off your seat and get out on the floor!" So here we go .... Merengue, Merengue baile, baile in the following sequence:

- Basic to Side: steps 1 to 8, two times, curving and straight.
- Box Step: steps 1 to 8, two times with turn.
- Side Breaks: steps 1 to 8, two times.
- Nightclub Basic Left Turn: steps 1 to 8, two times.
- Arm Slide: steps 1 to 8, two times.
- Repeat routine.

This routine is 80 beats of music, so dividing by Merengue's 4 beats per measure, you find this routine equals 20 measures of music. Your CD practice song is 29 measures of music per minute, so as a percentage, this routine will take 69 percent of a minute, or just over 41 seconds to repeat.

The Least You Need to Know

- Use a rolling action of the feet on all side steps in the Merengue.
- The eight beats of Merengue are all danced as Quicks.
- Most Merengue figures can be curved, danced in a semicircle or full circle.
- Practice dancing Merengue in very small spaces.

Chapter 21

Samba

In This Chapter

◆ African rhythms South American style

◆ Stay or move—Samba has it all

◆ Flex your knees and feel the bounce

◆ Keep on ticking

The Samba is a Brazilian dance with strong roots in African rhythms. The atmosphere evoked by Samba music is always festive, somewhat primal, and often quite provocative. During the festival period of Carnival, the country of Brazil celebrates throughout the streets of Rio de Janeiro displaying their native dance with pure joy, high energy, and extraordinary color!

Once you begin to master some of the characteristics of Samba, it will quickly become one of your favorite dances. Everyone finds something wonderful to *feel* about his or her Samba. The reason is simple: Samba uses characteristics that exist in every popular dance. It can be progressive like a Waltz and titillating like the Mambo, and at the same time, it possesses the party and bounce like the Swing. I hope you had a good night's sleep, because we are about to expend a lot of energy. To a dancer this means lots of fun!

The alignments of the dance figures in the Samba may be based on the couple's position relative to each other or a place in the room. Samba is both a progressive and a stationary dance. As a result, I will describe each alignment according to the previous position or by stating the preferable alignment of the couple. Please maintain the normal $^2/_4$ timing of the Samba and use the rhythm of Quick (1), Quick (a), Slow (2). The beat value of a Slow is 1, the beat value for the first Quick is $^1/_4$ of a beat, and the second Quick is $^3/_4$ of a beat. Your timing for each measure of music will be: count 1 (Quick), count -a- (Quick), count 2 (Slow). The first beat in a measure of Samba is syncopated. *Syncopated* means that a beat of music has been divided or fractionalized into two increments. You will maintain this rhythm throughout all of the Samba figures presented in this book.

The footwork throughout each Samba figure will be ball, flat (first weight change); ball (second weight change); ball, flat, ball (third weight change). The footwork for the third weight change is always used when continuing with another action. If you were stopping, there would be no need to use the second "ball" of the foot action. I will describe any additional techniques concerning footwork as we proceed.

Forward and Back Basic

Before you begin Samba, it is advisable to warm up your muscles. Try moving up and down rhythmically by bending and almost straightening both of your knees simultaneously using Samba music (as described in Chapter 7, "Music and More Music: About the Music on Your CD"). This is similar to the exercise described in Chapter 5, "Lifestyles Improve Socially, Psychologically, and Physically," in the section "Let's Get Physical … with Nonmovement Activity." I also describe a side-to-side exercise in Chapter 10, "The Quickstart Program© Progressive Movements," that will help you develop sideways energy with your partner. Use the following technique to develop the rhythmic bounce both with the "ball change" and without.

Technique

Technique (General for Both): You will dance the bounce action by stepping forward or back using the footwork of ball, flat with both knees flexed on count 1. Both of your knees will straighten slightly before flexing once more as your other foot closes very rapidly with firm pressure on just the ball of your foot. To be successful, this movement requires physicality. Be sure to keep your energy in the center of your quadriceps, hamstrings, and calves. It is much better to feel rise at the top of the hamstrings generating force up into your hips. I caution you to use the center of these muscles and *not* your ankles to create the lift or the bounce action!

The straightening of your knees occurs on the -a- count. You will then replace your weight by straightening both knees slightly before flexing once more to finish the weight transfer on beat 2. Dancers, in any dance form, often call these last two movements or weight changes a *ball change*.

Whether or not there is an -a- count stated in writing, the dancer must return to the ball of the foot and rise on either the -a- counts or between whole counts of music. This would occur for you between count 1 and count 2.

This method briefly lifts the entire torso between the stated beats. This is the moment when the free foot (the foot without weight) is placed to the next position. The duration of any -a- count can be defined as the least amount of time it takes to take your foot off the floor and transfer weight. When you are dancing the -a- count, your weight will momentarily be evenly dispersed between your feet. Strong control of your abdominal area is vital in order to be quick enough to enjoy success at this dance! The straightening and flexing of both your knees will cause your firm upper body and arm frame to rise and fall repeatedly.

Unlike the Rumba, where your supporting leg fully straightens while the nonsupporting leg releases its energy (the *peddling* action), the Samba finishes on the whole count 2 with both knees flexed. The knees will be very close together, with knee veer action during the first two Quicks—the counts of 1 -a-. The pelvis will actively tilt forward and back in what we call a *ticking action*. The ticking is generated by simple contractions of your abdominal wall. These characteristics of Samba give the dance a wonderful combination of swaying hips and rhythmic bounce.

I realize that this technique is complex, so it will take practice. As you continue with each of the dance figures, begin the choreography by first adding the bounce, and add the actions of the pelvis and abdomen later.

This dance figure will begin in closed position. Please use the standard footwork and rhythm. Your beginning alignment results from the finishing position of the previous figure.

Gentleman's Part: Forward and Back Basic

Details for the gentleman's Forward and Back Basic follow:

Step 1. Move forward on your left foot, turning up to $^1/_8$ counterclockwise between this step and step 3.

Step 2. Close your right foot to your left foot.

Step 3. Dance in place on your left foot.

Step 4. Move backward on your right foot, turning up to $^1/_8$ counterclockwise between this and step 6.

Step 5. Close your left foot to your right foot.

Step 6. Dance in place on your right foot, ending in closed position.

This figure may also be danced in double or single handholds. It is not necessary to use the rotation as described.

Step 1.

Step 2.

Step 3.

Lady's Part: Forward and Back Basic

Details for the lady's Forward and Back Basic follow:

Step 1. Move backward to your right foot, turning up to $^1/_8$ counterclockwise between this step and step 3.

Step 2. Close your left foot to your right foot.

Step 3. Dance in place on your right foot.

Step 4. Move forward to your left foot, turning up to $^1/_8$ counterclockwise between this step and step 6.

Step 5. Close your right foot to your left foot.

Step 6. Dance in place on your left foot.

CAUTION

Ballroom Bloopers

This is not the dance for you if you have any trouble with your knees. Like any physical activity that is new or untested, you should consult your physician if any of the techniques in this book include areas of your body that you have had problems with in the past! The Samba is also quite aerobic and requires you to get into shape to dance it for several minutes—so be smart and take it in small doses. If you are one of my wonderful "senior" students and want to experience some of the pure joy of this dance, I recommend that you keep your steps very small and flatten out or eliminate the bounce action. Keep it very understated and just enjoy yourself.

Side-to-Side Basic

This dance figure will begin in closed position. Please use the standard footwork and rhythm. Your beginning alignment results from your finishing position of the previous figure.

Gentleman's Part: Side-to-Side Basic

Details for the gentleman's Side-to-Side Basic follow:

Step 1. Move your left foot to the side, allowing a slight turn counterclockwise to occur between this step and step 6. This slight turn will make the figure more comfortable.

Step 2. Close your right foot to your left foot.

Step 3. Dance in place on your left foot.

Step 4. Move your right foot to the side.

Step 5. Close your left foot to your right foot.

Step 6. Dance in place on your right foot, finishing in closed position. This figure may also be danced in double or single handholds.

Step 1.

Step 2.

Step 3.

Lady's Part: Side-to-Side Basic

Details for the lady's Side-to-Side Basic follow:

Step 1. Move your right foot to the side, allowing a slight turn counterclockwise to occur between this step and step 6. This slight turn will make the figure more comfortable.

Step 2. Close your left foot to your right foot.

Step 3. Dance in place on your right foot.

Step 4. Move your left foot to the side.

Step 5. Close your right foot to your left foot.

Step 6. Dance in place on your left foot.

> **Technique**
>
> **Technique (General for Both):** It is advisable to make contact with the inside edge of your toe when initiating any side step. This allows the rolling action of the foot that I discussed in Chapter 19, "Rumba," for sidesteps for the Rumba.

Fifth Position

This dance figure will begin in closed position. Please use the standard footwork and rhythm. The beginning alignment is best when the gentleman is facing the wall.

Gentleman's Part: Fifth Position

Details for the gentleman's Fifth Position follow:

Step 1. Move your left foot to the side.

Step 2. Place your right foot behind your left foot.

Step 3. Dance in place on your left foot.

Step 4. Move your right foot to the side.

Step 5. Place your left foot behind your right foot.

Step 6. Dance in place on your right foot, ending in closed position.

This figure may also be danced in double or single handholds with slight rotation.

> **Technique**
>
> **Technique (Steps 2 and 3 for Both):** Your foot should be placed directly behind your supporting foot. Position the toe of the moving foot just behind the heel of the supporting foot. Use a "turned out" position, as I described in the Rumba. This will add to your flexibility and make it easier to generate the power necessary to support your body while on the ball of your foot.

Step 1.   *Step 2.*   *Step 3.*

Lady's Part: Fifth Position

Details for the lady's Fifth Position follow:

Step 1. Move your right foot to the side.

Step 2. Place your left foot behind your right foot.

Step 3. Dance in place on your right foot.

Step 4. Move your left foot to the side.

Step 5. Place your right foot behind your left foot.

Step 6. Dance in place on your left foot.

The Box

This dance figure will begin in closed position. Please use the standard footwork and rhythm. Your beginning alignment results from your finishing position of the previous figure.

Gentleman's Part: The Box

Details for the gentleman's The Box follow:

Step 1. Move forward on your left foot, turning up to $\frac{1}{4}$ counterclockwise between this step and step 3.

Step 2. Move your right foot to the side.

Step 3. Close your left foot to your right foot.

Step 4. Move backward on your right foot, turning up to $\frac{1}{4}$ counterclockwise between this step and step 6.

Step 5. Move your left foot to the side.

Step 6. Close your right foot to your left foot, ending in closed position.

This figure may be danced in double or single handholds. The rotation is optional.

Step 1.   *Step 2.*   *Step 3.*

Lady's Part: The Box

Details for the lady's The Box follow:

Step 1. Move backward on your right foot, turning up to ¹/₄ counterclockwise between this step and step 3.

Step 2. Move your left foot to the side.

Step 3. Close your right foot to your left foot.

Step 4. Move forward on your left foot, turning up to ¹/₄ counterclockwise between this step and step 6.

Step 5. Move your right foot to the side.

Step 6. Close your left foot to your right foot, ending in closed position.

Extended Box

This dance figure will begin in closed position. Please use the standard footwork, and your rhythm is as follows: 1a2, a3, a4, 5a6, a7, a8—for a total of four measures or eight beats. Your beginning alignment is determined from your finishing position of the previous figure.

Gentleman's Part: Extended Box

Details for the gentleman's Extended Box follow:

Step 1. Move forward on your left foot, turning up to ¹/₄ counterclockwise between this step and step 7.

Step 2. Move your right foot to the side.

Step 3. Close your left foot to your right foot.

Steps 4 to 7. Repeat steps 2 and 3 twice.

Step 8. Move backward on your right foot, turning up to ¼ counterclockwise between this step and step 14.

Step 9. Move your left foot to the side.

Step 10. Close your right foot to your left foot.

Steps 11 to 14. Repeat steps 9 and 10 twice, ending in closed position.

The rotation is optional. The Extended Box may sway left on steps 2 to 7 and then sway right on steps 9 to 14.

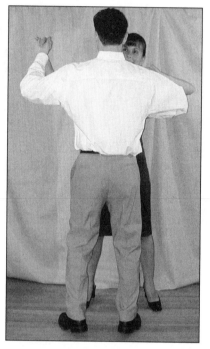

Step 4 Curving chassé.

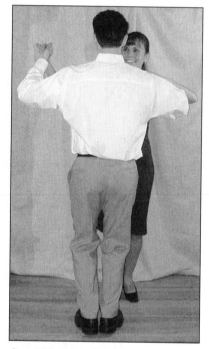

Step 5 Curving chassé.

Step 6 Curving chassé.

Step 7 Curving chassé.

Technique

Technique (General for Both): To maintain better control during steps 2 to 7 and 9 to 14, you should retain toe pressure with the floor on all of the closing steps. This technique will lend itself to a much smoother rise and fall and assist you in maintaining the compression in your upper legs rather than your ankles. This step is sometimes called a *continuous chassé*. Like all chassés described in this book, the closing action must be accomplished as quickly as possible to allow for continuity in time with your music.

The amount of curve can be increased from $1/4$ turn to almost $1/2$ on steps 2 to 7 and 9 to 14. This is possible when the leader employs the technique of inside and outside of curve—elongating his side steps slightly while increasing his amount of turn on steps 2 to 7 and then diminishing his side steps while he lets his partner travel on the outside of the curve around him.

Lady's Part: Extended Box

Details for the lady's Extended Box follow:

Step 1. Move backward on your right foot, turning up to $1/4$ counterclockwise between this step and step 7.

Step 2. Move your left foot to the side.

Step 3. Close your right foot to your left foot.

Steps 4 to 7. Repeat steps 2 and 3 twice.

Step 8. Move forward on your left foot, turning up to $1/4$ counterclockwise between this step and step 14.

Step 9. Move your right foot to the side.

Step 10. Close your left foot to your right foot.

Steps 11 to 14. Repeat steps 9 and 10 twice, ending in closed position.

Practice Routine: Samba Routine

A touch of Carnival is found in this high-energy Samba routine to be danced in the following sequence:

- Forward and Back Basic: steps 1 to 6 five times, allowing for counterclockwise rotation of up to $1/8$ turn. Start this figure facing LOD, finish almost facing the wall.
- Side-to-Side Basic: steps 1 to 6 two times, allowing for a slight turn counterclockwise to end facing the wall.
- Fifth Position: steps 1 to 6, two times, facing wall.
- The Box: steps 1 to 6, three times, to end backing LOD.
- Extended Box: steps 1 to 14, to end facing LOD.
- Repeat routine.

This routine is 54 beats of music, so dividing by Samba's 2 beats per measure, this routine equals 27 measures of music. Your CD practice song is 50 measures of music per minute. So as a percentage, this routine will take just over 54 percent of a minute, or just over 32 seconds to repeat.

Chapter 22

Cha-Cha

In This Chapter

◆ Golden Oldies to Top 40

◆ 2—3—Cha-Cha-Cha

◆ Cha-Cha is "jazz hot"

◆ Mix and match to double the fun

Cha-Cha enjoys a distinction as one of the most dominant "pop" rhythms of the last 30 to 40 years. Its closest rivals for rhythm supremacy would be the Swing and slow rhythm ballads. Just to reiterate what I covered in the history of dance, some of the largest-selling hits of all time have used this scintillating rhythm. You will have great fun listening to the radio or even going through your own musical archives and identifying how many of your favorite tunes are in Cha-Cha rhythm. What is even better is now you will know how to dance to them!

Cha-Cha lends itself to every dance nuance that finds itself in vogue! Steps like Little Eva's loco-motion, Jackson's moonwalk, Roger Rabbit, or Madonna's vogue are added to Cha-Cha's jazz-like dance versatility. Movements of ribcage and shoulder isolations, along with lots of cut rhythm steps work right into this playful, sexy Latin rhythm!

As in the Rumba, alignment of the dance figures in the Cha-Cha are based on the couple's position relative to each other and not on a place in the room. Please maintain the normal ⁴/₄ timing of the Cha-Cha and use the rhythm of Slow, Slow, Slow, Quick, Quick. The beat value of a Slow is 1, and the beat value for a Quick is ¹/₂. Your timing for each measure of music will be count one (Slow), count two (Slow), three (Slow), four (Quick), *and* (Quick). The fourth beat in a measure of Cha-Cha is syncopated. Syncopated means that a beat of music has been cut or fractionalized into two increments. Each of these increments has a time value of ¹/₂ beat of music. You will maintain this rhythm throughout all of the Cha-Cha figures presented in this book. The footwork throughout each Cha-Cha figure will be ball, flat. I will describe any additional techniques concerning footwork as we proceed.

Basic in Place—Nightclub Style

This dance figure will begin in close or closed Latin position. Please use the standard footwork and rhythm.

The major feature of this dance figure is its compact nature.

> **Bet You Didn't Know**
>
> The compact nature of this figure makes it absolutely perfect for dancing in the congested nightclub scenario. When teaching, I have often referred to this particular Cha-Cha step as using "salsa" styling. Salsa is a popular Latin nightclub dance that has its choreographic foundation in both Cha-Cha and Mambo. Using this compact form of Cha-Cha, along with many of the Mambo figures (also in compact form, which we will cover later), will allow you to dance the Salsa in its popular rhythm of Quick, Quick, Slow (like Rumba or Mambo) or the Cha-Cha Salsa rhythm (the same as the standard Cha-Cha rhythm). The Cha-Cha Salsa rhythm has been made particularly popular in the last couple of years! Check out Chapter 2, "Modern Ballroom Dancing Expressions: From 1900 to the Present," on modern expressions for examples.

Gentleman's Basic in Place

Details for the gentleman's Basic in Place follow:

Step 1. Move your left foot to the side.

Step 2. Backward to your right foot.

Step 3. Replace your weight forward to the left foot.

Step 4. Close your right foot to your left foot.

Step 5. Dance to your left foot in place.

Step 6. Dance to your right foot in place.

Technique

Technique (General for Both): Here is the essential technique for dancing any five weight changes or steps in the Cha-Cha Basic in Place using the nightclub style. The first step to the side is very small. This would be less than half the width of your torso. Steps 2 and 3, whether forward or back, are done exactly as described in the Rumba. They will be faster, because Cha-Cha is a faster tempo; however, the movement remains the same. The first three steps are one beat each, counted 1, 2, 3. Steps 4 and 5 are only $1/2$ beat each. The rhythm is expressed as Slow, Slow, Slow, Quick, Quick. I like to ask my students to say the rhythm out loud as they practice. When you reach count 4 *and* 1 for any pattern, say the following out loud: "Cha-Cha-Cha." Therefore, steps 6 to infinity would be counted out loud as follows: "Cha-Cha," 2, 3, "Cha-Cha-Cha," and so on. This will make life easier for you while dancing the Cha-Cha.

The body and leg action of the Cha-Cha-Cha (4 *and* 1) will be done as follows: Place your heels and ankles closer together than your toes to form a V. As you release your heels from the floor while doing the Cha-Cha-Cha, the balls of your feet will remain on the dance floor. As you lift your thigh, your knee bends and the heel of your foot will come off the floor, allowing your hip to settle backward. An effect of doing this will be to experience what is called "knee veer." The knee of the lifted foot will cross slightly in front of the knee of the standing foot. Once again, I use the analogy of standing in place impatiently while shifting your weight from one foot to the other. Or—think Elvis! You will find it quite easy to accomplish the speed necessary for this Cha-Cha-Cha if when saying each "Cha," your knees veer in and then straighten to normal position.

A side view of a solo dancer doing the Cha-Cha may resemble what you did as a child mimicking a locomotive. In fact, dancers call this "locomotion." The opposition arm and knee move ahead as the thigh rises up and down (for example, left arm with right leg). Locomotion can also be accompanied by ribcage isolation from side to side. Ribcage isolation does not effect the parallel alignment of the shoulders to the dance floor. This definitely takes practice, and for the time being should not be your priority—especially at the expense of losing balance!

Step 7. Move forward to your left foot taking a small step.

Step 8. Replace your weight back to your right foot.

Step 9. Close your left foot to your right foot.

Step 10. Dance to your right foot in place, ending in close or closed position.

Step 1 Count 1.

Step 2 Count 2.

Step 3 Count 3.

Step 4 Count 4.

Step 5 Count and.

Lady's Part: Basic in Place

Details for the lady's Basic in Place follow:

Step 1. Move your right foot to the side.

Step 2. Take a small step forward to your left foot.

Step 3. Replace your weight back to your right foot.

Step 4. Close your left foot to your right foot.

Step 5. Dance to your right foot in place.

Step 6. Dance to your left foot in place.

Step 7. Take a small step back to your right foot.

Step 8. Replace your weight forward to your left foot.

Step 9. Close your right foot to your left foot.

Step 10. Dance to your left foot in place, ending in close or closed position, apart, or in double handholds.

Cha-Cha Side Basic

This dance figure will begin in closed position. Please use the standard rhythm and footwork.

Gentleman's Cha-Cha Side Basic

Details for the gentleman's Cha-Cha Side Basic follow:

Step 1. Move your left foot to the side.

Step 2. Take a small step back on your right foot.

Step 3. Replace your weight forward to your left foot.

Steps 4 to 6. Dance your Cha-Cha Chassé, right, left, right.

Step 7. Take a small step forward on your left foot.

Step 8. Replace your weight back to your right foot.

Step 9. Move your left foot to the side.

Step 10. Close your right foot to your left foot.

Technique

Technique (General for Both): For all forward and backward steps, use the Rumba technique. Steps 4 to 6 are known as the Cha-Cha Chassé and are done by side stepping the size of half your torso.

The closing step of the Cha-Cha Chassé is quite possibly the fastest and most powerful dance step that exists! Close your foot as quickly as possible with the full pressure of your body weight added instantaneously. The least bit of hesitation will not allow you to keep up with the tempo of the Cha-Cha. You must accomplish the first side and close within one beat of music! Remember that your feet are in the V position, and you will continue to use knee veer throughout the Cha-Cha.

The second step to the side (which is step 1 again) allows you one beat of music to move and also prepare to either lead or follow the next step. The word Chassé in French means "to Chasé-Cha"—as in one foot chasing the other.

This figure can easily turn up to ¹/₄ counterclockwise during steps 1 to 10. As a leader, initiate the turn as you are stepping back on your right foot. You may also use a double handhold to replace closed position.

Step 4 Count 4.

Step 5 Count and.

Step 6 Count 1.

Lady's Part: Cha-Cha Side Basic

Details for the lady's Cha-Cha Side Basic follow:

Step 1. Move your right foot to the side.

Step 2. Take a small step forward on your left foot.

Step 3. Replace your weight back to your right foot.

Steps 4 to 6. Dance your Cha-Cha Chassé, left, right, left.

Step 7. Take a small step back on your right foot.

Step 8. Replace your weight forward to your left foot.

Step 9. Move your right foot to the side.

Step 10. Close your left foot to your right foot.

Progressive Cha-Cha Basic

This Cha-Cha figure, besides being a great deal of fun, is very versatile. You may begin this figure in closed position or in double handhold. Once you have begun to travel, the leader may release the handholds in apart or solo dance position using no hand contact. This is good training for visual leading.

Gentleman's Progressive Cha-Cha Basic

Details for the gentleman's Progressive Cha-Cha Basic follow:

Step 1. Move your left foot to the side.

Step 2. Take a small step back with your right foot.

Step 3. Replace your weight forward to your left foot.

Steps 4 to 6. Begin your running triple forward right, left, right.

Step 7. Take a small step forward on your left foot.

Step 8. Replace your weight back to your right foot.

Steps 9 to 11. Begin your running triple backward left, right, left.

Technique

Technique (General for Both): The forward, back, and replacement steps use exactly the same technique as the Rumba. Like the Side Basic it is best if you initiate rotation when stepping back on your right foot. This step can be danced in closed position but is more comfortable in open-facing position with double handhold. When releasing from double handhold to apart or solo position, it is advisable to complete the forward progression and release the handholds upon entering the back progression of the running triple. The running triple is also known as the *Progressive Chassé*.

Here are some important hints regarding the Progressive Chassé. First, use small steps! The size can vary between $1/2$ your foot length to a full foot length. You do not want to create interference with other couples on the dance floor. Second, large steps in Latin American dancing will have a tendency to negate your Cuban or hip motion. Lift your thighs to create a skimming action across the floor using locomotion rather than bouncing or shuffling. Maintain good vertical alignment of your torso and keep your eyes on your partner or on your horizon.

Steps 12 to 18. Repeat steps 2 to 8.

Step 19. Move your left foot to the side.

Step 20. Close your right foot to your left foot, ending in closed position.

Step 4 Count 4.

Step 5 Count and.

Step 6 Count 1.

Lady's Part: Progressive Cha-Cha Basic

Details for the lady's Progressive Cha-Cha Basic follow:

Step 1. Move your right foot to the side.

Step 2. Take a small step forward on your left foot.

Step 3. Replace your weight back to your right foot.

Steps 4 to 6. Begin your running triple backward left, right, left.

Step 7. Take a small step back on your right foot.

Step 8. Replace your weight forward to your left foot.

Steps 9 to 11. Begin your running triple forward right, left, right.

Steps 12 to 18. Repeat steps 2 to 8.

Step 19. Move your right foot to the side.

Step 20. Close your left foot to your right foot, ending in closed position.

Outside Partner

This dance figure will begin in closed position. Please use the standard rhythm and footwork.

Technique
Technique (Leading for Gentleman): Here is a simple step that has several variations. Using your standard Rumba leg action and Cha-Cha Chassé, you may release closed position and dance in double handholds, solo position, or alternating handholds (like a handshake). You may also create an Overturned Outside Partner by adding $1/8$ turn to the outside partner position and dancing steps 4 to 6 of the In-Place Basic.

Gentleman's Outside Partner

Details for the gentleman's Outside Partner follow:

Step 1. Move your left foot to the side, turning $1/8$ counterclockwise between this step and step 2.

Step 2. Place your right foot forward and across in left outside partner (OP) position.

Step 3. Replace your weight backward to your left foot, turning $1/8$ clockwise between this step and step 4.

Steps 4 to 6. Dance your side Chassé, right, left, right, turning $1/8$ clockwise between steps 6 and 7.

Step 7. Move forward and across on your left foot to right OP position (this is on your partner's left side).

Step 8. Replace your weight backward to your right foot, turning $1/8$ counterclockwise between this step and step 9.

Step 9. Move your left foot to the side.

Step 10. Close your right foot to your left foot, maintaining or regaining closed position. You may also finish in double handholds.

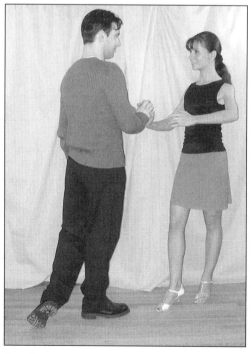

Step 2.

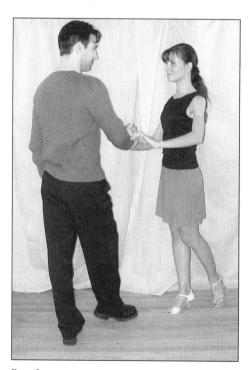

Step 3.

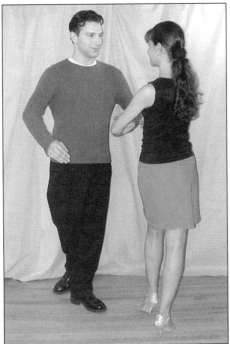

Step 7.

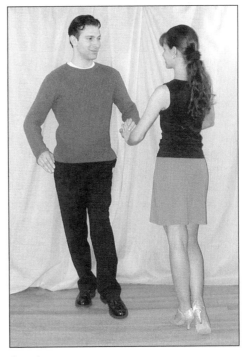

Step 8.

Lady's Part: Outside Partner

Details for the lady's Outside Partner follow:

Step 1. Move your right foot to the side, turning $\frac{1}{8}$ counterclockwise between this step and step 2.

Step 2. Take a small step back on your left foot.

Step 3. Replace your weight forward to your right foot, turning $\frac{1}{8}$ clockwise between this step and step 4.

Steps 4 to 6. Dance your side Chassé, left, right, left, turning $\frac{1}{8}$ clockwise between steps 6 and 7.

Step 7. Take a small step back on your right foot.

Step 8. Replace your weight forward to your left foot, turning $\frac{1}{8}$ counterclockwise between this step and step 9.

Step 9. Move your right foot to the side.

Step 10. Close your left foot to your right foot, ending in closed position.

Crossover Break with Spot Turn

This is certainly one of the most popular dance figures in the Cha-Cha. In this figure, the couple will turn 90 degrees from their closed position to a side-by-side position on both their left and right sides. The figure will conclude with what is known as a Spot or Walk Around Turn. This figure commences in closed position and is danced with the standard rhythm and footwork.

Technique

Technique (Leading for Gentleman): Your leads for the Crossover Break will be as follows. You will release your right hand from the lady's back after step 4, retaining your left-to-right handhold, to lead the first Crossover Break. At the conclusion of step 6 and to step 7, the couple will achieve left side-by-side position.

Between steps 9 and 10, you will switch to a right-to-left handhold to lead the second Crossover Break.

Between steps 14 and 15, you will switch back to the left-to-right handhold to lead the third Crossover Break.

Finally, as lead for the Spot turn, you will maintain your left-to-right handhold through step 19. Then on step 20, you will switch to a palm-to-palm handhold (your fingers pointing in the direction of the turn and the follower's pointing upward). Your left elbow and your partner's right elbow will point in the direction of the Spot turn. As a couple, you will achieve closed position between steps 25 and 26.

Gentleman's Crossover Break

Details for the gentleman's Crossover Break follow:

Step 1. Move your left foot to the side.

Step 2. Take a small step back with your right foot.

Step 3. Replace your weight forward to your left foot.

Steps 4 to 6. Dance your side Chassé, right, left, right, and turn $1/4$ clockwise on step 6. You will achieve left side-by-side position between steps 6 and 7.

Step 7. Take a small step forward on your left foot.

Step 8. Replace your weight back to your right foot, making a $1/4$ turn counterclockwise between this step and step 9.

Steps 9 to 11. Dance your side Chassé, left, right, left, turning $1/4$ counterclockwise on step 11. You will achieve right side-by-side position between steps 11 and 12.

Step 12. Take a small step forward on your right foot.

Step 13. Replace your weight back to your left foot, turning $1/4$ clockwise between this step and step 14.

Steps 14 to 16. Dance your side Chassé, right, left, right, turning $1/4$ clockwise on step 16. You will achieve left side-by-side position between this step and step 17.

Step 17. Take a small step forward on your left foot.

Step 18. Replace your weight back to your right foot, turning $1/4$ counterclockwise between this step and step 19.

Steps 19 to 21. Dance your side Chassé, left, right, left, commencing to turn counterclockwise.

Step 22. Place your right foot forward and across your left foot, turning $5/8$ counterclockwise between steps 22 and 23.

Step 23. Replace your weight forward to your left foot, continuing to turn $1/4$ counterclockwise on this step.

Steps 24 to 26. Dance your side Chassé, right, left, right, completing $1/8$ turn counterclockwise on the steps to end in closed position.

Step 27. Move forward to your left foot.

Step 28. Replace your weight back to your right foot.

Step 29. Move your left foot to the side.

Step 30. Close your right foot to your left foot.

Step 7.

Step 12.

Leading to Spot Turn.

Step 22.

Step 23.

Technique

Technique (General for Both): At this point, it is very important for both you and your partner to create what I call *foot swivel*. This is a twisting action of the foot while it remains on the floor. This means allowing your supporting foot to rotate. It becomes very difficult to turn unless this happens. In this case, foot swivel will occur on step 21, which includes the leader's left foot and the follower's right foot. Attempting this without foot swivel would be like trying to open a door without allowing the hinges to rotate. You may use a degree of foot swivel on every rotation! Use your hips and ribcage to generate the rotation of your body and your foot swivel. Beginners often fail with rotation because they attempt to create the turn with their legs and feet by "tossing," them across their body. Do not get caught in this optical illusion. Remember always that dancing is all about the use of the body.

Lady's Part: Crossover Break

Details for the lady's Crossover Break follow:

Step 1. Move your right foot to the side.

Step 2. Take a small step forward with your left foot.

Step 3. Replace your weight back to your right foot.

Steps 4 to 6. Dance your side Chassé, left, right, left, and turn $^1/_4$ counterclockwise on step 6.

Step 7. Take a small step forward on your right foot.

Step 8. Replace your weight back to your left foot, making a $^1/_4$ turn clockwise between this step and step 9.

Steps 9 to 11. Dance your side Chassé, right, left, right, turning $^1/_4$ clockwise on step 11.

Step 12. Take a small step forward on your left foot.

Step 13. Replace your weight back to your right foot, turning $^1/_4$ counterclockwise between this step and step 14.

Steps 14 to 16. Dance your side Chassé, left, right, left, turning $^1/_4$ counterclockwise on step 16.

Step 17. Take a small step forward on your right foot.

Step 18. Replace your weight back to your left foot, turning $^1/_4$ clockwise between this step and step 19.

Steps 19 to 21. Dance your side Chassé, right, left, right, commencing to turn clockwise.

Step 22. Place your left foot forward and across your left foot, turning $^5/_8$ clockwise between steps 22 and 23.

Step 23. Replace your weight forward to your right foot, continuing to turn $^1/_4$ clockwise on this step.

Steps 24 to 26. Dance your side Chassé, left, right, left, completing $^1/_8$ turn clockwise on the steps, to end in closed position.

Step 27. Move backward to your right foot.

Step 28. Replace your weight forward to your left foot.

Step 29. Move your right foot to the side.

Step 30. Close your left foot to your right foot.

Choreographed Routine: Cha-Cha Routine

The following is a sassy, fun-filled Cha-Cha routine to be danced in the following sequence:

◆ Basic in Place: steps 1 to 10, two times, allowing for counterclockwise rotation of up to ¼ turn.

◆ Side Basic: steps 1 to 10, two times, allowing for counterclockwise rotation of up to ¼ turn.

◆ Progressive Basic: steps 1 to 20; take double handholds after step 2 and regain closed position on steps 19 and 20.

◆ Outside Partner: steps 1 to 10, two times, one set in closed position and one set to start and finish in double handholds.

◆ Crossover Break: steps 1 to 30.

◆ Repeat routine.

This routine is 88 beats of music, so dividing by Cha-Cha's 4 beats per measure, this routine equals 22 measures of music. Your CD practice song is 30 measures of music per minute, so as a percentage, this routine will take just over 73 percent of a minute, or just around 44 seconds to the repeat.

The Least You Need to Know

◆ The footwork and technique in Cha-Cha is basically the same as in the Rumba.

◆ Small-sized steps, turned-out feet/legs, and the use of foot swivel will emphasize your Cuban motion.

◆ Turn is initiated with the body (ribcage and hips), not by flinging the free foot to a new position.

◆ You may extend the duration of your routine by repeating any of the figures in a row prior to the repeat.

Chapter 23

Mambo

In This Chapter

◆ Cuba's greatest export

◆ A slightly different start

◆ Body rhythm has its own beat

◆ Do the locomotion

Passionate participants and observers of Latin American music and dance have enjoyed a long love affair with the Mambo. It is truly the Latin dancer's Latin dance. Mambo is the national dance of Cuba. Mambo has its roots in the original "Danzón" (an original Afro-Cuban native ritual tribal dance) and has been personified by Hollywood, television, and Madison Avenue virtually since its introduction to the United States. Latin American orchestras and composers gained the status of royalty by being touted by "those in the know" as a "Mambo King."

In dance competitions at the professional level, the audience may swoon while watching the slower, romantic, and more difficult version of Rumba known as Bolero. But when Mambo is announced, the heat in the room skyrockets as the audience prepares to participate vicariously in the sensual sassiness of the Mambo. Come and live the Mambo with me.

The alignments of the dance figures in the Mambo are based on the couple's position relative to each other and not on a place in the room. Please maintain the normal $^4/_4$ timing of the Mambo and use the rhythm of Quick, Quick, Slow. The beat value of a Slow is two beats, and the beat value for a Quick is one beat. Your timing for each measure of music will be count 2 (Quick), count 3 (Quick), 4-1 (Slow). Yes, the first progressive movement of Mambo begins on beat number 2! There are three steps (weight changes) made in four beats of music. You will maintain this rhythm throughout all of the Mambo figures presented in this book. The footwork throughout each Mambo figure will be ball, flat. I will describe any additional techniques concerning footwork as we proceed.

A Different Start

Dancers call the first step in Mambo or any figure in Mambo a *break*. Breaks can move forward, backward, or sideways. In the standardized form of Mambo presented in this book, you will break on the second beat of music. This generally poses a problem that beginner dancers of Mambo must solve immediately in order to remain in time with the music.

I have purposely left this dance for the conclusion of the Latin American dances. Starting on an unfamiliar beat that is preceded by a rhythmic body and hip action has always posed a dilemma for beginners. This dilemma, combined with the inherent, sometimes frenzied, speed of the Mambo, is often a source of frustration—often enough to cause a student to give up! Do not be discouraged! Listen to the music. Mambo music points to the second beat as a starting point to break because of the heavy accent on the second beat.

The best way to begin, armed with this book's CD, is to find the first beat and count aloud from there—1, 2, 3, 4. Once you have established your tempo, begin to notice the accent on the second beat in the measure. This will help you to identify Mambo music in the future. Continue to count. Now I want you to release your starting foot (man's left, lady's right) from the floor by lifting your thigh from the hip joint on the fourth count. Now settle into your supporting leg's hip on the first count of the measure. You have now done what we dancers call *moving into the music*. You have made a preparation to begin with your appropriate starting foot.

As they say—this will be a test! The music is fast, so you will need to call upon many of the resources in your body that we have developed through the technique presented in this book. Remember that patience— especially with yourself—is a virtue!

Forward and Back Basic

This dance figure will begin in close or closed Latin position. Please use the standard footwork and rhythm.

The major feature of this dance figure is its compact nature.

Bet You Didn't Know

There is virtually no difference in the choreography of the Mambo and the Salsa. The Salsa of recent years also adds many of the movements from the Columbian dance the Cumbia. Keeping Mambo figures compact is the key to Salsa. This can be accomplished by converting many of the side movements on count 4, 1 to closes danced in place.

When teaching Salsa, I have often referred to this Forward and Back Basic as the *Mambo basic*. More good news: By altering the timing and weight changes, virtually every figure shown in the Rumba, Mambo, Merengue, and Cha-Cha in this book can be adapted to the other three dances.

Movement Memo

In Latin American dancing, a replacement step (see step 2 or 5) means the dancer's bodyweight returns to virtually the exact position that the body exited from on the former usage of that same foot. Therefore, no progressive (traveling) movement should occur. For example, on step 5, the dancer will return to the position of step 3. On step 2 the dancer returns to the figure's starting position.

Gentleman's Part: Forward and Back Basic

Details for the gentleman's Forward and Back Basic follow:

Step 1. Move forward on your left foot, turning up to $1/4$ counterclockwise between this step and step 6.

Step 2. Replace backward to your right foot.

Step 3. Take a small step backward on your left foot.

Step 4. Move backward on your right foot.

Step 5. Replace your weight forward to your left foot.

Step 6. Take a small step forward on your right foot, ending in close or closed position, apart, or in double handholds. By replacing steps 3 and 6 with a side step, this Forward and Back Basic takes on the characteristics of the original classical Mambo basic. You may also dance this figure in apart, solo, or open facing position with suitable handholds.

Technique

Technique (General for Both): Here is the essential technique for dancing any three weight changes or steps in the Forward and Back Basic. Step 1, whether forward or back, is done exactly as described in the Rumba. The step will be faster because Mambo is a much faster tempo; however, the movement remains the same. The first three steps are one beat each—counted 2, 3, 4. Then count 1 is paused in place. Your body and arm movements on count 1 can be very expressive. This is due to the delayed movement of the hips from count 4 to count 1. The rhythm is expressed as Quick, Quick, Slow for every four beats of music. I always ask my students to say the rhythm out loud as they practice. When you reach count 1 for any pattern, say the following out loud: "hip." This word signifies the deepening of pressure felt in the legs and hip as you prepare to move again on count 2.

The body and leg action of the Mambo 4, 1 will be done as follows. Place your heels and ankles closer together than your toes to form a V. As you release your heels from the floor while doing the Mambo, the balls of your feet will remain on the dance floor. As you lift your thigh, your knee bends and the heel of your foot comes off the floor, allowing your hip to settle backward. The action that results from doing this is called *knee veer*. The knee of the lifted foot will cross slightly in front of the knee of the standing foot. Once again, I use the analogy of standing in place impatiently while shifting weight from one foot to the other. Or—think Elvis! Using this technique, you will find it quite easy to accomplish the speed necessary for the approaching count 2. When saying each "hip" or "hold," your knees veer in and then straighten to normal position.

A side view of a solo dancer doing the Mambo may resemble what you did as a child mimicking a locomotive with a delay on count 1. In fact, dancers call this "locomotion." The opposition arm and knee move ahead as the thigh rises up and down (for example, left arm with right leg). Locomotion can also be accompanied by ribcage isolation from side to side. Ribcage isolation does not affect the parallel alignment of the shoulders to the dance floor. This definitely takes practice and for the time being should not be your priority—especially at the expense of losing balance!

Step 1.

Step 2.

Step 3.

Lady's Part: Forward and Back Basic

Details for the lady's Forward and Back Basic follow:

Step 1. Move backward on your right foot, turning up to $^1/_4$ counterclockwise between this and step 6.

Step 2. Replace your weight forward to your left foot.

Step 3. Take a small step forward on your right foot.

Step 4. Move forward on your left foot.

Step 5. Replace your weight back to your right foot.

Step 6. Take a small step backward on your left foot, ending in close or closed position, apart, or in double handholds.

Side Breaks

This dance figure will begin in closed position. Please use the standard rhythm and footwork. The Side Break here in the Mambo is the example of the Second Position Break (also known as the Cucarachas; we mentioned in Chapter 20, "Merengue") as a universal figure. It is a major component of the interchangeable nightclub version of Mambo known as Salsa!

Technique

Technique (General for Both): The technique used for this step will be the same for all figures in the Mambo that contain a side movement. As you take a side step, endeavor to touch the inside edge of your foot to the floor first. As you take weight into the ball of the foot, you will feel a rolling action beginning at that outside edge and moving across the bottom of your foot. Be careful not to roll to the outside edge of the foot. Stop rolling when your foot is flat and all your body weight covers all of the foot. This action will allow for rhythmic body movement particularly through the hips. Stepping too quickly on the whole foot during a side step will cause your body to finish the weight change too quickly and too abruptly.

The closing action and weight transfer feels very much like peddling a bicycle. While maintaining good carriage of the body and support from the foot that contains your weight, pressurize the standing leg as you release the free leg upward in the same way that you peddle a bicycle. As your thighs move while you are peddling, it is easy to feel the action of your hips and pelvis. As you take the downward stroke of your peddle, feel your quadriceps flex and the back of your knee stretch. At the same time, or with coincidence, the other thigh raises, releasing its energy and allowing the knee to bend. Even though you are releasing energy here, the good cyclists do not take their feet off the pedals. Some part of the foot must remain on the floor through all the steps of the Mambo. Draw the feet toward and under the body with slight pressure on the floor. The peddling action of the knees and thighs is what actually creates Cuban motion or hip action—not the hips! This sequence of events is vital for Latin American dancing.

Another helpful device for perfecting hip action is to divide your timing. In place of Quick, Quick use Quick *and*, Quick *and*. The Quick represents $^1/_2$ of a beat. Use this to complete the leg action and weight change. The *and* represents $^1/_2$ of a beat to allow your hip to settle while releasing the former foot from the floor. Imagine yourself standing outside an elevator impatiently settling your hip from one leg to another. Now try it. This often works as a physical analogy.

Gentleman's Part: Side Breaks

Details for the gentleman's Side Breaks follow:

Step 1. Take a small step side with your left foot.

Step 2. Replace your weight side on your right foot.

Step 3. Close your left foot to your right foot.

Step 4. Take a small step side with your right foot.

Step 5. Replace your weight side on your left foot.

Step 6. Close your right foot to your left foot, ending in closed or open position using any suitable handholds.

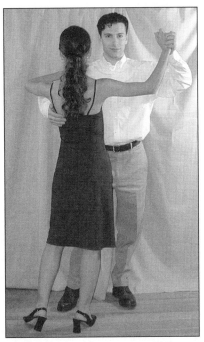

Step 1.

Step 2.

Step 3.

Lady's Part: Side Breaks

Details for the lady's Side Breaks follow:

Step 1. Take a small step side on your right foot.

Step 2. Replace your weight side on your left foot.

Step 3. Close your right foot to your left foot.

Step 4. Take a small step side on your left foot.

Step 5. Replace your weight side on your right foot.

Step 6. Close your left foot to your right foot.

Side Breaks and Cross

You may begin this figure in closed position or in double handhold. Double is actually easier, as closed requires a promenade movement. Once you have begun to travel, the leader may release the handholds in apart or solo dance position using no hand contact. This is good training for visual leading.

Gentleman's Part: Side Breaks and Cross

Details for the gentleman's Side Breaks and Cross follow:

Step 1. Take a small step side on your left foot.

Step 2. Replace your weight side on your right foot.

Step 3. Move forward and across on your left foot.

Step 4. Move your right foot to the side.

Step 5. Replace your weight side on your left foot.

Step 6. Move forward and across on your right foot, ending in closed position.

This figure will require all of the general Mambo techniques as previously detailed throughout this chapter.

Step 2.   *Step 3.*   *Step 6.*

Lady's Part: Side Breaks and Cross

Details for the lady's Side Breaks and Cross follow:

Step 1. Move your right foot to the side.

Step 2. Replace your weight side on your left foot.

Step 3. Move forward and across on your right foot.

Step 4. Move your left foot to the side.

Step 5. Replace your weight side on your right foot.

Step 6. Move forward and across on your left foot.

Cross Body Lead

This dance figure will begin in closed position. It may also begin with double handholds. Please use the standard rhythm and footwork. This figure is the most important transitional figure used in Mambo or in Salsa, please take your time with it and it will return dividends.

Gentleman's Part: Cross Body Lead

Details for the gentleman's Cross Body Lead follow:

Step 1. Move forward on your left foot.

Step 2. Replace your weight back to your right foot, turning up to $^1/_4$ counterclockwise between this step and step 3.

Step 3. Move your left foot to the side.

Step 4. Take a small step back on your right foot, turning up to $^1/_4$ counterclockwise between this step and step 5.

Step 5. Replace your weight forward to your left foot.

Step 6. Take a small step forward on your right foot, maintaining or regaining closed position. You may also finish in double handholds.

Step 6 may also be taken to the side.

Technique
Technique (General for Both): Again, I must emphasize to please observe the rule of "step then turn!" There are many foot swivels in this and subsequent figures. You may find the following advice helpful. Footwork for the Mambo begins with the ball of the foot (the metatarsal). While the weight remains on the ball, the rest of the foot is lowered in a very controlled manner. Be careful not to just drop into the heel. The action of swiveling on your foot occurs as your heel is lowering and just to the point of grazing the floor, but before weight is taken into the whole foot. Virtually all rotations in dance begin with weight on the ball of the foot.

Step 2.

Step 3.

Step 5.   *Step 6.*

Lady's Part: Cross Body Lead

Details for the lady's Cross Body Lead follow:

Step 1. Move backward on your right foot.

Step 2. Replace your weight forward to your left foot.

Step 3. Move forward on your right foot.

Step 4. Move forward on your left foot and pivot up to $\frac{1}{2}$ counterclockwise at the end of this step.

Step 5. Move backward on your right foot.

Step 6. Take a small step back on your left foot.

Technique

Technique (Leading for Gentleman): The lead for this step will be the release of your arm from the lady's back on step 6. This is followed by gentle but consistent pressure to lead the lady away from you on step 7. On step 9, you will raise your left arm to lead the lady's spot turn by circling the handholds over and around the lady's head for steps 10 and 11. I often call this making a halo over your angel! Regain closed position at the end of step 12.

Open Break Underarm Turn

This is certainly one of the most popular dance figures in the Mambo. In this figure, the man will dance virtually in place as the lady concludes with a Spot or Walk Around Turn. This figure commences in closed position and is danced with the standard rhythm and footwork.

Gentleman's Part: Open Break Underarm Turn

Details for the gentleman's Open Break Underarm Turn follow:

Steps 1 through 6. Perform dance steps 1 through 6 of the Cross Body Lead.

Step 7. Take a small step back and on your left foot.

Step 8. Replace your weight forward to your right foot.

Step 9. Move your left foot to the side.

Step 10. Take a small step back on your right foot.

Step 11. Replace your weight forward to your left foot.

Step 12. Move your right foot to the side.

The Cross Body Lead may turn up to ½ counterclockwise.

Step 9.

Step 10.

Step 11.

Step 12.

Lady's Part: Open Break Underarm Turn

Details for the lady's Open Break Underarm Turn follow:

Steps 1 through 6. Perform dance steps to 1 through 6 of the Cross Body Lead.

Step 7. Take a small step back on your right foot.

Step 8. Replace your weight forward to your left foot.

Step 9. Move your right foot to the side.

Step 10. Move forward and across on your left foot, turning ¼ clockwise on this step.

Step 11. Replace your weight forward to your right foot and continue to turn ½ clockwise on this step.

Step 12. Move your left foot to the side, completing ¼ turn clockwise on this step.

Technique
Technique (General for Lady): Success in the spot turn is assured when *foot swivel* is used. Foot swivel is a twisting action of the foot while it remains on the floor. This means you must allow your supporting foot to rotate. It becomes very difficult to turn unless this happens. In this figure, foot swivel will occur on steps 10, 11, and 12. Attempting the full rotation clockwise without foot swivel would be like trying to open a door without allowing the hinges to rotate. You may use a degree of foot swivel on every rotation! Use your hips and ribcage to generate the rotation of your body and your foot swivel. Beginners often fail with rotation because they attempt to create the turn with their legs and feet by "tossing" them across their body. Do not get caught in this optical illusion. Always remember that dancing is all about the use of the body.

Choreographed Routine: Mambo Routine

A feisty action-packed Mambo routine should be danced in the following sequence:

- Forward and Back Basic: steps 1 through 6, three times, allowing for counterclockwise rotation of up to ¼ turn.
- Side Breaks: steps 1 through 6, two times; first set in closed position and second set in double handholds.
- Side Breaks and Cross: steps 1 through 6, three times in double handholds, regaining closed position after the third set.
- Forward and Back Basic: steps 1 through 6, ending side on step 6.
- Cross Body Lead: steps 1 through 6.
- Open Break Underarm Turn: steps 1 through 12, two times.
- Repeat routine.

This routine is 96 beats of music, so dividing by Mambo's 4 beats per measure, this routine equals 24 measures of music. Your CD practice song is 47 measures of music per minute, so as a percentage, this routine will take just over 51 percent of a minute—or just over 31 seconds—to the repeat.

The Least You Need to Know

- The footwork and technique in Mambo is basically the same as in the Rumba and Cha-Cha.
- Small-sized steps, turned-out feet/legs, and the use of foot swivel will emphasize your Cuban motion or hip action.
- All figures presented in Mambo, Rumba, Cha-Cha, and Merengue can be used interchangeably in all these dances with appropriate adjustments for the rhythm, timing, and characteristic of each.
- You may extend the duration of your routine by repeating any of the figures in a row prior to the repeat.

Chapter 24

East Coast Swing

In This Chapter

♦ The all-American dance
♦ Three units will make it simple
♦ The Swing Rock—the end and the beginning
♦ Always observe the eleventh commandment

Swing dancing is by far the most versatile dance in the world. The rhythm is infectious and as natural to us as our heartbeat! Swing has many forms and varieties that are enjoyed everywhere there is music. We are going to work on the variety of Swing known as the East Coast or Triple Swing. This form of Swing provides the best foundation from which the dancer can grow into Swing's numerous varieties, and that is why I have chosen it just for you!

In my book *Quickstart to Swing*, I present four Swing rhythms with over a hundred interchangeable figures. East Coast is just one of the rhythms presented there, but I feel it is the most important. It lends itself to cumulative growth in all of Swing dancing. The fundamentals learned in East Coast Swing allow its practitioners to make much easier entry into other varieties, like Jive, Lindy Hop, West Coast, Shag, and so on.

The cover of *Quickstart to Swing* says it is "The all-American dance that has the whole world Jumpin' Jivin' and Wailin'!" Come join the fun. This book presents five important and action-packed figure patterns that will get you out on the dance floor. So what are you waiting for?

Quickstart to Swing's© Unit Method for Easy Learning

At this very early stage of your Swing dance experience, all your figures will include three units—each unit containing two beats. There are eight weight changes (steps) in six beats of music. This allows me to describe a pattern or figure in a more concise and standard fashion and allows you to concentrate on that figure's direction, rotation, leads and follows, and so on.

The following descriptions of the two Chassé movements and Swing Rock are the "nuts and bolts" of the dance. If you were taking private lessons with me, our first mission would be to work on your three units until you could do them with the proverbial "blindfold and hands tied behind your back" level of ease! The three units of Swing that I present here must be thought of as your "mode of transportation" for this dance, in the same way as walking is your mode of transportation in your daily life. These three units are also the best technical starting points for other forms of Swing. They provide the basis for hundreds of additional figures with literally millions of combinations. The time required to perfect the three units can be as quick as a few minutes or as long as many hours. This will depend on your physical resolve and athleticism. The good news is once you own the movement and do it without thinking, it is just like any other of your physical activities—you will never forget it, and the rest is easy.

I should note that although Swing can become easy to learn, it will always remain one of the most physical things you have ever done. You do not have to be a great athlete to be a good Swing dancer, but you will have to exhibit a great deal of athleticism. You will need to use all the major muscle groups of your body in a combined effort for several minutes at a time—it is a workout! Take it slow at first and build up your endurance and stamina.

Gentleman's Part: East Coast Swing

The gentleman's (leader) East Coast Swing steps for every figure follow:

- ◆ **1st Unit Steps:** Left side step, close the right to the left, left side step. The beat value is $\frac{1}{2}$, $\frac{1}{2}$, 1 or Quick, Quick, Slow. There are three weight changes during beats 1, 2. This is known as a *left Chassé*.
- ◆ **2nd Unit Steps:** Right side step, close the left to the right, right side step. The beat value is $\frac{1}{2}$, $\frac{1}{2}$, 1 or Quick, Quick, Slow. There are three weight changes during beats 3, 4. This is known as a *right Chassé*.
- ◆ **3rd Unit Steps:** Back on left, replace weight forward on the right. The beat value is 1, 1 or Slow, Slow. There are two weight changes during beats 5, 6. This is a transitional movement known as a *Swing Rock*. Consider this unit as the link from one Swing figure to another rather than the ending of movement.

Lady's Part: East Coast Swing

The lady's (follower) East Coast Swing steps for every figure follow:

- ◆ **1st Unit Steps:** Right side step, close the left to the right, right side step. The beat value is $\frac{1}{2}$, $\frac{1}{2}$, 1 or Quick, Quick, Slow. There are three weight changes during beats 1, 2. This is known as a *right Chassé*.
- ◆ **2nd Unit Steps:** Left side step, close the right to the left, left side step. The beat value is $\frac{1}{2}$, $\frac{1}{2}$, 1 or Quick, Quick, Slow. There are three weight changes during beats 3, 4. This is known as a *left Chassé*.
- ◆ **3rd Unit Steps:** Back on right, replace weight forward on left. The beat value is 1, 1 or Slow, Slow. There are two weight changes during beats 5, 6. This is a transitional movement known as a *Swing Rock*. Consider this unit as the link from one Swing figure to another rather than the ending of movement.

1st Unit Swing Technique

The gentleman (leader) will begin a Swing figure with his weight on his right foot. When he desires to move, he must create a flexing action into his right knee. In this way, both the lower and upper torso will move simultaneously over his left foot as he changes weight. The actual position of his left foot should be in line or directly under the left side of his pelvis. This will ensure a complete weight change to his left foot. It is extremely important that as the weight of the leader's body is consummated over the left foot, the right foot is simultaneously removed from the floor by lifting the thigh—in the same way a staircase is ascended. He should use this same type of movement to continue from his left to his right foot and then finally to his right to left foot. This triple step is known as a *Swing Chassé*. Throughout this chapter, the 1st Unit for the leader will always start by moving to his left foot.

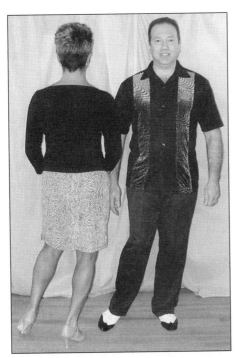

Step 1 1st Unit Solo Position.

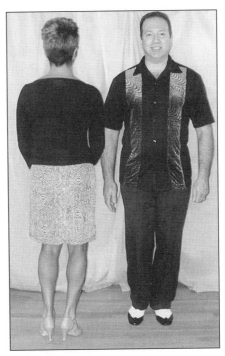

Step 2 1st Unit Solo Position.

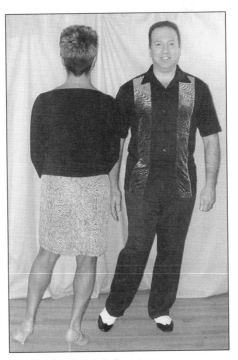

Step 3 1st Unit Solo Position.

The 1st Unit for the lady (follower) is the same series of physical movements described for the leader. The difference is that the supporting and moving legs are used in opposition to that of the leader (i.e., follower's right to the leader's left). Throughout this text, the 1st Unit for the follower will always start by moving to her right foot.

2nd Unit Swing Technique

The leader will begin the 2nd Unit of any Swing figure with his weight on his left foot. During the concluding moments of the 1st Unit's second beat, he will begin the compression into the left knee. From that point on, the series of physical actions described in the 1st Unit is repeated using the opposite feet. Throughout this chapter, the 2nd Unit for the leader will always start by moving to his right foot.

Step 1 2nd Unit Solo Position.

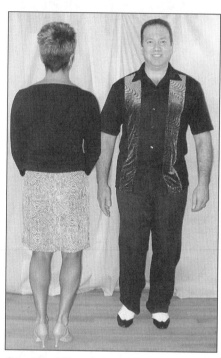

Step 2 2nd Unit Solo Position.

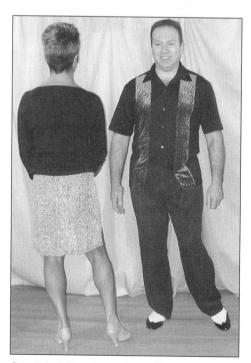

Step 3 2nd Unit Solo Position.

The 2nd Unit for the follower will be the entire set of physical movements as described for the leader. The difference is that the supporting and moving legs are used in opposition (for example, the follower's left to the leader's right). Throughout this chapter, the 2nd Unit for the follower will always start by moving to her left foot.

Technique

Technique (General for Both): Your motto: "Jeff Allen is the teacher that trains me to take my feet off the floor for success in Swing dancing!" At this early stage of a beginner's Swing experience, I recommend that whenever you change weight, the free foot should rise at least a couple of inches from the dance surface. This action will ensure a complete weight change and prevent undesirable upper-body sway or undue momentum throughout the shoulders. The removal of any foot from the dance floor during a Swing dance should be accomplished by lifting the upper thigh with a light and swift movement of the hip (for example, the ball socket joint at the top of your leg). This would be quite similar to the harmony of leg movement created by pedaling a bicycle or ascending a staircase. During Swing dancing, the poise of your entire torso will be erect and inclined slightly forward. You will know you are in the correct posture when you feel the weight of your body over the balls of your feet. To help accommodate this, there will be a flex in the knees throughout all body movements and action of the legs in all figures of the Swing.

Muscles and Joints Are Key to Good Swing Dancing

The supporting leg will always feel much more compression in the upper thigh than the leg of the free foot. Additionally, the knee of the free or nonsupporting leg will move to an elevation that is always slightly higher than the knee of the supporting leg. Allow your ankles to remain soft and pliable so that foot pressure and stability can be maximized. While dancing Swing, the knees should be and remain closer together than the ankles. Keeping the knees closer together than the ankles will allow the entry of the weight into the dancer's feet to be continuously controlled, smooth, and rolling. As the knees bend, accepting the body weight into the feet, they will converge or move even closer to each other. This technique is known as dancing with *knee veer*. The movement of the hips in Swing dancing is also influenced and accommodated by knee veer. A slight lowering of the pelvis in coincidence with the moving leg helps the balance of the dancer's center. Additionally, focusing on the use of the pelvis is a great aid in keeping the power and weight of the dancer out of the shoulders.

The pelvis will tilt slightly to the side and downward each time the weight is taken into the moving foot on the progressive side. Flexing the middle and lower abdominal area will allow you to control the use of the pelvis. Using the abdominal area isolates the hips from the ribcage. During Swing dancing, the lower abdominal area of the body is highly active, facilitating balance, movement, and rotation.

Unfortunately, many new Swing dancers are not taught this properly. They are not taught to isolate the hips from their ribcage by using the abdominal muscles. When these beginners attempt to mimic the actions of good Swing dancing, they erroneously include rocking or swaying of the ribcage instead of tilting of the pelvis. The ribcage drops or lowers from side to side, producing a very heavy, awkward, and unbalanced Swing dancer. These dancers become difficult and often unpleasant to have as a partner. As you attempt to develop, correct, or even teach Swing dancing, take great care to isolate the rhythmic tilting of the pelvis so as to *not* compromise the lift and support that should always be felt in the ribcage!

Swing dancing is extremely physical. The energy from the body into the legs should be maximized in the lowering movements (bending of the knee) rather than the movements considered as rise (straightening of the knee)! Strong down—light up. It is the proper use of your vertical energy (lowering and rising) that produces the smoothness found only in very good Swing dancers.

The maximum distance a Swing dancer should separate the moving foot from the supporting foot approximates the width of their hips. As a rule of thumb, this width is certainly less than the width of the shoulders and would closer approximate the width of the pelvis. Frankly, the Swing dancer should be more concerned with driving the body away from the supporting foot. This is accomplished by releasing the compression built up in the thigh of the supporting leg through the knee of the same leg. Feel that you are pushing away from your knee. This will produce a powerful step, but not a wide step! Whenever you are directed in this text or on a lesson to take a step, this distance becomes your innate benchmark, which will allow for maximum stability, good rotational skills, and a fluid approach to the art of partner dancing. When you see a good Swing Chassé from a forward or back view, it should look as if the lower torso is tracing the letter W.

Technique

Technique (General for Both): Now let us examine another very common physical analogy you can use to develop the movement needed for East Coast or Triple Swing—Pedaling Swing: pedaling a bicycle! Pedaling a bicycle demonstrates the use of two feet rather than just one step at a time. It is important to note that a dance step always includes two feet. One foot is for support and lift, and the other creates inclination and a target for the body. We maintain a coincidental gain and loss of pressure as we pedal. The physical logic of left, then right is lost when we stop with both feet on the floor. The important technique to remember here is that it is like pedaling a bike: The finish of your Swing steps with one foot off the dance floor (up) and one foot on the dance floor (down) and is only a brief moment. The brain likes it best this way, as we are naturally moving to the free foot without the need to choose which foot is next. The choice is always simple: The free foot is next. The eleventh commandant for dancers: Never stop with both feet on the floor and your weight evenly distributed. While pedaling, the rotation of the hip joints is continuous, allowing free and unimpeded movement for the designated muscles of the legs and hips. The feet do their work according to the speed we desire to travel.

Important: The Swing Chassé may be danced in any direction, including rotations clockwise or counterclockwise, or moving forward, backward, sideways, promenade, or remaining in place (no traveling).

The common footwork for the Chassé is ball, flat; ball; ball, flat. Other varieties are permissible according to tempo and style.

3rd Unit: The Swing Technique (Rock)

The Swing Rock is your most important moment and movement in Swing dancing! In the six-count rhythms of Swing (six beats of music), the Rock is used to both conclude and begin the vast majority of your six-count figures.

The Swing Rock (the third of the two beat units) can be described as a step back and a replacement step forward. The rocking action is felt primarily in the trunk area or lower torso and is generated by a flexing of both knees. The leader will lower into his right leg while moving the left foot back into position. The leader will then remove his right foot from the floor by lifting the right thigh, which results in a total transfer of weight to his left foot. The follower will use a similar procedure, moving from her left to her right foot. As always, the ball socket joint at the hip will be used to generate the lifting movement of the thigh. I recommend that you remove the right foot at least two inches from the floor while keeping the entirety of the bottom surface of your foot parallel with the dance floor. This method will ensure that dancers will not have the problem of their weight and the subsequent momentum moving up into their shoulders. This sequence described is completed on one beat of music.

Back Step Swing Rock Solo Position. *Replacement Step Swing Rock Solo Position.*

As soon as this back movement is completed, flexing begins again through the leader's left knee (the follower's right knee), and the replacement foot is positioned on the dance floor. This flexing energy will create an immediate and fluid response of the body, moving the leader back to the right foot and the follower's left. The total time of the couple's replacement step—including the body flight and the moment of transition to conclude the rocking action—will be one beat of music.

When you see a good Swing Rock from a side view, it should look as if the lower torso is tracing the letter U. This Swing Rock swings! Throughout this chapter, the leader and follower's 3rd Unit will begin with their left and right feet, respectively.

The common footwork for the Swing Rock is ball (back step), then ball flat (forward replacement step). Other varieties are permissible according to tempo and style.

Closed Basic in Promenade Position

Promenade position is simply defined as a closed dance position where both the leader and the follower travel to the same theoretic point on the dance floor. The inside or center of the couple's frame finds the bodies in or nearly in contact with each other. The couple's ribcages form a 90-degree angle at the point of contact. To form promenade position, the partners will stand with the shoulders and hips of each parallel to each other. The leader will rotate $^1/_8$ of a turn counterclockwise, and the follower will rotate $^1/_8$ of a turn clockwise from the parallel stance. The couple will form their frame with a closed handhold—leader's left to follower's right. The leader's right arm will be on the follower's left shoulder blade for closed position or on their right shoulder blade for a closer position called *Closed Position*. The follower's left arm will be in a normal closed frame position, except her left hand will be placed in front of the leader's shoulder, palm facing him. Please be careful not to "grip" your partner! The arms must be allowed to move in order to accommodate the bodies' movements. One important note concerning the dancer's feet: While dancing forward and backward movements in Closed Promenade Position, the feet never alter their position or direction.

Gentleman's Part: Closed Basic in Promenade Position

The gentleman's details for the Closed Basic in Promenade Position follow:

Steps 1 to 3. 1st Unit Chassé forward in Promenade Position.

Steps 4 to 6. 2nd Unit Chassé backward in Promenade Position.

Steps 7 and 8. 3rd Unit Swing Rock, finishing in Promenade.

1st Unit in Closed PP.

2nd Unit in Closed PP.

3rd Unit Back Step in Closed PP.

3rd Unit Fwd Replacement in Closed PP.

Lady's Part: Closed Basic in Promenade Position

The lady's details for the Closed Basic in Promenade Position follow:

Steps 1 to 3. 1st Unit Chassé forward in Promenade Position.

Steps 4 to 6. 2nd Unit Chassé backward in Promenade Position.

Steps 7 and 8. 3rd Unit Swing Rock, finishing in Promenade.

Outside (Arch) Turn from Closed Promenade Position to Finish in Open Facing Position

This is a follower's underarm turn that rotates clockwise. Ladies, please observe that the arm you travel under is his, not yours! It may be wise to refer to the section about rotation in Chapter 13, "The Interactions of the Dance Couple."

Gentleman's Part: Outside (Arch) Turn from Closed Promenade Position to Finish in Open Facing Position

The gentleman's details for the Outside (Arch) Turn from Closed Promenade Position to Finish in Open Facing Position follow:

Steps 1 to 3. 1st Unit Chassé forward from promenade position, raising your left hand and leading your partner forward under the arch.

Steps 4 to 6. 2nd Unit Chassé closing toward the lady, having released his right hand from her shoulder blade while circling his left like a halo over her head for one full rotation clockwise, allowing the joined hands to lower at the turn's completion. You will make $1/4$ rotation counterclockwise.

Step 7 and 8. 3rd Unit Swing Rock, finishing in Open Facing Position.

1st Unit Lead to Arch Turn.

Lady's Underarm Turn.

Open Facing Position.

Lady's Part: Outside (Arch) Turn from Closed Promenade Position to Finish in Open Facing Position

The lady's details for the Outside (Arch) Turn from Closed Promenade Position to finish in Open Facing Position as follows:

Steps 1 to 3. 1st Unit Chassé forward and slightly left from Promenade Position, passing under the arch.

Steps 4 to 6. 2nd Unit Chassé, rotating up to $^3/_4$ turn clockwise.

Steps 7 and 8. 3rd Unit Swing Rock, finishing in Open Facing Position.

The Basic Figure in Open Facing Position

This figure has been thoroughly described technically at the introduction to this chapter. Use the pictures of the 1st and 2nd Units provided with the intro technique for this figure's development. Photos for the 3rd Unit can be found in the next section.

Gentleman's Part: The Basic Figure in Open Facing Position

The gentleman's details for the Basic in Open Facing Position follow:

Steps 1 to 3. 1st Unit Chassé sideways in Open Facing Position.

Steps 4 to 6. 2nd Unit Chassé sideways in Open Facing Position.

Steps 7 and 8. 3rd Unit Swing Rock, finishing in Open Facing Position.

Rock Back 3rd Unit.

Fwd Replacement 3rd Unit.

Lady's Part: The Basic Figure in Open Facing Position

The lady's details for the Basic in Open Facing Position follow:

Steps 1 to 3. 1st Unit Chassé sideways in Open Facing Position.

Steps 4 to 6. 2nd Unit Chassé sideways in Open Facing Position.

Steps 7 and 8. 3rd Unit Swing Rock, finishing in Open Facing Position.

Inside Turn (Loop Turn) from Open Facing Position Finishing in Open Facing Position

This figure will cause the partners to trade places with each other. Good Swing dancers find this figure to be one of the most effective and space-saving figures in their repertoire. While inexperienced dancers, slingshot and yank away from each other, you'll stay with your partner cool, calm, and collected!

Gentleman's Part: Inside Turn (Loop Turn) from Open Facing Position Finishing in Open Facing Position

The gentleman's details for the Inside Turn (Loop Turn) from Open Facing Position, finishing in Open Facing Position, follow:

Steps 1 to 3. 1st Unit Chassé is danced sideways. Pivot $^1/_4$ clockwise between the 3rd Unit replacement step (right foot) and the 1st Unit of this figure. You will raise the joined left-to-right handhold toward your right shoulder as the pivot is completed. Your partner's back is now facing your chest.

Steps 4 to 6. 2nd Unit Chassé sideways. The joined handhold will be looped over the follower's head and then downward to her waist level. The leader will continue to turn $^1/_4$ clockwise in Open Facing Position between the former 1st and this 2nd Unit.

Steps 7 and 8. 3rd Unit Swing Rock, finishing in Open Facing Position.

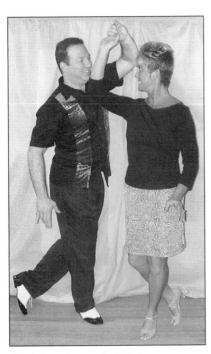

Lead from former 3rd Unit.   *Loop finished end of 1st Unit.*   *3rd Unit Open Facing Position.*

Lady's Part: Inside Turn (Loop Turn) from Open Facing Position Finishing in Open Facing Position

The lady's details for the Inside Turn (Loop Turn) from Open Facing Position, finishing in Open Facing Position, follow:

Steps 1 to 3. 1st Unit Chassé sideways, pivoting $\frac{1}{4}$ counterclockwise between your former 3rd Unit replacement step (left foot) and this 1st Unit.

Steps 4 to 6. 2nd Unit Chassé sideways in Open Facing Position. Turn $\frac{1}{4}$ counterclockwise between the 1st Unit and this 2nd Unit.

Steps 7 and 8. 3rd Unit Swing Rock, finishing in Open Facing Position.

Leader's Underarm Turn from Open Facing Position to Closed Promenade Position

Okay guys, it is your turn to do what the lady's love, an underarm turn. This figure is your hardest, so practicing it alone is a good idea!

Gentleman's Part: Leader's Underarm Turn from Open Facing Position to Closed Promenade Position

The gentleman's details for the leader's Underarm Turn (Arch) from Open Facing Position to Closed Promenade Position follow:

Steps 1 to 3. 1st Unit Chassé forward and left in Open Facing Position so that both you and your partner's right shoulders will pass very close to each other. At this moment, the leader will raise the joined left-to-right handhold.

Steps 4 to 6. 2nd Unit Chassé in place, turning one full turn counterclockwise in Open Facing Position, passing under the arch with your back by the follower's chest between the 1st and this 2nd Unit. Your rotation must be completed before your partner's. Use strong CBM. Any unfinished amount of rotation to conclude in promenade position may occur through steps 7 and 8.

Steps 7 and 8. 3rd Unit Swing Rock, finishing in promenade position.

Lady's Part: Leader's Underarm Turn from Open Facing Position to Closed Promenade Position

The lady's details for the leader's underarm turn (arch) from Open Facing Position to Closed Promenade Position follow:

Steps 1 to 3. 1st Unit Chassé slightly forward in Open Facing Position.

Steps 4 to 6. 2nd Unit Chassé in place, turning $\frac{1}{4}$ clockwise between the 1st Unit and this 2nd Unit.

Steps 7 and 8. 3rd Unit Swing Rock, finishing in Promenade Position.

End of 1st Unit.   *Man's Lead of Underarm Turn.*   *2nd Unit entry to P.P.*

Choreographed Routine: Swing Routine

Hey, lil' sister and big daddy-O! Swing out with this routine on the golden hardwood to be danced in the following sequence:

◆ Closed Basic in Promenade Position: At least two times to get into the groove. You may find that you can turn it clockwise.

◆ Outside (Arch) Turn from Closed Promenade Position to Finish in Open Facing Position.

◆ The Basic in Open Facing Position: Two times.

◆ Inside Turn (Loop Turn) from Open Facing Position, Finishing in Open Facing Position: Two times.

◆ Leader's Underarm Turn from Open Facing Position to Closed Promenade Position.

◆ Repeat routine.

This routine is 48 beats of music, so dividing by Swing's 4 beats per measure, this routine equals 12 measures of music. Your CD practice song is 32 measures of music per minute. As a percentage, this routine will take 37.5 percent of a minute, or just over 22 seconds to the repeat.

The Least You Need to Know

◆ East Coast Swing provides the best foundation from which to progress to other varieties of Swing dancing.

◆ Using the Three Unit Method will increase your learning curve.

◆ Never stop with both feet on the floor or your weight evenly distributed.

◆ Throughout Swing dancing, your knees should be closer together than your ankles, producing good knee veer and more hip flexibility.

Hustle

In This Chapter

◆ Hustle fever

◆ Four steps in three beats

◆ Use those magic feet!

◆ Lift those thighs

Hustle? No, not the line dance, but the most popular partner dance during the mid-1970s to mid-1980s! The dance romanticized in the hugely popular motion picture *Saturday Night Fever* and that kept TV audiences mesmerized once every week on the hit show *Dance Fever* is making a huge comeback! With its roots in New York City, this dance is as easy as walking tall and marching in place to a consistent cadence. If dance history repeats itself, and it will, then the resurgence in Swing and Lindy Hop, the Tango and Latin, will sow the seeds for the growth of the Hustle communities!

In 1960 the Twist nearly destroyed ballroom dancing. No more "touching" resulted in a generation that gave up on the notion of having to "learn how to dance." Clearly, it was the Hustle in the 1970s that not only saved what was known as ballroom dancing but also added huge numbers to its corps after the initial fad died down. Youth had no interest in their grandparents' form of dancing and yet longed unknowingly for the pleasures and natural chemistries that only ballroom dancing could provide. The Hustle brought us back "together again" and now, as ballroom dancing is enthusiastically embraced on campuses throughout our nation, interest in this great dance has been rekindled. After all, how often is it that Broadway produces a show from a movie as it has with *Saturday Night Fever?* The Hustle completes the complement of dances in this book by truly providing something for everyone and for every mood!

Hustling the Technique

At this early stage of your Hustle dance experience, all your figures will include four weight changes (completed dance steps)—two half beats and two whole beats. This is a total of three beats per figure. The alignment is based on the couple's position relative to each other rather than some spot in the room. Please maintain the normal $^4/_4$ timing of the Hustle.

Connecting with the Rhythm

Face your partner in Open Facing Position with a double handhold. The hands form a hook, or what I call the *universal handhold position.* To create actions toward the man, he must draw the lady's hook on the inside of his fingers to the inside of her fingers. To create actions away from the man, he must send the lady away from the backs of his fingers to her palms. The dancers must not clamp the fingers closed on their partner. Such clamping is restrictive to hand changes and underarm turns, plus it can be quite uncomfortable. Ladies, you will be a much more effective and responsive partner if you remember to tone your wrists and keep them just below the level of your palms.

A natural tendency for beginners is to let the wrists become sloppy and too loose. I call this "puppy dog begging" style. The lack of tone in the wrists is improperly replaced with too much power from the biceps. This type of power has a tendency to "launch" the lighter of the two partners from the floor, spoiling foot pressure, balance, and timing. In addition, the shoulders and clavicle, which always should be kept down on the ribcage, become "flighty," making the qualities of good leading and following unusually difficult. Your arms are released from your shoulders and apart from your ribcage throughout the development exercise and the dance in total.

Now begin to march in place with a strong, noncollapsing ribcage for four steps. Try this first without music by counting aloud. Then add the music and repeat, still counting aloud. Now repeat again with only the music on the book's CD (no counting aloud). Repeat this until you can do it instinctively.

- Your rhythm is "&," 1, 2, 3 during the four complete weight changes.
- The beat value of each step in this sequence is ½ beat, one beat, one beat, ½ beat.
- Your directions are back, forward, in place, in place.

Back double handholds.

Forward double handholds.

Let's Get the "Disco Action" from Your Legs

Like Swing, Hustle can be easy to learn. However, it, too, requires continuing physical focus with strong control from within, especially the abdominal area and the upper legs. You don't have to be a great athlete to be a good Hustle dancer, but you will have to exhibit a great deal of athleticism. You will need to combine all the major muscle groups of your body into a combined effort for several minutes at a time—it is a workout! Take it slow at first and build up your endurance and stamina. It is a terrific way to lose inches and pounds!

Do not "slingshot" your partner with your hands or arms. Instead, exit from your supporting foot with sustained lift in your body. Enter your moving foot smoothly while incrementally increasing the energy in that foot until it maximizes during the exit from the foot.

When taking a forward step, the energy should be felt at three main places:

1. The foot that you stand on—by way of strong pressure against the dance floor.
2. From your back—at the center of your shoulder blades.
3. At the base of your skull—at the atlas axis joint.

When taking a backward step, the energy should come from three main places:

1. The foot that you stand on—by way of strong pressure against the dance floor.
2. Drawing your tummy against your spinal column.
3. Holding your head and neck above your shoulders.

To move sideways, observe all of the above and accelerate from the left side of the body when moving right and the right side of the body when moving left.

"Magic Part of the Foot"

The 1st "&" count of each basic step in the Hustle is the most important! This is your transition movement—ending one figure and beginning the next. Uniformly, the "&" (and) count begins and ends with only the ball of the foot. Although not described in the step patterns, the first point at which to feel contact for the back step in the Hustle is "The Magic Part of the Foot." I first introduced this contact point in my book *Quickstart to Swing.*

I defined the magic part of the foot as a theoretical point located equidistant between the ball of the foot and the big toe. Using this contact point prevents the difficulty a dancer experiences when trying to stop "dead center" on the bottom of the ball of the foot and missing contact with the toes altogether. Trying to stop on any ball is hard enough—just ask a circus performer! But in the Hustle, dropping out of control to the heel from the ball of the foot with only $1/2$ beat to manage the back flight of the body and prepare for forward acceleration is deadly.

The point is magic because, "like magic," many of my students across the country enjoy immediate improvement in their dancing. Contact is made by compressing your big toe on the floor while maintaining the elevation of your heel. This exposes part of the ball of the foot closest to the big toe. When simultaneous contact is made at this point, it creates a stoppage of backward momentum, allowing for smooth transition through the knees, hips, and pelvis. Energy is immediately sent right back up the leg, assisting the dancer in the change of direction from backward to forward.

Remember Jeff's Nickname—"Off the Floor!"

Once again, I must point out the application of an important technique you learned in the Quickstart Program© that will continue to serve you well in the Hustle: lifting the upper thigh with a light and swift movement of the hip (i.e., the ball socket joint at the top of your leg) to take your feet off the floor. This would be quite similar to the harmony of leg movement created by pedaling a bicycle or ascending a staircase.

Frankly, the Hustle dancer should be more concerned with driving the body away from the supporting foot with both legs straightening while the body is moving. This is accomplished by releasing the compression built up in the thigh of the supporting leg through the knee of the same leg. Feel that you are "pushing away" from your knee and foot. This will produce a powerful and proportionate step!

Remember the eleventh commandment for dancers: Never *stop* with both feet on the floor and weight evenly distributed.

Basic (Slotted) Right Turn

This figure will begin in Open Facing Position with double handhold. The partners pass to each other's right side. The notation of "slotted" means that you will trade places with your partner. Please use the standard timing.

Gentleman's Part: Basic (Slotted) Right Turn

The gentleman's details for the Basic (Slotted) Right Turn follow:

Step 1. Place your left toe to your right heel using the footwork of ball.

Step 2. Move your right foot forward and slightly across. With your right side leading, commence to turn clockwise. Your footwork is heel (although you will use your whole foot, the footwork of heel denotes no rise).

Step 3. Move your left foot to the side using the footwork of ball, flat, and turning ¼ clockwise.

Step 4. Move your right foot back and slightly across using the footwork of ball, flat, and turning ¼ clockwise.

Step 2.

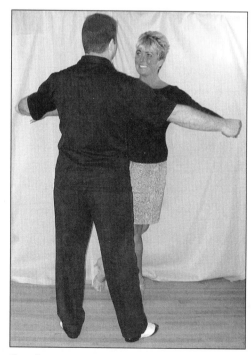

Step 3.

Step 4.

Lady's Part: Basic (Slotted) Right Turn

The lady's details for the Basic (Slotted) Right Turn follow:

Step 1. Place your right toe to your left heel using the footwork of ball.

Step 2. Move your left foot forward and slightly to the side. Use the footwork of heel (although you will use your whole foot, the footwork of heel denotes no rise) with your right side leading.

Step 3. Move your right foot forward and turn $^1/_8$ clockwise using the footwork of heel.

Step 4. Move your left foot to the side and back. Use the footwork of ball, flat, and turn $^3/_8$ clockwise.

Lady's Left Underarm Turn (Slotted)

This figure begins in Open Facing Position with a double handhold. The man will be turning clockwise, while the lady turns counterclockwise passing to the man's right side.

Gentleman's Part: Lady's Left Underarm Turn (Slotted)

The gentleman's details for the Lady's Left Underarm Turn (Slotted) follow:

Steps 1 through 4. Use exactly the same description of movements as found in the gentleman's basic step. On step 2, the man will lift his left arm to allow his partner to pass under. Additionally, he can check her movement by placing her left hand on her waist with his right. This will keep her at the inside of the curve, making it easier for her to complete the rotation. Retaining light contact with the lady's body and arms will allow the double handhold to be naturally regained.

Step 2.

Step 3.

Step 4.

Lady's Part: Lady's Left Underarm Turn (Slotted)

The lady's details for the Lady's Left Underarm Turn (Slotted) follow:

Step 1. Place your right toe to your left heel using the footwork of ball.

Step 2. Move forward and slightly across on the heel of your left foot, with your left side leading. Commence to turn counterclockwise.

Step 3. Move your right foot to the side using the footwork of ball, flat, and making ¼ turn counterclockwise while passing under the joined handhold.

Step 4. Move your left foot slightly back and across using the footwork of ball, flat, and turning ¼ counterclockwise.

Man's Left Underarm Turn (Slotted)

This figure begins in Open Facing Position with a double handhold. The man will be turning counterclockwise, while the lady turns clockwise. Each partner will pass by the other's right side.

Gentleman's Part: Man's Left Underarm Turn (Slotted)

The gentleman's details for the Man's Left Underarm Turn (Slotted) follow:

Step 1. Place your left toe to your right heel using the footwork of ball.

Step 2. Move forward and across on your right foot leading with your right side using the footwork of ball, flat. Lift your right arm, and with your left, place the lady's right hand on your right hip.

Step 3. Move forward on the heel of your left foot turning ⅛ counterclockwise. Allow the lady's right hand to slide along your waist while passing under the joined handhold.

Step 4. Move backward on your right foot using the footwork ball, flat, continuing to turn ⅜ counterclockwise while regaining double handholds.

Step 2.

Step 3.

Step 4.

Lady's Part: Man's Left Underarm Turn (Slotted)

The lady's details for the Man's Left Underarm Turn (Slotted) follow:

Steps 1 through 4. Use exactly the same description of movements as found in the Lady's Part: Basic (Slotted) Right Turn. On step 3, maintain contact with the leader's waist.

Open to Side Closed Position

This figure will cause the partners to return to Side Closed Position, allowing for what will become the normal starting position of the Hustle. Begin in Open Facing Position with a normal left-to-right single hand-hold.

Gentleman's Part: Open to Side Closed Position

The gentleman's details for the Open to Side Closed Position follow:

Step 1. Move your left foot slightly across your right foot using the footwork ball, flat. This is called a check action variation versus the normal back step. It is used to establish the man's position early in the figure.

Step 2. Move your right foot slightly back, using the footwork all flat while turning $\frac{1}{8}$ clockwise. Lead the lady forward.

Step 3. Move your left foot to the side using the footwork ball, flat while turning $\frac{1}{8}$ clockwise. Lead the lady in front of you almost at a right angle to your body while preparing to cradle her with your right arm. Your left arm moves forward toward the lady as she passes you.

Step 4. Close your right foot to your left foot using the footwork of ball, flat, establishing the Side Closed Position.

Step 1.

Step 2.

Step 3.

Step 4.

Lady's Part: Open to Side Closed Position

The lady's details for the Open to Side Closed Position follow:

Step 1. Place your right toe to your left heel using the footwork of ball.

Step 2. Move forward and slightly across with your left foot, retaining the right side leading using the footwork of heel.

Step 3. Move forward and slightly across on your right foot using the footwork of heel while turning $^1/_8$ clockwise.

Step 4. Move your left foot to the side and slightly back using the footwork ball, flat, while turning $^3/_8$ clockwise and finishing in the Side Closed Position.

Throw Out

Well gals, we would certainly never throw you out because we love dancing with you. However to begin or continue the dance we have to find a way to move from closed position to open single or double handholds position. Perhaps some "wiseguy," named this pattern after an argument with his girl!

Gentleman's Part: Throw Out

The gentleman's details for the Throw Out follow:

Step 1. Move your left foot to the side using the inside edge of the ball of the foot. Lead the lady to step back by rotating your body and arms toward the lady's position.

Step 2. Dance with your right foot in place, sending your partner forward across your body in almost a perpendicular position. Your footwork is ball, flat, and your left hand moves toward your left side.

Step 3. Cross your left foot in front of your right foot using the footwork ball, flat, turning $\frac{1}{8}$ counterclockwise. You may begin to acquire double handholds at this point by skimming your right hand along the lady's back and left arm.

Step 4. Move your right foot to the side and back in the footwork ball, flat. Turn up to $\frac{1}{8}$ counterclockwise to finish in Open Facing Position with double handholds.

Step 1.

Step 2.

Step 3.

Step 4

Lady's Part: Throw Out

The lady's details for the Throw Out follow:

Step 1. Place your right toe to your left heel using the footwork of ball turning $^1/_8$ clockwise to generate torque for the following movement.

Step 2. Move your left foot forward and slightly across with the left side leading. Use the footwork heel and turn $^1/_8$ counterclockwise.

Step 3. Move your right foot to the side using the footwork ball, flat, turning $^1/_4$ counterclockwise.

Step 4. Move backward on your left foot and slightly across your right. Use the footwork of ball, flat. Turn $^1/_4$ counterclockwise to finish in Open Facing Position.

Choreographed Routine: Hustle Routine

With the disco ball spinning and lights flashing, dance the Hustle in the following sequence:

- Throw Out: steps 1 to 4, ending in double handholds.
- Lady's Left Underarm Turn (Slotted): steps 1 to 4, two times.
- Basic (Slotted) Right Turn: steps 1 to 4, two times.
- Man's Left Underarm Turn (Slotted): steps 1 through 4.
- Basic (Slotted) Right Turn: steps 1 to 4, two times.
- Open to Side Closed Position: steps 1 through 4.
- Repeat routine.

This routine is 27 beats of music, so dividing by Hustle's 4 beats per measure, this routine equals 6.75 measures of music. Your CD practice song is 28 measures of music per minute. As a percentage, this routine will take 24 percent of a minute, or just over 14 seconds to the repeat.

The Least You Need to Know

- Perfect the basic timing and movements of the Hustle.
- Use "the magic part of the foot" to transition smoothly from backward to forward movement.
- Remember the eleventh commandment: Never *stop* with both feet on the floor and weight evenly distributed.
- Take your feet off the floor by using your upper thigh.

Appendix A

Glossary

alignment   The direction of the feet in relation to the line of dance and its varied room-orientated descriptions.

amalgamation   Combining individual dance figures into a predetermined sequence.

apart   A couple's position in which the partners make no contact. Also called *solo position*.

back-to-back   A couple's position in which the leader and follower have their backs facing each other.

balance   The ability to control and maintain the body's center when moving to music.

basic figure   The template of movement for any dance that generally becomes a physically and visually recognizable component of the majority of dance's figures.

beats of music   A systematic method of counting musical notes in a musical composition. Most dancing is written in ⁴/₄ timing (four beats to each bar of music), making a quarter note's value one beat of music.

Chassé (the triple step)   One foot following or chasing the other becomes the foundation dance movement of the East Coast Swing and Cha-Cha. A Chassé may travel in any direction, including a rotation.

clockwise rotation   Turning the body in the direction the hands of a clock move.

closing action   Bringing the free or unsupported foot next to the standing or supporting foot and transferring the body's weight to it. The closing action is also called a *close* or *closing step* and is nonprogressive.

connection   The point of contact between partners made from one partner's hands and fingers to the other partner's hands, arms, shoulder blades, etc. This type of contact must allow the transmission of *feeling* to occur when the rhythmic weight change is made.

contra body movement (CBM)   Portions of rotation that the various assemblies of the body make in preparation to turn, spin, or pivot as a whole. Generally CBM is the leader's first indication of changing direction. CBM begins with the opposite side of the body rotating toward the moving leg.

contrary body movement position (CBMP)   Positioning the foot across the plane or directional line of the supporting foot in either a forward or backward direction.

counterclockwise rotation   Turning the body in the opposite direction in which a clock's hands move.

cross body position   A couple's position in which the follower is at a right angle to the leader on the leader's right side.

Cuban motion or Latin hip movement   The pelvis is allowed to gently move sideways and then rotate backward toward the supporting leg as a result of flexing and straightening the knees. The thigh of the non-supporting foot is lifted, allowing the inside edge of the toe and ball of the foot to be placed into position with soft pressure at first. Then as the weight is transferred incrementally to that foot, there is a proportionate lowering of the heel and straightening of that same leg. With even and complete reciprocity, the opposite foot, leg, and pelvis are released, allowing the action to begin again on the opposing side.

double handholds   The leader's left hand joins the follower's right hand while the leader's right hand joins the follower's left hand.

fallaway rock or fallaway position   A couple's position in which the leader and follower both move backward in promenade position.

figure   A series of dance steps or directional movements that form a consistent reusable and recognizable pattern.

follower   The partner who responds to and resolves the initiation of the lead during a dance.

footwork   The various contact points made between the dancer's foot and the floor. In the Smooth dances, the usage of the ball of the foot is generally unwritten.

hip action or movement   *See* Cuban motion or Latin hip movement.

inside turn or loop turn   An underarm or solo turn with the rotation initiated toward the partner.

leader   The partner who logistically directs the dance couple and maintains relative proximity through the follower's resolve.

left over right   The leader's left hand is joined with the follower's left hand; their arms are held over the leader's right hand joined with the follower's right hand.

Left Side-by-Side Position   A couple's position in which the follower is on the leader's left side, and both partners are facing the same direction.

left-to-left   The leader's left hand joins the follower's left hand. Also called a *reverse handhold*.

magic part of the foot   The point of contact under the dancer's foot equidistant from the center of both the ball of the foot and the big toe.

moving foot   The foot that will next carry the dancer's weight. The moving foot is also called the *free foot*, *stepping foot*, *target foot*, *unsupported foot*, and *traveling foot*.

no-foot rise (NFR)   When stepping back during the inside portion of a turn, the heel of the supporting foot remains in contact with the floor until the following step's weight change is complete. The rise or elevation changes are created through the knees and body.

normal handhold   The leader's left hand is joined with the follower's right hand. This is also called a *single handhold*, a *natural handhold*, or a *basic handhold*.

open-facing position   A couple's position in which the partners are facing each other and are apart with a left-to-right handhold, a right-to-right hold, a double hold, a crossed double handhold, or a solo position.

outside partner position   A couple's position comparable to the closed position but longer in the normal alignment. The similar foot of the leader (or follower) takes a step forward and to the outside of their partner's similar foot. In the case of the right feet, this position is called *right outside partner*. In the case of the left feet, it is called *left outside partner*. Also known as *parallel position*.

outside turn or arch turn An underarm or solo turn with the rotation initiated away from the partner.

pivot or swivel The act of rotating through the later portion of a weight change—generally one-half turn or less. During a pivot or swivel, there should be weight on one foot with a contact point of the free foot skimming the dance floor. The body's vertical alignment should be carried over the ball of the foot during these rotations.

poise, lady The vertically erect position of the ballroom dancer, including center body control, with balance inclined between the arch and ball of the supporting foot and the knees flexed to represent the character of the dance. In the Smooth dances, the inclination and alignment of the lady is slightly leftward. On any backward movement, her shoulders should not be allowed to initiate the action or fall backward.

poise, man The vertically erect position of the ballroom dancer, including center body control, with balance inclined toward the ball of the supporting foot and the knees flexed to represent the character of the dance. In the Smooth dances, the inclination and alignment of the man's body is slightly leftward.

pressure The incremental increase or decrease of feeling a connection, created by the suppleness of joints and the activity of muscle. Pressure exists between each of the partners and through the dance floor.

promenade position (PP) A dance position created by the partners rotating $\frac{1}{8}$ of a turn away from each other, where the partners face and move toward the same theoretic place on the dance floor. PP can move forward, backward, or in a circle.

pulling The negative use of pressure through connection, which renders a partner's balance, timing, and position on the dance floor ineffective.

right-over-left The leader's right hand is joined with the follower's right hand; their arms are held over the leader's left hand joined with the partner's left hand.

Right Side-by-Side Position A couple's position in which the follower is on the leader's right side and both partners are facing the same direction.

right-to-left The leader's right hand is joined with the follower's left hand. This is also called a *cross-handhold* or a *handshake handhold*.

side leading (left or right) A position of the body in which either the left or right side of the ribcage and/or shoulder is advanced ahead of the alternate side during a forward or backward step. This can also occur on a side step.

supporting foot or leg The foot or leg that carries the body's weight using an act of compression or flexing through its muscles and joints. The supporting foot or supporting leg is also known as the *standing* foot or leg.

syncopation (split or fractions of beats) The act of splitting music from its normal structure to a weaker one.

unit or unit method My Quickstart's method of isolating two beats of music and their respective directional movements. This was developed to coincidentally describe similar choreography for any of the swing rhythms.

Further Reading

Other Books by Jeff Allen

Quickstart to Social Dancing, Second Edition. Cranston, RI: QQS Publications, 1997, ISBN 0-9654423-1-4.

Quickstart to Swing. Cranston, RI: QQS Publications, 2000, ISBN 0-9654423-3-0.

Quickstart to Tango. Cranston, RI: QQS Publication, 1998, ISBN 0-9654423-2-2.

The Complete Guide to Slow Dancing booklet and video. Cranston, RI: QQS Publications, 1997.

Wedding Details: 101 FAQs. Jeff Allen, Jack Benoff, Edith Gilbert, Sherri Goodall, Lois Pearce, and Pat Taylor. Pennythought Press and wd web. co, www.weddingdetails.com

Additional Reading Materials

American Style Rhythm Bronze Manual. W.D. Eng, Inc. d/b/a Dance Vision, 2000, www. dancevision.com.

American Style Smooth Bronze Manual. W.D. Eng, Inc. d/b/a Dance Vision, 2000, www. dancevision.com.

Dance: A Very Social History. Carol Wallace, Don McDonagh, Jean L. Druesedow, Laurence Libin, and Constance Old. The Metropolitan Museum of Art, 1986, ISBN 0-8478-0819-X.

Dance Fever. Don McDonagh. Quarto Marketing Ltd., 1979, ISBN 0-394-73667-0.

Dancing USA Magazine. 200 N. York Road, Elmhurst, IL 60126

Hustle. Neil Shell and John P. Nyemchek. Nyemchek's Dance Center, 55 East Central Ave., Pearl River, New York 10965, 1999, ISBN 1-929574-00-2.

Dance Resources on the Web

www.quickstartbooks.com
Jeff Allen's Quickstart Books
JeffAllen@quickstartbooks.com

www.dancevision.com
Dance Vision International Dancer's Association (DVIDA)
Dance Vision—Dance Videos and Music, 1-800-851-2813

www.dancingusa.com
Dancing USA: The Art of Ballroom Dance Magazine

National Governing Organizations

www.ndca.org
Professional: National Dance Council of America, Inc. (NDCA)

www.usabda.org
Amateur: United States Amateur Ballroom Dancers Association (USABDA)

Index

Check Out These
Best-Selling
COMPLETE IDIOT'S GUIDES®

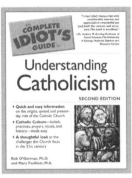

Understanding Catholicism
SECOND EDITION

Bob O'Gorman, Ph.D. and Mary Faulkner, M.A.

1-59257-085-2
$18.95

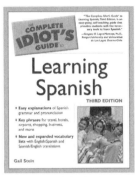

Learning Spanish
THIRD EDITION

Gail Stein

0-02-864451-4
$18.95

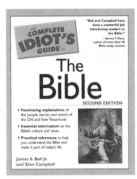

The Bible
SECOND EDITION

James S. Bell Jr. and Stan Campbell

0-02-864382-8
$18.95

Being a Groom
SECOND EDITION

Jennifer Lata Rung and Mark Rung

0-02-864456-5
$9.95

Grammar and Style
SECOND EDITION

Laurie E. Rozakis, Ph.D.

1-59257-115-8
$16.95

Playing the Guitar
SECOND EDITION

Frederick Noad

0-02-864244-9
$21.95 w/CD

Personal Finance in Your 20s & 30s
SECOND EDITION

Sarah Young Fisher and Susan Shelly

0-02-864374-7
$19.95

Knitting and Crocheting
SECOND EDITION
Illustrated

Barbara Breiter and Gail Diven

1-59257-089-5
$16.95

The Perfect Resume
THIRD EDITION

Susan Ireland

0-02-864440-9
$14.95

Buying and Selling a Home
FOURTH EDITION

Shelley O'Hara and Nancy D. Lewis

1-59257-120-4
$18.95

Low-Carb Meals

Lucy Beale and Sandy G. Couvillon, M.S., L.D.N., R.D.

1-59257-180-8
$18.95

Calculus

W. Michael Kelley

0-02-864365-8
$18.95

More than *450 titles* in *30 different categories*
Available at booksellers everywhere

ALPHA

About the Author

Jeff Allen is a graduate of the University of Rhode Island and has been self-employed since 1972. He is the author of *Quickstart to Social Dancing*© (the USA's number-one selling social dance book), *Quickstart to Tango*©, *The Complete Guide to Slow Dancing*©, and *Quickstart to Swing*© and presently resides in Cranston, Rhode Island.

Jeff, a Rhode Island native, stresses basic and advanced partnering skills, along with the teaching and learning of each major dance's characteristics. One of Jeff's specialties is what he calls "partnering kinesiology," which includes the use and control of the dancer's body and their partner's body in conjunction with the physical sciences and music.

Additionally, Jeff stresses physical and mental attitudes as an approach to partner dancing. He has taught and coached beginners through professionals, as well as teachers, in Rhode Island and throughout the USA for 18 years. He is the recipient of more than 30 NDCA (National Dance Council of America) top teacher awards and holds both amateur and professional championships in the American and International styles.

Jeff holds Membership credentials with the North American Dance Teachers Association, Inc., and the Pan American Teachers Association, and he is a columnist for *Dancing USA* magazine. He is an Associate Member of the Imperial Society of Teachers of Dance and is a Regional Examiner for Dance Vision International Dancers Association.

To contact Jeff for information on teaching, coaching, speaking, special corporate events, or teacher examinations, go to JeffAllen@quickstartbooks.com or call 1-888-254-3162.